Praise for *Global Te*

'In this book, Jo Owen provides not only a thorough understanding of what makes a "global" organisation effective, but also ideas and reflections on how to go about it, in a way that is neither simplistic nor dogmatic. Great read.'

Bertrand Lavayssiere, Ayres and Co. Strategy Consultancy

'A perk of my job is that I get paid to read and review books. Nothing thrills me more than to know that one of my favourite management authors, Mr Jo Owen, has another book published.

I enjoyed reading his perspectives on the various aspects of management as he provides insights that can be easily digested by anybody, yet has the necessary depth to help you with the skills needed in management.

His latest offering showcases research that he has extensively carried out and provides astute insights that will benefit any executive from any level of management, be it middle or senior.

Quickly bookmark this for your "to-read list" as it is a useful, insightful read.'

Sadie Jane Nunis, Publications Manager, Singapore Institute of Management

'Jo Owen has done it again – spotted a big gap in the literature and filled it elegantly and effectively with this splendidly readable, comprehensive, practical and evidence-based treatment of a topic that is really challenging to our globalising business world. Packed with great examples and quotes, Owen leads the reader through the toughest and most interesting challenges in cross-cultural management: leadership, team dynamics, business context and systems, cultural intelligence and conflict resolution. This should be the first item for global managers to put in their hand luggage.'

Nigel Nicholson, Professor, London Business School. author, *The 'I' of Leadership: Strategies for Seeing Being and Doing*

'Original and practical book on a vital topic which no one has looked at in depth before; simple and clear to read, with lots of real world case examples, it escapes the normal orthodoxy where globalisation means spreading western practice.'

Alberto Forchielli, Managing Partner, Mandarin Capital Partners

GLOBAL TEAMS

PEARSON

At Pearson, we believe in learning – all kinds of learning for all kinds of people. Whether it's at home, in the classroom or in the workplace, learning is the key to improving our life chances.

That's why we're working with leading authors to bring you the latest thinking and best practices, so you can get better at the things that are important to you. You can learn on the page or on the move, and with content that's always crafted to help you understand quickly and apply what you've learned.

If you want to upgrade your personal skills or accelerate your career, become a more effective leader or more powerful communicator, discover new opportunities or simply find more inspiration, we can help you make progress in your work and life.

Every day our work helps learning flourish, and wherever learning flourishes, so do people.

To learn more, please visit us at **www.pearson.com/uk**

Global
Teams

How the best teams achieve high performance

JO OWEN

Harlow, England • London • New York • Boston • San Francisco • Toronto • Sydney • Auckland • Singapore • Hong Kong
Tokyo • Seoul • Taipei • New Delhi • Cape Town • São Paulo • Mexico City • Madrid • Amsterdam • Munich • Paris • Milan

PEARSON EDUCATION LIMITED
Edinburgh Gate
Harlow CM20 2JE
United Kingdom
Tel: +44 (0)1279 623623
Web: **www.pearson.com/uk**

First edition published 2017 (print and electronic)

ISBN: 978-1-292-17191-3 (print)
     978-1-292-17192-0 (PDF)
     978-1-292-17193-7 (ePub)

British Library Cataloguing-in-Publication Data
A catalogue record for the print edition is available from the British Library

Library of Congress Cataloging-in-Publication Data
A catalog record for the print edition is available from the Library of Congress

10 9 8 7 6 5 4 3 2 1
20 19 18 17 16

Cover design by Two Associates
Cover image © iStock

Print edition typeset in 9.5 pt and ITC Giovanni Std by iEnergizer Aptara® Ltd
Printed by Ashford Colour Press Ltd, Gosport

NOTE THAT ANY PAGE CROSS REFERENCES REFER TO THE PRINT EDITION

Contents

About the author

Jo Owen worked with and researched over a hundred of the best, and one or two of the worst, organisations on our planet for *Global Teams* over thirty years.

He has built a business in Japan, and has led businesses in Europe and North America; he is a co-founder of eight not-for-profit organisations with a collective turnover of nearly $200 million a year. He is co-founder of Teach First, the largest graduate recruiter in the UK. He also started a bank. He began his career in brand management at P&G.

An award-winning author, Jo has written 15 books which have been published in nearly 100 editions globally. His titles include *How to Lead*, *How to Manage* and *Tribal Business School*.

He is in demand as a speaker on leadership, tribes and global teams and can be reached at jo@ilead.guru

Acknowledgements

This is a book I have been wanting to write for many years. But I was nervous about starting. Before beginning this research programme I had a huge fear: why on earth would anyone want to invest their time in helping out? Would they think that global teams represented a worthwhile challenge? The reaction I received was astonishing. Time and again I found that firms and executives were more than willing to take part: they see that global teams are important, challenging and poorly understood. It is clearly a hot issue for global firms and global managers.

I am hugely grateful to the many executives around the world who have contributed to this book, which draws on their collective wisdom, knowledge and experience. In particular, I would like to thank the 80 plus firms where I was able to work or conduct formal research with individuals or teams:

Accenture, Aegon, AIG, Airbus, ALICO, Allen & Overy, Amex, ANZ Bank, Apple, Armstrong Industries, AstraZeneca, Aviva, BAML, Bank Indonesia, Barclays, BASF, BNYMellon, British Council, Canon, Cap Gemini, Citi, Dentons, Deutsche Bank, Dow, EBRD, EDS, Electrolux, Facebook, Financial Times, Fujitsu, Google, HCA, Hiscox Re, Hitachi, HSBC, IBM, Ito Chu, JAL, Laird, MetLife, Mitsubishi Chemical, Mitsui OSK Lines, Mitsui Sumitomo Insurance, Monsanto, Nationwide, Nokia, Nomura, Nordea, NRI, NTT, P&G, Pearson, Pepsico, Philip Morris, Philips, Premier Foods, Qualcomm, RBS, RELX, Rentokil, Rolls Royce, SABIC, San Miguel, SECOM, Social Media,[394] Standard Chartered Bank, SWIFT, Symantec, Tetrapak, Tokyo Marine, UBS, Unilever, Visa, World Bank, Zurich Insurance as well as many smaller companies and NGOs including: Ares & Co, Arrowgrass, CRU, The Groove, HERE, House, Mandarin Capital, Modern Tribe, Opportunity Network, STIR, Vastari and World Faith.

I gained greatly from their insight: I hope they enjoyed the process and got some value from it as well. Throughout the book I quote individual executives who took part in the structured interviews: my thanks to each of them for letting me quote them.

None of this would have been possible without a vast army of people in the background who made it possible. Pearson were, as ever, thoroughly professional in supporting this project from the start. In particular, Richard Stagg once again showed the level of insight, realism and support that an author needs; Eloise Cook quickly took over a challenging project at a challenging time as editor and saw it through. My long-standing agent Frances Kelly once again ensured I was not distracted by contracts and was, as ever, a source of strength and support whenever I needed it.

Finding the initial interviewees is always a challenge: you have little to offer to the first guinea pigs. It was definitely a matter of pulling in favours and using networks and contacts. My wife, Hiromi, went above and beyond in tracking down many executives from Japan who stepped up and helped out. She also became a book widow for months while I researched and wrote.

Any book is at risk of containing errors of fact or judgement, especially one which relies so heavily on original research. Any errors are mine entirely: I could not have asked for better support from so many people in bringing this book to fruition.

CHAPTER ONE

Introduction

Why *Global Teams* is needed

Much has been written about globalisation. Much less has been written about global teams. Globalisation depends on small teams of people from across the world making things happen. These teams may be working on supply chains or R&D, serving a global customer, building a global service or product, running IT, risk, finance or HR for the firm. Global teams are the oil that helps global firms work.

Making teams succeed within one country is hard enough. Succeeding across borders is far harder. The challenges of making decisions, setting goals, communicating, building trust and managing the team are far harder when you are separated by time, language, culture and priorities.

If you look for practical help on how to run cross-border teams, you will find there is little help. There is plenty of advice on culture. That is useful, but it is not enough. You can learn how to exchange *meishi* (business cards) in Japan and that will help smooth your introductions, but it will not make your global team succeed.

The focus of *Global Teams* is to deal with the challenges which practising managers face:

▶ How can I influence decisions in a head office thousands of miles away where they speak a different language?

▶ How do I trade off our local goals and priorities versus the global priorities?

▶ Can I trust my peers in other countries to deliver on their commitments to me?

▶ How do I find out what is really going on and how it will affect me?

▶ Can I trust top management to support my agenda and me personally?

▶ How can I lead people who I do not see and are not like me?

The need for effective global teams is growing as globalisation grows. It will be increasingly hard for managers to succeed unless they have some global experience: the world is simply becoming more interconnected. A few simple facts will make the point:

▶ World GDP has grown at 3.5 per cent annually from 1972 to 2014: 2014 GDP is 4.4 times larger than it was in 1972.[1]

▶ World trade has grown at 6.1 per cent annually from 1973 to 2011:[2] trade has grown tenfold in less than forty years. Trade growth has been consistently faster than GDP growth.[3]

▶ Growth in trade and GDP has been driven by the arrival of China on to the global market. Exports from China were just $249 billion in 2000; by 2014 China exports reached $2,342 billion: nearly a tenfold increase which saw it leapfrog the United States to become the largest global exporter. Over the same period, exports from the United States rose from $780 billion to $1,620 billion.[4]

▶ Growth in global communications has been faster than growth in GDP or trade. International telecoms traffic has grown in 20 years (1995 to 2015) from 70 billion minutes to 560 billion minutes.[5] Nearly half of that traffic now comes from VOIP traffic, which was virtually non-existent 20 years ago.

▶ The growth in global communications has been mirrored by explosive growth in internet usage. In 1996 there were just 45 million internet users. By 2015 there were 3.4 billion internet users who now have the world at their fingertips.[6]

The need is now greater than ever for managers to know how to manage in a global economy. In the past, globalisation was a code word for spreading

In the past, globalisation was a code word for spreading western practices around the world.

western practices around the world. First, the rise of Japan put paid to the idea that western management was the default mode of management. Now the rise of China means that there is more than one perspective on how to make things happen. The rise of India and the rest of Asia is not far behind. Global now means global, not western practice spread around the world.

Why *Global Teams* is different

Global Teams fills a gap in our knowledge about globalisation. Most of the work on globalisation looks at challenges for the firm or the individual. *Global Teams* bridges the gap between firm and individual by focusing clearly on the challenges of the global team.

Early work on globalisation by Bartlett and Ghoshal looked at the firm-wide trade-off between global integration and local responsiveness.[7] They then explored how that trade-off varied across the value chain. This is valuable work when looking at high-level organisation design and strategy, but it does not help team leaders and members in their day-to-day practice. Every day, team leaders face the challenge of bridging global and local needs. Bartlett and Ghoshal look at globalisation from the perspective of the firm: *Global Teams* looks at global working from the perspective of the team. Global teams soon discover that there is no trade-off between global integration and local responsiveness: they are expected to achieve both goals, even if they appear to pull the team in opposite directions.

More recently, Erin Meyer[8] has produced invaluable work on cultural differences across the world, and has shown how they affect individuals.[9] This helps individuals, but still leaves unasked questions about how the team can operate effectively. Culture is only one aspect of making a global team work. Global teams also have to work out how to build trust; how to communicate effectively; how to make decisions amid uncertainty, ambiguity and conflict; how to create clear and shared goals for the team; how to build a team with the right skills and values.

Global Teams fills the gap between the firm-wide challenges of global working (Bartlett and Ghoshal) and the individual challenges of global working (Erin Meyer). Helping global teams work is at the heart of making global firms work: this book represents a modest first step in addressing that need.

About the research

Global Teams is based on original research for a simple reason: there is no other substantive research to draw on. It has been a woefully neglected subject.

The book is based on work and original research with individuals and teams at over 80 global firms including:[10]

Accenture, Aegon, AIG, Airbus, ALICO, Allen & Overy, Amex, ANZ Bank, Apple, Armstrong Industries, AstraZeneca, Aviva, BAML, Bank Indonesia, Barclays, BASF, BNYMellon, British Council, Canon, Cap Gemini, Citi, Dentons, Deutsche Bank, Dow, EBRD, EDS, Education Development Trust, Electrolux, Facebook, Financial Times, Fujitsu, Google, HCA, Hiscox Re, Hitachi, HSBC, IBM, Ito Chu, JAL, Laird, MetLife, Mitsubishi Chemical, Mitsui OSK Lines, Mitsui Sumitomo Insurance, Monsanto, Nationwide, Nokia, Nomura, Nordea, NRI, NTT, P&G, Pearson, Pepsico, Philip Morris, Philips, Premier Foods, Qualcomm, RBS, RELX, Rentokil, Rolls Royce, SABIC, San Miguel, SECOM, Social Media,[11] Standard Chartered Bank, SWIFT, Symantec, Tetrapak, Tokyo Marine, UBS, Unilever, Visa, Warner Music, World Bank, Zurich Insurance as well as many smaller companies and NGOs including: Ares & Co, Arrowgrass, CRU, The Groove, HERE, House, Mandarin Capital, Modern Tribe, Opportunity Network, STIR, Vastari, World Faith.

In total, the research draws on research, work and experience from over 100 countries in a deliberate attempt to counter the western bias of most work on globalisation.

There were three elements to the research:

▶ Structured in-depth interviews with people working on global teams
▶ A short survey on global team effectiveness
▶ Workshops with select partner firms to find out how to improve global team working.

Throughout the research, the focus was on practical experience and real-life examples of what works and what does not. I was not looking for people's opinions or theories on global teams: I wanted the day-to-day reality of global teams.

Achieving a rounded view on global teams requires looking at them from different perspectives. The main perspectives of the research were:

▶ Hub versus spoke
▶ Team leader versus team member

► Western versus non-western

► Small versus large firms.

Each of these is explained briefly below.

Hub versus spoke

Global teams normally have a hub and several spokes. The hub is the centre of power, decisions and communications. This causes problems for people who are in the remote spokes. We are all the centre of our own universes, and everyone else is a bit player in our own life story. So it can be difficult when you discover that you are a bit player in someone else's world. Suddenly, you feel the challenges of trust, decision making and communications more acutely. Meanwhile people in the hub wonder whether they can really trust people on the spokes to deliver, and whether they can make the right decisions when the hub is asleep. Understanding both perspectives was central to this research.

Team leader versus team member

The team leader is often at the nexus of the global–local trade-off. He or she faces the challenge of bridging the distance between team members across time zones, language, culture, skills and expectations; bridging the distance between global and local demands; understanding and influencing decisions which affect the team but over which there is little control; shielding the team from the distractions which the ambiguity and uncertainty of global work bring. These are huge challenges.

In contrast, each team member relies on the rest of the team to perform, which raises questions about mutual trust, communication, decision making and accountability within the team. The team leader and team members may be working to a common goal, but they have very different perspectives on what matters and what they personally need to achieve.

Western versus non-western

Looking at much of the literature on globalisation, and on management, there is a clear western bias. As one Japanese interviewee put it: 'many western management books are translated into Japanese, so we have some idea about western ways. How many Japanese management books are translated

How many American managers have read a Japanese management book?

into English?' How many American managers have read a Japanese management book?[12] This can have devastating consequences. The Japanese rode to success largely on the back of absorbing and adopting Deming's work on quality, which only came back to the West too late.[13]

In the past, globalisation was a code word for spreading western practices and business around the world. The rise of East Asia has firmly consigned that idea to history, but the literature is yet to catch up with reality. *Global Teams* starts that catch up process.

The research confirms many of the cultural differences explored by Meyer and others. But it also shows that many of the challenges of making global teams work are universal. The book explores the differences and similarities across the world. The research is intended to make sure that this is not another western-biased book on the challenges of globalisation.

Small versus large firms

The temptation in researching global firms is to focus on the big global firms. They are important and prestigious. But the future of globalisation does not belong to them alone. The future may well be with small start-ups. Facebook was a start-up at Harvard in 2004;[14] by 2015 it had reached 1.6 billion monthly users.[15]

Research with smaller firms revealed highly innovative ways of working globally; they also brought into sharp relief some of the challenges of working across borders. Working without all the corporate life support systems that both enable and imprison us is a mixed blessing. Smaller firms are resource constrained. This makes them focus very clearly what they can gain from being global, and it makes them focus on how they can best manage across borders. They all make mistakes, but learn fast from them. This book captures that learning so that you can accelerate your learning process. It is less painful to learn from others' mistakes than your own.

Sources

Throughout I have relied heavily on original research and I am hugely grateful to the many contributors who gave their time and insight. Wherever possible, I have identified them with their permission. In quite a number of cases, the contributors have asked to stay anonymous. This is particularly true in banking where getting permission for saying anything requires approval from compliance, risk, corporate communications, legal, PR, and both product and geographic line management. That may say something about the current state of banking. I am grateful for the off-the-record interviews, and I flag these up as anonymous where I have to. In every case, an anonymous source is an original source.

I have also made anonymous any quotations or examples which could prove contentious for the individual or the firm.

Continuing the research

Understanding how global teams work is a huge task – there are a vast number of variables: nationality and culture of the team and firm; functionality and focus of the team; standing versus project teams; type of industry; type and size of firm; type of issue and challenge. If you put all the variables together and wanted to have a statistically valid database for each variable, you would need at least one billion data points. Big data helps, but only if you can generate the initial data points. So this research is likely to be work in progress for years to come. But even at this stage, the main themes and main challenges are clear enough to allow practising managers to see how they can raise their game with their global teams.

The next phase of research has two priorities:

▶ Understand how firms can move from current practice to best practice
▶ Deepen the level of understanding by geography and region.

Research will continue with a research partner programme which gives participating organisations simple and valuable tools to help them improve the working of their global teams. If you are interested in taking part, visit the www.teams.world website. I am also always interested in talking to individuals from around the world with relevant experience. Again, you can contact me at www.teams.world.

About the language

Globalisation is full of words which have quite precise meanings for people who care about them: global firms, transnationals, internationals, multinationals, MNCs, MNEs, multilocals and many more besides. This research has shown that it is not necessary to worry about these different forms and names. Once you dig down to the practical level of a team working across borders, these differences no longer matter greatly. Teams in all these types of organisation are struggling with the same issues of leadership, trust, decision making and communications. The one place these names do make a difference is when looking at structures: Chapter 10 (Structure) explores the significance of these differences for global teams.

For this reason, I use the word 'global' to cover every type of firm which works across borders. It is a shorthand designed to make the book easier to read. In the interests of precision, I could refer to both global and cross-border teams: most teams that work cross border are not fully global. But 'global' is the word most people use, and so I follow common usage. Ease of reading trumps intellectual precision.

I also use the word 'firm' loosely. Where the case explicitly involves an NGO or not-for-profit organisation, I say so. Otherwise 'firm' is another simple form of shorthand to cover all the types of organisation which have been involved in this research effort.

There are myriad cultural perspectives globally, which require some simplification. One of the key differences is between what I have labelled the Anglo world and the rest. The Anglo world broadly encompasses North America, the UK and other English speaking nations. While there are significant differences within the Anglo world, I use this shorthand to point up differences with other cultures. Europe comprises several different cultural groups in management terms: Anglo, Germanic, Latin, Nordic and arguably France all have their own unique way of doing things. Similarly, it would be lazy and inappropriate to refer to an 'Asian' culture, when there are major differences between Japan, China, India, the Philippines and the many other cultures of Asia.

Finally, I describe two types of global firm: hub and spoke versus network. The hub and spoke has a powerful centre (the hub) with spokes that are largely independent of each other. All the communication goes through the hub. The alternative is the network where the hub (centre) is not so strong and all nodes in the network are more explicitly dependent on each other. The reality is that no global firm is exclusively hub and spoke or exclusively network: every firm is a hybrid between the two extremes. For the purposes of this book, the contrast helps to highlight some of the challenges and opportunities of different forms of organisation structure.

I have added a short glossary at the end of the book as a handy reference for you.

The structure and outline of *Global Teams*

By its nature, a book on global teams involves a wide variety of perspectives: different nationalities; hub versus spokes; team leader versus team member; different types of team. Exploring every perspective would be exhaustive, exhausting and ultimately confusing. There has to be some degree of simplification.

The book is divided into four parts. The first three parts offer a different perspective on the global team. Part four is a short conclusion about how you can improve the working of your global teams. If you want to cheat, read Chapter 2, 'What is special about global teams' and the conclusions first: they will give you a high-level picture of the book.

The book has been written so that each chapter stands on its own feet: you can read the book in any order you want. The figure below is an overview of the key themes and the structure of the book.

Emerging leadership framework for managing global teams

- Technical
- Personal
- Mix

People

Systems

- Decision making
- Processes and protocols
- Management information

Goals

Trust and communication

Outcomes

- Clear
- Shared
- Group and local

- Accountability
- Rewards and measures

Structure

Values

- Hub and spoke
- Network

- Common languages
- Common beliefs

Part one of *Global Teams* looks at the perspective of the team leader, who is concerned with every part of the leadership framework in the figure above.

Part two takes the perspective of team members, who are in the middle bubble of the chart. Individual team members take the overall framework as a given, regardless of whether they approve of it or not. Their main concern is about trust (Chapter 4) and communications (Chapter 5) within the team.

Part three takes the perspective of the firm which has to create the context for the team to succeed. That means deciding on:

▶ Goals: clear goals and shared goals. Chapter 6

▶ Systems: decision making, accountability, learning and innovation. Chapter 7

▶ People: recruiting and developing the best talent. Chapter 8

▶ Values and culture: managing cultural distance. Chapter 9

▶ Structure: complexity, co-ordination and conflict. Chapter 10.

Part four pulls together the findings and conclusions from the rest of the book: Chapter 11.

Global Teams comes with a complimentary Skill Pill: 'I am... Global Team Leader'.

Not only will you have a quick reference to the book's key insights, you will also take away useful, actionable exercises, leadership tools and techniques to aid you as you form your global team.

A Skill Pill is a short motivational video that you can view on your smartphone, tablet or computer. Use the QR code below to access the skill pill directly or visit: www.skillpill.com/globalteams

2

What is special about global teams

Working on a global team accelerates your personal and professional growth. You meet different people and work across different cultures. You are also likely to be working on important and worthwhile initiatives: global teams are not created for trivial matters. Global teams are a huge opportunity, and a huge responsibility.

You learn fast on a global team because everything is different. What works locally does not work around the world. Working with people you do not see, who think, act, talk and look different and live in a different time zone, means that even simple tasks become complex.

You have to replace tried and tested ways of working domestically with new and unfamiliar ways of working: this is a chance to learn and an obligation to learn. A new context requires a new way of working if you are to succeed.

Why global teams are different

There is plenty of guidance on how to make domestic teams work, but none on how to make global teams work. The rules of survival and success are different for global teams. The basic tasks of making a team work are harder in a global context. Four examples will make the point.

Communicating: Communicating within a domestic team is tough. There are always misunderstandings. But at least it is obvious when the person in front of you does not understand or agree, and you can quickly resolve any differences. On global teams, culture and distance make communication a far harder challenge.

Misunderstandings arise more easily, and they are harder to spot and harder to resolve on global teams. Distance means you cannot see the body language; you cannot see when there is misunderstanding or disagreement. Cultural noise means that what you say and what is heard may be different. Other cultures will choose to communicate or not communicate in ways that are unfamiliar. Small differences unintentionally become big differences.

Decision making: Within a domestic team you know who the stakeholders are, you know their interests, you can access them relatively easily and you know the context in which the decision is being made. Even then, decision making can be contentious and time-consuming. In a global team you may not know who all the stakeholders are or what their interests are; you do not have easy access to people in different time zones, cultures and languages, and you are not part of the flow of office gossip which gives you all the context about what the decision is and how it is being made. You are flying blind, but still you have to find ways of influencing decisions and stakeholders effectively.

Delegating: Delegating is an act of trust: you have to trust that someone else can complete the task you have given them. If you are in the same office, you can see when they are struggling and you can have a real-time conversation which keeps things on track. The trust bar is far higher on a global team because you cannot see when the team is struggling and you cannot have real-time conversations with everyone around the world. In addition, cultural issues means you may not hear about bad news or problems until it is too late. On global teams the trust bar is higher and the barriers to building trust are higher: how easily do you trust people you do not see, are not like you and you rarely see?

How easily do you trust people you do not see, are not like you and you rarely see?

Goal setting: You can read many articles about the global–local trade-off: should a firm focus on global goals and needs, or local ones? At the top of the firm, global needs come first. On the front line, local needs are the immediate needs which have to be dealt with. In between, there are global teams who find themselves in the cross-fire between global priorities and local needs. Somehow, they have to find the balance, despite the challenges of communicating and decision making which global teams face.

In practice, almost everything is harder on a global team. Global teams find that they are working across different regulatory and legal environments; different parts of the team may have incompatible systems and

Everything is harder on a global team.

different communication platforms; performance will be managed in different ways, even if the formal performance management systems look the same; the way team members relate to each other and to the team leader differs by culture.

These challenges mean that the way the team leader, the team and the firm work together has to be different on a global team compared to a domestic team, as follows:

▶ The team leader: global teams raise the leadership bar. The global team leader needs a distinct mindset which is open, adaptable and inquisitive. A team leader who sticks to their domestic success model will fail, because what works in one country does not work across every country. The global team leader needs an ability to influence people and decisions remotely, to motivate and manage at a distance. These are skills which are not learned domestically where you can see the people you need to influence, manage or motivate on a daily basis.

▶ Team members: the challenge of trust and communication is far more acute on a global team than on a domestic team. It is easier to trust people you see and can talk to, especially when they come from a similar cultural background. Building trust with people you see and talk to less and are very different from you is far harder. Rising to the challenge requires more methodical ways of communicating and of building trust. It also requires developing deep cultural intelligence across the team. Team members need a distinct mindset which is open, adaptable, positive and accountable.

▶ The firm has to put in the support framework for global teams which looks the same as for a domestic team: recruiting and developing people; performance management; relevant processes and systems. Although the headlines look the same, the reality is far more complicated when dealing with many countries and cultures.

Global Teams is organised around these three perspectives. The book shows how the team leader, team members and the wider firm have to raise their game and change their game to make global teams work.

Part one: The team leader's perspective
Chapter 3: The global leadership challenge

Globalisation is forcing a radical change in the way leaders lead. Global teams need a new sort of leader with a different set of skills and a different mindset from domestic team leaders. They need to:

▶ exercise power without authority

▶ influence decisions from a distance

▶ balance multiple and conflicting stakeholders and goals

▶ motivate and involve team members who they rarely see

▶ build trust with people who think and act differently from them

▶ have cultural intelligence to adapt their style to different contexts.

This is extreme leadership: it raises the bar for leaders. It is also leadership of the future, far removed from the comforting past of command and control within a domestic setting.

Part two: The global team member's perspective

At the heart of high-performing global teams are trust and communications. These are the two topics which came up time and again from team members. They are the glue which holds a highly dispersed team together.

Chapter 4: Trust: the glue that binds the team

Trust was rated by 72 per cent of global teams as one of their top five challenges. Trust is essential for a team to drive delegation, autonomy, accountability, honest and open communications and motivation. High-trust teams enable differing views and conflict to be aired and resolved productively. High trust improves communications, and good communications build trust in a virtuous spiral.

Trust is harder to build in global teams because of the challenges of cultural and physical distance, and because the high stakes involved in global teams means higher levels of trust are required.

Teams need two types of trust: personal and professional. Anglo, Germanic and Nordic cultures focus on professional trust; other cultures focus on building personal trust first. Global teams need both personal and professional trust.

Personal trust comes from finding common interests, experiences and values. Professional trust requires aligning agendas; finding common ways of communicating, deciding and acting; building credibility through consistent delivery and reliability. And the whole team needs to build cultural intelligence: breaking down national stereotypes and celebrating the best of what each culture brings to the team.

Chapter 5: Communications: less noise, more understanding

In an age of hyper-communication, communication is as hard as ever. It is easier than ever to communicate across borders; it is as hard as ever to be understood across borders. Communicating and understanding are different.

It is easier than ever to communicate across borders; it is as hard as ever to be understood across borders.

The communications challenge is about noise: what we say may not be what is heard or understood. The noise in global teams is much higher than in domestic teams because messages get lost in translation: this is a mixture of language, cultural assumptions and distance. Distance makes it hard to have the frequent and informal conversations which happen naturally in an office and help avoid or remedy misunderstandings.

Technology helps with transactional messaging, but can stand in the way of building relationships and trust. In particular, global teams find that email is open to misuse and misinterpretation: it is a good vehicle for destroying trust.

Smaller firms are using technology highly innovatively to improve communications and to increase autonomy and accountability. They use technology to deliver high transparency and low privacy. This makes use of communications as a cultural choice: high transparency can be used to increase support or increase control. If the balance goes too far to control, communications and trust break down. To deal with this, even the most high tech firms realise that trust comes from meeting face to face: these individual, team and corporate meetings are high cost but a good investment.

Part three: Creating the firm-wide context for success

Chapters 6 to 10 show how the firm can create the context in which global teams can thrive.

Chapter 6: Goals: clear goals or shared goals?

The views from the top of the firm and the team are very different. The top usually believes the goals are clear. Teams routinely complain that they are not clear. About 65 per cent of managers rated clear goals as one of their top challenges; nearer 80 per cent of managers outside the hub rated it a top five challenge for their team.

At first, it seems a mystery that clear goals can be a problem: most firms are awash with targets, key performance indicators and goals. Goal setting is one of the basics of good management. But global teams consistently find goal setting to be a challenge for two reasons:

▶ Goals are not clear. What appears simple at the top of the firm becomes very unclear for the global team which is having to manage the trade-offs between serving global needs and meeting local needs. In practice, every global team represents a wide range of perspectives, interests and stakeholders. The global team has to find a way of navigating through these differences to find a common way forward.

▶ Goals are not shared or owned. It is not enough for the goal to be clear: it has to be shared by every member of the team, and they need to understand both the goal (the 'what') and the context for the goal (the 'why' and 'how'). This leads to challenges around decision making: balancing the need for effectiveness with the need for fair process. The Anglo culture is often efficient at making decisions, but poor at fair process: they do not create ownership of the decision. Asian cultures are the reverse: they seem to have slow and inefficient decision-making processes, but they are very effective at building buy-in.

Chapter 7: Systems and processes: the building blocks of success

Plumbing is not glamorous, but it is vital.

Plumbing is not glamorous, but it is vital. This chapter examines the processes and systems which help or hinder global teams. These are largely hygiene factors: if done wrong they will demotivate the team. If done well, they are taken for granted.

Firms need to focus on four key areas:

► Roles and responsibilities: if these are not clear, then accountability will also be unclear. In a domestic team it is possible to see who does what, so accountability is relatively easy to assign. On a global team you cannot see who does what, so greater clarity of accountability is required. Once you have clear accountability, it is easier to delegate. The more you delegate, the more you drive autonomy and motivation. Delegation does not rely only on systems and processes: it also relies on trust. You only delegate tasks to people you trust.

► Processes and protocols: global teams need predictable routines for communicating, deciding and reporting. These disciplines need to be stronger on a global team, because the challenges of time, language and culture make it hard to have the flexibility which domestic teams enjoy. Typically, senior management expressed low concern about processes and protocols. Front-line team members expressed great concern about this, because they have to live with the consequences when incompatible processes cause problems.

► Decision making: global teams face the challenge of influencing decisions in a different time zone, different culture and different language where they may not know all the key stakeholders and they are not in the loop on all the latest gossip about what agendas are emerging, who wants what and who really has influence. All global teams need an insider, a sponsor, who can help them navigate their way through unfamiliar decision-making territory.

► Learning and innovation. The best global firms harness global knowledge and learning, both within and beyond the firm. Learning and innovation requires a fundamental cultural shift for many firms: they have to move from a closed to an open system. The closed system believes that head office knows best. The open system believes that the ecosystem is smarter than any of us. With the right culture in place it, the firm, has to build the technology, processes and infrastructure to enable learning and innovation to happen.

Chapter 8: People and skills: global talent, global mindset

Global teams need people with special skills and a special mindset. Even the most skilled person will not succeed on a global team without a global mindset, which reaches beyond any one culture.

This chapter explores how firms can identify and nurture global talent. This starts from the top: if there is a pyramid of passports in which only the home nation can rise to the top, then it becomes hard to attract the A* players who are needed on global teams. Global teams need exceptional talent with three characteristics:

▶ Different skill set from purely domestic talent: global team members, like team leaders, need to have strong influencing skills, high cultural intelligence and excellent communications. Communication skills are about outstanding listening skills, not about broadcasting skills.

▶ Higher skill set than domestic talent: global teams tend to work on high stakes projects. And if you work outside your home country you will be an expensive asset, and the local talent will need to be convinced that they can learn from you.

▶ Different mindset from the domestic mindset. The global mindset is comfortable with ambiguity, seeks autonomy and accountability, and is constantly curious about new cultures and new ways of doing things. It is constantly learning, growing and adapting. A fixed mindset and way of doing things causes clashes between cultures.

In practice, global talent is often self-selecting: global managers want to stay global, and reintegrating them into domestic work is awkward. Once you have tasted the freedom, autonomy and variety of global working, it is hard to go back to the familiar routines of a domestic team.

Chapter 9: Culture: building cultural intelligence

Rising to the global challenge requires a new way of thinking. Rising to the global challenge requires a new way of thinking. We are used to being at the centre of our own small universes: we have assumptions about how things should work and find other ways mysterious, baffling and ineffective. To others, we are the people with mysterious, baffling and ineffective ways of working. This is especially hard for managers from the Anglo world: most of the business literature is written from this perspective. That means other cultures have some idea how the Anglo world works, but the Anglo world is offered little insight into other cultures.

To succeed culturally, global managers need to suspend judgement. You have to understand and respect other ways of working. There is no right or wrong culture: there are only different cultures. The twenty main cultural differences fall into five categories:

► Attitudes to authority and hierarchy. Two sharp divides exist here. The first is between hierarchical and egalitarian cultures which affects how decisions are made, who speaks to who and how much autonomy teams have. The second divide is between individualistic and collective cultures. This affects decision making again, and also affects how much autonomy managers feel comfortable having.

► How team members communicate with each other. There are as many different ways of communicating as there are human beings. Even small differences can lead to big misunderstandings. To simplify, for global teams there are four areas where differences matter and these are consistent differences across cultures:

  ► Persuasion: principles, logic and reason versus pragmatic and practical

  ► Dealing with problems: open and rational versus private and personal

  ► Body language: expressive and open versus restrained and closed

  ► Style: direct and simple versus layered and nuanced.

► How team members relate to each other. Two obvious divides exist in trust and status. Some cultures focus on building personal trust, others focus on professional trust. Some cultures value status and respect more than others, which affects who talks to who and when.

► Mindset and beliefs. Cultures have beliefs which are deep enough that no one challenges the assumptions, until they come up against people with different beliefs. Four of these stand out:

  ► Optimists versus pragmatists

  ► Task focused versus people focused

  ► Growth versus fixed mindsets

  ► Tolerate or eliminate ambiguity.

▶ Cultural differences are about the way society works at large. Attitudes to time, law and openness not only change personal behaviour, but also affect the way the team works.

A team leader requires cultural intelligence, not cultural knowledge. As a team leader, you do not need to learn all the cultural differences of the team. You are not an anthropologist building deep cultural knowledge. You are a team leader and that requires cultural intelligence, not cultural knowledge. You have to have a mindset which is open, and learns and adapts very fast. Global team leaders cannot afford to be fixed in their ways.

Chapter 10: Structure: co-ordination and conflict

Any global structure leads to complexity and balances co-ordination and conflict across the firm. Global teams are often caught in the middle of this.

The structural challenge for global firms has been seen as balancing the need for global integration with local responsiveness. This is not a trade-off for most global teams: they are expected to achieve both outcomes. In doing so, they find they are often serving multiple internal and external stakeholders with competing agendas.

Managers see the world from where they stand. That means all structures contain completely different perspectives and agendas: that is a recipe for the conflict all firms face. This conflict can be a constructive way of deciding priorities and creating new ideas; it can also be destructive. Global teams experience this conflict in two ways.

First, the hub and the spokes of the firm have a mutual but asymmetric lack of trust in each other. The spokes are not sure they trust the hub to look after their interests; the hub does not trust that the spokes can deliver for them.

Second, there is a gulf between the top of the firm and the team. At the top, the goals are clear, decision making is fair and communications are good. The opposite is true for global teams. Decision making is seen to be opaque and communication from the top is seen to be incomplete and inadequate. Goals are also muddy because the team has to trade off multiple stakeholders. Building a sense of shared ownership around goals is a challenge.

There is no magic wand: any form of structure is a compromise between competing priorities. But any structure can be made to work well if the right people, systems and culture are in place.

Part four: Rising to the global challenge
Chapter 11: Conclusions

Making global teams succeed is hard work and it is complicated. But we are all busy and we do not have the time to absorb long and complicated arguments. So Chapter 11 offers you a short and simple summary of the key themes and messages from this book. At the risk of over-simplifying the core messages, you can look at global teams from three perspectives:

▶ Team leaders. Global team leaders need higher skills, different skills and a different mindset from domestic team leaders.

▶ Team members. Team members also need similar skills and mindset to the team leader. The main concern of team members is building trust and communication across the team.

> **Global team leaders need higher skills, different skills and a different mindset from domestic team leaders.**

▶ Firm. The challenge for the firm is to create the context for success. Successful teams and firms must be cohesive, and firms have a choice about how they build cohesion: do they integrate around the home nation culture and talent, or do they build a culture and grow talent which transcends borders? Once this is clear, the hard work can start on creating the processes, systems, structures and talent management that the firm requires.

Global teams are only going to grow in importance. Globalisation means that firms have to seek the best talent, ideas and value from around the world. Global teams are the integrating mechanism for the talent, values and ideas. Survival and success will rely increasingly on how well firms make their global teams work.

PART ONE
Leading the team

CHAPTER THREE

The global leadership challenge

New skills, new mindset

Global teams require exceptional leaders. Global team leaders have to overcome the distance challenges of time, culture, language, and differing agendas and capabilities. This raises the bar in terms of all the traditional skills of a leader: managing and motivating the team, managing performance and making decisions. But it also requires a new set of skills and a new mindset. The global team leader needs to have high influencing skills: command and control does not work well at distance. Global team leaders also need to learn and adapt fast: a leader who is stuck with a success model carefully honed over the years in a domestic setting will struggle with the different challenges of the global context.

Global leaders need three characteristics, which this chapter will explore in detail:

▶ High IQ (intelligence quotient). This is not about having academic qualifications. It is about pattern recognition. In a global context, familiar patterns are replaced with unfamiliar patterns of behaviour and success. You have to learn and adapt fast to these unfamiliar patterns and challenges.

▶ High EQ (emotional quotient).[16] Leading global teams means making things happen through people who do not think like you. You need high cultural intelligence to pick up the signals and respond appropriately to different cultures and different ways of thinking and working.

▶ High PQ (political quotient).[17] Navigating decision-making systems and influencing networks remotely is also vital, and requires strong political skills or PQ: political quotient. You cannot rely on traditional command and control skill. You need a new set of skills around influencing, motivating, building commitment and ownership, learning fast, adapting to different ways and leading without formal power. This is leadership of the future, not the past.

It is not just the global team leader who faces new challenges. The top leadership of the firm faces a paradox: the best performing global teams often see global leadership from the centre as being irrelevant. But top leadership is not irrelevant. In practice, the best global teams work because the leadership in the centre has created the conditions in which global teams can flourish. The hand of the leader may be invisible, but it is vital.

In this chapter we will show how leaders of global teams and leadership in the centre make the difference between failure and success.

1. The global leadership challenge: raising the bar
2. The global leadership challenge: IQ, EQ and PQ
3. Global team leaders: deploying IQ, EQ and PQ in a global context
4. Global leadership challenge and the gender agenda
5. Leadership from the centre: the invisible puppet master
6. Are you ready for the global leadership challenge?

1. The global leadership challenge: raising the bar

Global team leaders need to master leadership skills to an exceptionally high level.

The skills bar rises for global leaders for three reasons:

▶ Firms select from a global talent pool, so the competition is greater.
▶ Global team members expect more from a global team leader.
▶ The intrinsic challenges of the job are greater.

Global team leaders need excellence in most leadership skills, in addition to developing the unique skills required to manage across the distance of time, culture and language. If this seems like an exceptional challenge, it is. It is also worth it, both for the organisation and for the individual. As you face these challenges, recall President Kennedy's words on why America should go to the moon: 'we do these things, not because they are easy, but because they are hard,

26

because that goal will serve to organize and measure the best of our energies and skills'.[18] As a global team leader, you will develop exceptional leadership skills.

Below are the three reasons why the skills bar rises so much for global team leaders.

Firms select from a global talent pool, so the competition is greater

Firms are able to select from a much wider talent pool when looking for a global team leader. Central management in most global firms exploit and develop their global talent pool deliberately and consistently:

▶ 'Being global is not an objective, but it is a tool to hiring some of the best people'.[19]

▶ 'We don't just have to recruit from one geography, so that means we can recruit better and cheaper'.[20]

▶ 'In Japan, there are only 16,000 graduates who majored in computer science. There are 60,000 in the US and 300,000 in China. I assume there are more than that in India. If I'm asked whether I want to hire engineers from a pool of 16,000 or a pool of more than a million, the answer is self-evident.'[21]

> **'Being global is not an objective, but it is a tool to hiring some of the best people.**

This puts particular pressure on people from higher cost countries: they have to prove that they are worth the premium salary they extract.

Not all firms make the most of the global skills market. Many have a home nation bias where they have a pyramid of passports, which normally works like this:

▶ Top of the pyramid jobs go to the home nation

▶ Second-tier jobs go to western nations

▶ Bottom of the pyramid jobs (dirty, dull, dangerous and demeaning) go to nationals of select Asian countries.

These firms have global reach, but not a global mindset. They pay a heavy price for this bias. The best global talent is ambitious and wants to reach the top. When they see a firm which has a glass ceiling to stop foreigners rising to the top, they look elsewhere. This becomes a vicious circle where the firm finds it cannot recruit the best foreign talent, so it persists with its bias of favouring home country nationals. Home country nationals have many in-built advantages: they have their networks of influence; they understand how to make things happen; they understand the culture and how to make the network work for them.

Firms which are very prestigious in their home markets are prone to home country bias, especially if their home country is a large market such as China, Japan or the United States. Hitachi recognised this: 'The relationship was Japan saying "make this many" or "sell this many". The control towers were all located in Japan.'[22] This is a common challenge for global firms. Hitachi's response is to consider the heresy of moving its headquarters away from Japan: 'globalisation is in transition'.[23] It is no longer about taking the home country model and team around the world. It is about being a truly global team and global organisation.

Global team members expect more from a global team leader

The team itself does not want an overseas team leader unless the leader can make a real difference. If the talent already exists locally, then there is no point from the local team's perspective of bringing in overseas capability. Typically, non-domestic staff have high costs and they take time to become effective as they need to learn how things work locally. Their presence can also be resented if they are seen to be taking up a post which could be filled by a local manager. If you want to be a global team leader, you will be under the spotlight, and people will expect you to be exceptionally good at your craft skills as well as at your leadership skills.

Deep skills levels matter externally as well as internally, where the team leader is likely to have to negotiate with external stakeholders. Credibility and deep skills go together. In the words of Graham Sheffield:[24] 'We need experienced professionals in their specialist fields, colleagues who have credibility with their peers, and who have earned respect through their career journey'. Having an amateur negotiating with film producers and publishers is not wise.

Intrinsic challenges of the job are greater

Everything is harder at a distance. You do not see your colleagues in person day to day, and you may be on different time zones with different languages and culture. This makes decision making, delegation, motivation, performance management and all the other basics of management a real challenge. The first person to work out how to motivate by email and phone will make a fortune. It is a fortune which is unlikely to be made.

The first person to work out how to motivate by email and phone will make a fortune. It is a fortune which is unlikely to be made.

For the team leader, building trust at a distance is especially hard. All teams need affective trust and communication to function well. When working within an office, building trust and maintaining good communication is challenging enough. Misunderstandings arise spontaneously. At least in the office, you can quickly spot and deal with these misunderstandings so that trust is not destroyed. Working across borders, the likelihood of misunderstanding rises because it is harder to communicate at all, and messages get lost in translation. So misunderstandings fester and then trust erodes.

Global teams can fall into negative feedback loops fast. Here is how one hedge fund described the relatively limited challenge of managing between New York and London: 'A natural reaction is that we need tighter controls to manage America but then that shows that we don't trust them which doesn't engender the right response either. In London there is a constant conversation so we can keep on adjusting, but in New York it is much more about formal communications with London. You really miss the water cooler communications which allow constant adapting.'[25]

It is impossible to micro-manage a global team: you cannot micro-manage when you are asleep and your team works in a language you don't speak and a culture you don't understand. You have to find a different way of leading. You have to build trust, delegate, make decisions and manage performance at a distance.

2. The global leadership challenge: IQ, EQ and PQ

Global team leaders don't just need high skills: they need a different set of skills. Global teams demand a new sort of leadership.

Leading a global team instead of a domestic team changes everything. To understand why, it is worth looking at how management has evolved, and how global leadership now represents the future of leadership.

Nineteenth century: the IQ era

In the past, management was the art of making things happen through other people. Managers had to get ideas out of their heads and into the hands of workers, who were not that well educated or trained. Managers were meant to be smart, and have relatively high IQ. That expectation creates two traps for leaders today. First, many experts stumble into the trap of thinking that leading is about being smart. This means that they find it very hard to let go. They want to demonstrate their expertise by doing the work themselves instead of delegating to their team. On a global team, this trap is bigger because the global team leader is expected to have expertise. But expertise is not enough. Vastari, which connects museums and collectors, clearly needs deep art expertise, but even it recognises that 'it is not enough to have a PhD; you also have to have the business skills, interpersonal skills and the integrity. You need the human touch. We look for the hunger to achieve our shared mission.'[26]

Second, team members are now better educated and better trained. They can do more, but they also expect more. Managers have had to learn to manage people as individuals, not as unreliable machines. This is the 'human touch' which Vastari referred to. Being smart is not enough: managing people requires EQ, or emotional quotient.

Twentieth century: the rise of EQ

Times have moved on and the EQ challenge has grown. In the past, managers were making things happen through people they controlled. Now managers are meant to make things happen through people who they may not control. That is the joy of working in a matrix organisation. Unlike in the past, where your authority equalled your responsibility, in a matrix your responsibility routinely exceeds your authority. That means managers have to learn a whole new set of skills around influencing and motivating people to make things happen.

Global teams raise the stakes even further for EQ. In global teams you have to make things happen through people you don't control, may not understand and may not even have met because they are dispersed around the world. In-country managers have the benefit of working with people who probably have a similar education, values and even social background. Such cohesiveness makes communication and decision making relatively easy, even though there is much that gets lost in translation between IT and marketing, or finance and sales. Global managers lose the benefits of cohesiveness and easy communication. If you cannot communicate well, then motivating, delegating, performance managing, decision making and all the other basics of management become very hard. This is extreme management.

As a global leader, you need more than EQ: you need cultural intelligence. This is the ability to learn, grow and adapt fast to new situations and new cultures. Being fixed in your ways may work domestically where the context is stable and familiar; when the context has changed, you have to change.

Twenty-first century: the advent of PQ

Global management requires learning another layer of skills, in addition to the intellectual and emotional (IQ and EQ) skills that in-country managers have to learn. Global managers need to learn another whole skill set: the art of politics. We might call this 'political quotient' (PQ), to go alongside the traditional skills of IQ and EQ.

Politics is sometimes seen as a grubby subject in firms: it is seen to be about who is climbing the greasy pole and who is falling off it. But politics is not grubby. It is the essence of how organisations work. To make things happen through people you do not control, you have to forge alliances, align agendas, negotiate for resources, influence decisions, build top-management support, and work trade-offs and conflicts. That puts politics at the heart of making the organisation work for you and with you. Perhaps inevitably, these are precisely the skills which business schools and training courses ignore, but managers cannot afford to ignore.

These political skills are essential in most matrix and flat organisations where you do not control all the resources you need.

Managing politics is always hard: managing politics remotely is far harder. You have to manage decision-making processes which may be in a different time zone and different language, where you have no chance of bumping into key executives for those informal five-minute conversations

Global team leadership is extreme leadership: if you can lead a global team, you can lead any team.

which can help sell an idea and give valuable insight into who is thinking and saying what.

Global team leadership is extreme leadership: if you can lead a global team, you can lead any team.

3. Global team leaders: deploying IQ, EQ and PQ in a global context

IQ

The old paradigm of leadership was that the bosses had the brains and the workers had the hands. The job of the boss was to get the idea out of their head and into the hands of the workers. The boss was the brain on legs. As team members have more education and better qualifications, some bosses have tried to stay ahead of their team by being even smarter and more technically knowledgeable. This is a dead end, because ultimately there will always be someone younger, hungrier and with more up-to-date skills waiting to fill your shoes. In a global team, that smarter and hungrier person may come from a low-cost country and work on one-quarter of your income. If you rely on being smarter than everyone else, be ready to see your job 'best shored' somewhere else.

There will always be someone younger, hungrier and with more up-to-date skills waiting to fill your shoes.

For the global team leader, IQ is not about being the smartest person on the team. Your job as global team leader is to liberate the talent of the team. The mindset is different. The global team leader has to 'believe that the ecosystem is smarter than any of us', in the words of Purnima Kochikar, Head of Games and Apps at Google.

For a global leader, as with any modern leader, IQ is not about the number of degrees you hold. IQ is not academic: it is practical. Ultimately, IQ for managers is about pattern recognition. You learn from experience what works and what does not work. You can then build your own personal success formula which works in your unique context. As soon as you go global, everything changes. Conditions vary from country to country and from task to task which makes it hard to spot consistent patterns of success.

This is where there is a role for both the individual and the firm. The firm should see the patterns of success among its global leadership teams: a true learning organisation will package and disseminate this so that team leaders can accelerate their learning (see the text box on learning from experience fast). Your role is to take responsibility for your learning journey: stay curious and learn actively.

How to build your leadership IQ

In workshops, I ask people how they have learned to lead. I let them select two of the following six factors as their main sources of learning, and you might see which two you select:

▶ Books

▶ Courses

▶ Peers

▶ Role models (inside or outside work)

▶ Bosses (positive or negative lessons)

▶ Experience.

Virtually no one choose books or courses, which could be bad news for an author who delivers workshops. Nearly everyone chooses personal experience first, and then some form of second-hand experience: bosses, peers and role models. This is natural, but problematic, especially for global team leaders. There are two problems. First, experience is often a random walk. A random walk of learning can be painful if you find you are learning from negative role models and experience. Second, it is a slow way to learn. If 'experience' is the entry ticket to global leadership, then that is a good way of locking out the young and the talented.

You need a way of accelerating and structuring your learning. That is where, to this author's personal relief, books and courses come into play. Books may not transform you into a global leader on page 298, but they help you make sense of the nonsense you see and help you structure your journey to leadership.

We have already noted that pattern recognition is the vital ingredient which lies behind ideas like 'business judgement', 'experience' and even 'IQ'. Books are not the only way of acquiring pattern recognition. Firms can help package and structure experience so that managers can learn the intuition of what works. This is different from training, which is generic: it is customised and packaged experience based on the unique context of the firm. The text box on the following page shows how this can be achieved.

Learning from experience fast: the power of pattern recognition

Advertising is notoriously hard to judge. In the words of John Wanamaker,[27] one of the pioneers of advertising and marketing: 'Half the money I spend on advertising is wasted; the trouble is I don't know which half.' This is the challenge of traditional TV and print advertising where you cannot gauge consumer responses directly. It takes years of experience to judge how well new advertising might work. So how can you package this intuitive experience and become an expert fast?

It does not take years to acquire judgement about advertising: it takes one afternoon. As a new brand manager, I was faced with the challenge of working out whether Daz advertising would work or not. I spent an afternoon looking through every piece of Daz advertising for 50 years in the P&G library. Alongside each piece of advertising were the key performance metrics achieved by the advertising, which at that time was Day After Recall (DAR).[28] By the end of the afternoon, I had seen an entire social history of Britain over 50 years: commercials went from 90-second black and white mini dramas to 30-second bold and colourful blitzes. I had also seen enough patterns in the advertising that I could predict closely what the performance metrics would be for any piece of Daz advertising.

Good global leaders need endless curiosity. Good global leaders need endless curiosity about the people around them, about new cultures and about how things work. You should not wait for the years of the random walk of experience to build your success model. Look at other success models; look for where patterns of success have been bottled for you: this book helps on that learning journey.

The biggest challenge for global leaders is to recognise that they need to learn and adapt to new patterns of success. The more successful a leader has been in a domestic context, the harder it is for them to adapt. Once they have built up their personal success model based on familiar patterns of failure and success, they are reluctant to give it up. What works in Baltimore does not necessarily work in Berlin, Bangalore or Beijing.

EQ[29]

EQ is about knowing how to deal with people: other people and yourself. Neither is easy, and both are harder in a global context.

Churchill said of Russia that it 'is a riddle wrapped in a mystery inside an enigma'.[30] People are even more of a riddle, mystery and enigma. The challenge facing practising managers is to find workable answers to that riddle, mystery and enigma, knowing that the answer will be different for each person they encounter. That is why EQ is so hard. Churchill sniffed the answer to the Russian riddle: 'perhaps there is a key. That key is Russian national interest.' As with Russia, so with people: the key is personal interest because ultimately we are all the heroes of our own life stories.

It is hard to deal with people across the office, but even harder to deal with people across the world, for the same reasons that it is hard to influence them remotely: we do not see them day to day; we lack common bonds of interests, values and experiences; we think and act differently.

If EQ is hard within a local office, it is far harder with a global team. The core EQ skills encompass:[31]

▶ Self-awareness: this is not about being in touch with your inner self, but being aware of how you affect other people. Knowing how you affect people you do not see and may not understand is hard. Global EQ is harder than domestic EQ because you are not getting all the visual cues which tell you how others are responding to you.

▶ Self-regulation: we are all good at self-regulation when times are good. Self-regulation becomes important in times of stress, ambiguity and uncertainty. That is when you need to be positive and professional. The need to exercise self-regulation increases dramatically when you are faced with the complexity, uncertainty and ambiguity of global working.

▶ Internal motivation, which creates a passion for work that goes beyond external rewards.[32]

▶ Empathy: you have to understand your team members if you are to manage them well. But if you cannot see them and find talking to them hard, your relationship is going to be transactional rather than personal: creating empathy at a distance is an unknown art.

▶ Social skills: these are normally built by personal interaction which cannot happen remotely. Learning how to motivate, encourage, build trust and build relationships remotely again raises the EQ bar dramatically for global managers.

For the global manager we can add two more essential EQ skills, which are also mindset skills: curiosity and accountability.

Curiosity and EQ

Curiosity is essential: managers lacking curiosity have a fixed mindset which can be a 'my way or no way' approach. That leads to team conflict. From around the world, there was a consistent view that a good team leader or team member has to have curiosity:

▶ China: 'They should truly want to explore new cultures and new ways of doing things'[33]

▶ United States: 'We look for four things in the people we recruit: happy, helpful, curious and accountable'[34]

▶ United Kingdom: 'We look to employ people who are intellectually rigorous and naturally curious'[35]

▶ India: 'You need to have an interest in global things: politics, arts, travel, food'[36]

▶ Europe: 'The passion to learn and the passion for the craft is very important'[37]

▶ Japan: 'Global team members must be open minded. They must be flexible like a football team, not a baseball team'.[38]

Curiosity is vital for two reasons. In a global team it is very easy to judge others and to judge them negatively, especially when the unexpected or unwanted happens. The curious mindset does not try to judge: it tries to understand and learn. If we judge, we set up conflict. If we attempt to understand and learn, then we can build trust and make progress. On good days, most managers have the time and space to be open to learning and understanding. On tough days when there are tight deadlines and things are going awry, learning and understanding can go out of the window.

Curiosity is also vital to making the most of the team. Making the most of the talents of the team does not mean imposing your own way. That is the traditional style of leadership where the boss has the brains and the team has the hands. In the words of one Japanese insurance executive, 'You cannot do things solely in a Japanese way and you cannot do things solely in an English way. We might decide in an English way and execute in a Japanese way. Or we might decide in a Japanese way and execute in an English way. This unique blend could be the differentiator against competitors and also a strength of ours'. Each team has to make the most of its diverse talents, and that requires curiosity and openness from the team leader who must discover and develop the talents of the team.

'Good leaders must adapt, not copy and paste their previous experience into the new firm'.[39] This runs against the instincts of most managers: if something works, you do more of it. Don't change a winning formula. In a domestic context, where the context is relatively stable, that makes good sense. In the global context, it can be a very dangerous instinct because when the context changes, then the

> **Good leaders must adapt, not copy and paste their previous experience into the new firm.**

success formula also has to change. Global team leaders have to be open, flexible and adaptable. You need curiosity and the courage to learn and to change how you work. This is a very different profile of leader from domestic leaders.

Accountability and EQ

The accountability mindset can be elusive in a global team. When things go wrong it is easy to blame others who are not present. When the team cannot influence decisions at head office which affect them, it is natural to grumble about the iniquity and arrogance of head office. Grumbling and blaming are classic symptoms of the victim mindset, not the accountable mindset. The victim mindset believes that the locus of control is elsewhere: the victim is at the mercy of events, people and a largely unfair world.

The accountability mindset does not blame others when things go wrong. Instead of blaming remote colleagues, you need what one organisation calls 'positive regard'. Work on the assumption that the other party is doing their best. You then work together to find a way forward, instead of conducting an inquisition to find out what went wrong.

Instead of grumbling about head office, the accountability mindset means that you take responsibility for influencing decisions, finding out what networks work, making contact and if necessary finding the budget to go and meet the key stakeholders. As we will see in the section on PQ, this is very hard to do in a global context.

The accountability mindset is also different from the traditional corporate mindset. The corporate mindset links control to formal authority and focuses on performing well within a clearly defined role. This may work on a domestic team, but not on a global team. The global team leader has to influence decisions, people and events beyond their immediate area of formal control.

The differences between the corporate, victim and accountable mindsets are summarised in the table below. Each mindset is based on different beliefs about where the locus control lies and how much self-efficacy the leader has. As a global team leader, you need the accountable mindset and have to foster it in the rest of the team.

The accountability mindset

Factor	Corporate mindset	Accountable mindset	Victim mindset
Locus of control	You believe your control is defined by your formal responsibilities, role and authority	You believe you can control your destiny and your environment	You believe you are shaped by events around you which you cannot control
Self-efficacy	You focus on performing well within your area of responsibility	You take on new challenges beyond your remit and learn and grow	You avoid new challenges and stick with a stable and familiar role

Even high-flying global team leaders can fall into the victim mindset. It is commonplace to hear them complaining about not being understood, not being able to influence decisions and feeling left out of the loop. That is understandable in a global organisation. But it is also a victim mindset. As the COO of one high-powered financial services firm put it: 'people will say that they cannot get access to someone and they can't meet so-and-so. But then I say: why don't you just fly over and meet them? I would happily pay for their flight. If they fly over they can get more connected. Instead of complaining and feeling like a victim they should take responsibility and make the connection themselves.'[40]

PQ

PQ[41] is about making the global network work for you, extending your sphere of influence and impact far beyond your formal budget and authority. PQ is fairly natural and easy in an office environment because you:

▶ see everyone else more or less daily

▶ build bonds of trust (and occasionally mistrust) naturally over the years

▶ understand each manager's agenda and style by working with them

▶ know who counts and who does not count for different decisions

▶ speak the same language as everyone else

▶ share broadly similar backgrounds in terms of education and culture with your colleagues.

Even with all these advantages, managing internal politics is widely seen as a huge drain of time and effort, but people do it because they have to if they are to perform well.

The global team leader has none of these advantages when they are distant from head office. This is one reason global team leaders often come from the home nation: they already have the networks of trust and knowledge which will let them protect and support their global team.

In practical terms, global managers need two strong PQ skills: influencing skills and trust skills. Building trust is so important that it merits a chapter all of its own. Trust does not arise spontaneously. You can learn how to build and sustain trust systematically, and the chapter on trust shows how.

Influencing skills can also be learned. Influence is different from persuasion. Persuasion is about a transaction; influence is about a relationship. And they push against each other. If I am very persuasive, I might persuade you to do or buy something you later regret. Next time you see me, I will probably find my ability to persuade you

Persuasion is about a transaction; influence is about a relationship.

has evaporated. In contrast, when you influence someone successfully, then they willingly want to work with you, and will actively seek you out. Influence is a subtler art than persuasion, but pays far greater dividends in the long term.

Global managers have to learn how to influence people, decisions and events remotely. This is the subject of another book: *How to Influence and*

Persuade.[42] At the risk of trivialising the book, some of the ideas of how to influence people and decisions are captured below.

Ten principles for building personal influence

1 **Build rapport**
   Find common ground, common interests, common experience.

2 **Align your agendas**
   Find out how they see the world, what they need, want and fear. Work your agenda to fit with theirs: don't start with your agenda and mindlessly inflict it on them.

3 **Listen**
   The more you listen, the more you find out about them and the more they relax. Smart questions work better than smart ideas.

4 **Flatter**

   > **There is no point at which flattery becomes counterproductive.**

   There is no point at which flattery becomes counterproductive:[43] no one thinks they are over-promoted, over-recognised and over-paid. If you recognise their innate genius, diligence and humanity, they will be in awe of your very fine judgement and will reciprocate.

5 **Build commitment incrementally**
   Don't ask for everything all at once: don't scare them. Ask for small commitments and limited involvement. Let the commitments build.

6 **Build your trust and credibility**
   Always deliver on your commitments and always set expectations clearly.

7 **Manage risk**
   People are risk averse. Remove perceived risk and personal risk; show that you can be trusted to deliver on commitments.

8 **Put scarcity to work**
   Find something they want which you can give. And then make them work for it: they will value it more than if you give it away.

9 **Something for something: reciprocity works**
   Don't give something for nothing: it sets the wrong expectations.

10 Act the part: the partnership principle

Act as their partner and equal, not as a supplicant. You want an adult-to-adult conversation, not a parent–child conversation.[44]

As you read the ten principles of influence, you will recognise a familiar pattern: these skills are far harder to deploy in a global context than they are in a domestic context. Take just the second principle: aligning agendas. This requires understanding who is thinking what, who has what priorities and what they might object to. Discovering this within the same office takes time and frequent contact with the key stakeholders. Discovering this when you are not in the flow of small talk and big talk is harder. It is far easier for leaders at the hub to deploy PQ to align agendas than it is for leaders at the spokes. Power naturally flows into the centre and stays there.

But if leaders at the spokes have the accountability mindset, they will not assume that they are powerless to influence their destiny. The example of the LBGT film festival shows how a global leader with a clear vision and a strong sense of accountability can influence and align agendas to achieve their desired goal.

The LBGT film festival[45]

Alan Gemmell, Country Director Israel, decided that he wanted to run a global LBGT campaign based on a film festival for the British Council. The British Council operates in 110 countries with its main HQ in London. Alan was aware this would be a 'first' for the British Council and technically as a Country Director he didn't have the remit, budget or authority to create a global campaign.

The idea was not without challenges. The British Council is not a campaigning organisation and there were certain sensitivities to be considered, including the fact that the British Council operates in countries where LGBT rights and even being gay can lead to imprisonment or violence against individuals. Additionally, promoting an LBGT film festival could wreck the British Council's own reputation in some countries. Also, Alan had set himself the goal of launching the festival in two months which meant arranging everything from film rights to building the technical platform to enable global participation.

So Alan put PQ to work. He worked with his networks to show key decision makers how the festival might support their agenda, while carefully pre-empting the many potential objections. He did what in Japanese is known as *kuuki o yomu*: he read the air. Some executives wanted to promote digital capabilities, others wanted to focus on the human rights issues and others again believed in the core LBGT mission. For doubters, he was able to show that it was low cost, the content would be suitable, LBGT groups supported it and it would be easy to roll out globally because the collateral was available; countries could choose their level of engagement to respect local laws and culture; the UK government supported it. The key was that each stakeholder had a different agenda: Alan had to show that the film festival either supported their agenda or at least did not violate it.

Leaders in complex organisations will recognise that this is standard operating procedure, albeit under extreme circumstances. PQ is about aligning agendas and making the network work to achieve things well beyond your formal sphere of influence. Alan had the advantage that he personally knew much of the network from prior experience: that is an advantage many global team leaders do not have.

Following the success of the campaign, Five Films for Freedom[46] became a staple in the British Council calendar and Alan took charge of India in what was a major promotion. PQ works for the group and the individual.

4. Leadership from the centre: the invisible puppet master

A leadership paradox emerged in the research: a vocal minority of interviewees did not see a great need for leadership. Some went further and saw too much leadership as positively dangerous:

▶ 'Some teams can work despite having no team leader or sponsor.'[47]

▶ 'I have worked on projects with rubbish leadership, but they have worked.'[48]

▶ 'Some of our team wants leadership like a drug: they rely on their leader, not on their own accountability. The more you give leadership, the more you reduce their autonomy and leadership.'[49]

The statement about too much leadership reducing autonomy and accountability points the way to resolving the paradox; it also points towards the desired role of the global leader. The role of the global leader is not to direct and manage things day to day. In the words of John Ridding, the CEO of the Financial Times: 'as someone smart once said, the clock has three hands, second, minute and hour, and you need to be aware of all three simultaneously – the immediate, the medium term and the long term.' Many leaders get stuck watching the second hand: they are micro-managing day-to-day activities. The global leader cannot ignore the second hand but also has to keep an eye on the hour hand: the leader has to see into the future and create the conditions for the team to succeed.

Effective global leaders see their role as enabling, not directing:

▶ 'You cannot micro-manage people when you are working across borders, because you will always be behind.'[50]

▶ 'I see my role as a connector of people and ideas.'[51]

▶ 'I need to protect my direct reports ... I prepare the ladder for them to climb up.'[52]

▶ 'I have to exercise leadership without authority.'[53]

▶ 'You should always work with a boss who takes care of you and who helps you to learn and to grow.'[54]

This is not the traditional view of leadership: the visible, lone hero guiding the army to triumph. It is less about directing people and more about enabling people. Enabling the team and creating the conditions for success is not a leadership cop-out: it is both vital and difficult to achieve. The requirements for making the global team succeed are outlined in the diagram below:

Global teams leadership agenda

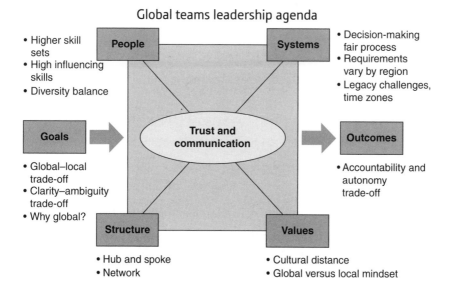

• Higher skill sets
• High influencing skills
• Diversity balance

People

Systems

• Decision-making fair process
• Requirements vary by region
• Legacy challenges, time zones

Goals

Trust and communication

Outcomes

• Global–local trade-off
• Clarity–ambiguity trade-off
• Why global?

• Accountability and autonomy trade-off

Structure

Values

• Hub and spoke
• Network

• Cultural distance
• Global versus local mindset

Each element of this leadership agenda raises questions and challenges for the global team leader:

Goals

▶ How can I manage the trade-off between global needs and local needs?

▶ How can I make sure everyone understands the goals, their context and why they are relevant in each location?

▶ How can I make sure the goals are shared across geographies, rather than just mandated from the centre?

▶ How can I align everyone's disparate skills and perspectives in one direction?

People

▶ How can I find team members with the right skills, values and mindset for working on a global team?

▶ How can I motivate and support people I do not see often, who are not like me and who I may not fully understand?

▶ How can I ensure individuals are treated equitably wherever they are based?

Systems

▶ How can I influence global decisions when I am far from the decision makers and may not speak their language?

▶ How can I protect the vital interests of the team?

▶ How do I manage the different technical and management systems across the world?

Values

▶ How can I create a common language, understanding and way of working across the team?

▶ What are the core values that all team members must have?

▶ How can I build a global mindset of mutual respect across the team?

▶ How can the team bridge very different cultures and mindsets?

Structure

▶ What is the right team structure?

▶ How can we manage decisions effectively within the team?

▶ How can we bridge the different perspectives and agendas of hub and rim?

▶ How can we create clear roles and responsibilities without creating geographic silos?

Trust

▶ How can I build credibility, intimacy and trust with people I do not see and who are different from me?

▶ How can I build trust between team members who rely on each other but do not see or know each other?

▶ How can I build trust between the centre and the team, so that the team is properly empowered and supported?

Communications

▶ How do I manage communications across time zones, languages and cultures?

▶ What are the right technologies and protocols for communicating with and across the team?

▶ How can we avoid misunderstandings and build a culture of positive regard in communications?

Outcomes

▶ How can I performance manage people when I cannot see how they are working?

▶ How do I give feedback effectively in different cultures?

▶ How can I encourage appropriate levels of autonomy across the team?

▶ How can I encourage accountability, rather than delegating problems upwards?

The value of the global leader is not in micro-managing. The challenges of people, values, systems, structure and communications are faced by all leaders. But the nature of the challenge is different and more intense for the global leader. The value of the global leader is not in micro-managing; it is in creating the conditions for success. The hand of the leader may be invisible to the team, but it is vital.

5. The global leadership agenda and the gender agenda

The research on global teams did not set out with a gender agenda. But it soon hit us fairly forcibly. Nearly all the people who were working on global teams outside the centre were male. Overall, 25 per cent of interviewees were female. Just 6 per cent of the interviewees with P&L responsibility were female. The pipeline of future global leaders is male dominated.

The purpose of this book is not to argue about whether gender balance is desirable in its own right; instead, it is to look at what makes a global team work well. And in this chapter we have seen that global leadership requires a particular set of skills. A quick comparison of two types of leader below will make the point:

Type Y leader	Type X leader
Command	Influence
Control	Collaborate
Task focus	People focus
Risk taking	Risk management
IQ	EQ

Type X fits the traditional mould of leadership; type Y fits the new world of global leadership.

Type Y also fits the normal stereotype of males: we might call it type XY in homage to the male chromosomes. Type X (or type XX for the female chromosomes) fits more neatly with the stereotype of female behaviour. There is, of course, huge risk in stereotyping any group based on gender, nationality, race, religion or anything else. Trade books tend to trumpet gender differences and make out that male and female leadership styles are fundamentally different. The academic research does not support this, although it does detect some differences.

Professor Alice H Eagly[55] conducted a meta-analysis of the available research and found:

'Sex-related differences are present in leadership style. However, these differences take the form of highly overlapping distributions of women and men — in other words, the differences are small. One of these differences is that female leaders, on the average, are more democratic and participative than their male counterparts.'[56]

To the extent that there are differences, they seem to favour the female stereotype. That should be good news in the long term for creating gender balance at the top levels of global organisations. But females are not appearing on global teams. Only 4 per cent of all interviewees were females working outside their home country. Given the random nature of the sample, this data may not be statistically significant but it fits with the patterns perceived by most interviewees.

The global lifestyle does not sit easily with family life. Depending on where you are, conference calls may start regularly at 10pm and/or 6am. Travel is a constant: some global managers relish their platinum cards from airlines and hotels. They are testament to time devoted to work, not family. Juggling work and home in a demanding job is hard enough. The global dimension to that challenge makes the juggling act more or less impossible and forces a choice between family and work. The evidence we saw in who was available for interview was that the choice still splits on traditional lines: men prioritise being the breadwinner over being the home maker.

The pipeline of future global leaders is being filled by men, even though global teams could benefit from more female leadership.

The pipeline of future global leaders is being filled by men, even though global teams could benefit from more female leadership.

6. Are you ready for the global leadership challenge?

To rise to the global leadership challenge you need both skill and will. Skills can be learned, but will has to come from within, and that is a very personal decision. During the research, it soon became clear that global work attracts a different sort of person who is strongly motivated to work globally. This was expressed in three ways:

Learning and global outlook

Most already had global experience, and had enjoyed it and learned from it. They had embraced local culture and local ways of working. This stands in contrast to 'some executives with vast global experience have not learned anything: they just impose their views on the environment and are very domineering'.[57] In one extreme case, executives lived in a *gaijin* (foreigners') area in Tokyo; they were chauffeured to their office to avoid encountering locals on the metro; they went to the floor where all the other foreign executives worked; after work they returned to the Tokyo American club. They lived in a bubble which minimised their contact with Japan. They were domestic managers who had no interest in global work. The firm was a global leader in photography. It is now bankrupt.

Global experience means immersing yourself in the local culture and business: effective global leaders relish this. Ineffective global leaders try to replicate their domestic experience wherever they are in the world.

To succeed globally, you need a global outlook. Truly global firms look for leaders who can see beyond their home country perspective. Laird, a specialist global technology company, is clear about this: 'You must have a senior team that does not see the world by country.'[58]

Personal enjoyment

In some firms, enthusiasm is seen as a certifiable disease. But if you are going to put in the extra effort and the anti-social hours required to succeed on the global stage, you need to enjoy what you do. You only succeed at what you enjoy. Nearly all the global leaders expressed a strong and positive preference for continuing to work globally, for the sheer fun of it:

▶ 'I always enjoy different cultures and meeting exotic people and being able to visit exotic places: that's where you get different ideas.'[59]

▶ 'It's fun to work in a global job to expand the business.'[60]

▶ 'It's fascinating, it's interesting and it's exciting for the business. My most interesting experiences have always been at global companies, for instance at MI6 and McKinsey.'[61]

▶ 'Working globally just broadens your mind and challenges everything you take for granted. It sharpens your mind and makes you learn different ways of dealing with people.'[62]

▶ 'Visiting new countries is like tourism: you see new cultures. Tourism is just pictures for one week, but doing real business is much more interesting. You find out much more about the local culture.'[63]

Fear of the alternative

Their desire to continuing to work globally was matched by a fear of returning to head office, which was generally seen negatively. Partly this was about becoming a small fish in a big pond, which is an awkward transition to make if you have been used to being a big fish in a small pond. But head office was also seen as a place where small-minded people with limited world views play politics with each other. In contrast, global working gives leaders the chance to test themselves, to see the difference they make, and to learn and to grow fast.

For many leaders, global working is not just a career choice; it is a lifestyle choice as well. Wanting the global lifestyle is one thing: having the ability to succeed is another. This chapter has shown that global leaders need to be exceptionally good at the core leadership skills which all managers need to have; they also need a deeper set of skills and beliefs if they are to succeed. These beliefs are set out below:

Domestic manager	Global manager
Clarity and focus are vital to effectiveness and efficiency	Ambiguity and uncertainty creates great opportunities
I need control to succeed	I influence people, events and decisions to succeed

▶

Domestic manager	Global manager
Overseas colleagues need to do more to understand how we operate successfully	How can I learn more and achieve more with our overseas colleagues?
Can I really trust my overseas colleagues to deliver?	How can I earn the trust of my overseas colleagues?
I have mastery of my craft	I have mastery of my craft – and people regularly turn to me for advice
I prefer familiar food, music, films and holidays	I prefer to try new food, music, films and holidays

The profile of the domestic manager is that of a traditional domestic manager. In practice, domestic management is moving in the direction of global management. Domestic managers are having to become much more comfortable with ambiguity; they have to have a growth mindset which is open to learning; they have to be able to control through influence, not power. The difference between global and local leadership is more a question of degree than a comparison of opposites.

Use the checklist on the previous page to see how closely you fit the global or local leadership paradigm. Global leadership is not for everyone: global leaders will have no doubt where they stand. Doubt is a sign of someone who is probably more effective as a local leader.

Taking on a global leadership role is a huge leap into the unknown for most people. It poses huge personal, family and career questions:

▶ Will I succeed in a new role in a new country?

▶ How will my family cope with a different culture, different language, and no network of friends and family in close support?

▶ Will there still be a job for me if and when I return to my home base? Can I believe that the promises made to me will be honoured by someone else in three years' time?

▶ What if it does not work out for professional or personal reasons?

These are deeply personal decisions about career and lifestyle. Rising to the global leadership challenge is a one-way leap: once you have made the leap from local to global, you may find it very hard to make the leap back from global to local.

Conclusions

Leading a global team is a great test and a great opportunity for any leader: if you can lead a global team, you can lead any team. The skills you acquire as a global leader are the skills that all leaders of the future will need. The three skill sets of IQ, EQ and PQ are a combination of traditional leadership skills and new leadership skills.

Leading a global team raises the bar in terms of skills. Even traditional skills are harder to deliver in a context where you have to overcome the challenges of distance: you are separated in terms of time, culture, language and geography from the people you lead and from the stakeholders you need to influence. When you cannot see people day to day, the challenges of motivation, performance management, decision making, problem solving and delegation become far greater.

In addition to traditional leadership skills, you need new skills: these new skills are the skills of global leaders and of all future leaders. As a global leader, you learn to acquire and use influence, not just authority; deal with ambiguity, variety and complexity; lead remotely, not face to face, and build commitment, not just compliance across your team.

Success as a global leader is Darwinian. Success is not about being the smartest person in the firm, or even in the room. Success is about how fast you can learn, grow and adapt to a new context. Working in a new and diverse environment means that any success model you built up in a domestic environment will have limited use in the global environment.

Success is about how fast you can learn, grow and adapt to a new context.

For the firm, the challenge is to identify and develop these global leaders. Identifying global team leaders is about finding people with the right mindset. You can train skills, but you cannot train mindset. Firms which are superficially global develop leaders from a very limited pot: their own home nation. This deters the best global talent from joining the firm, however prestigious it may be in its home nation. Truly global firms find, retain, develop and promote the best talent wherever it is in the world. To succeed globally, you need global talent.

PART TWO
Teams without borders

4

CHAPTER FOUR

Trust

The glue that binds the team

Trust is the invisible glue that keeps teams, families and society together. Only when it is missing do we discover how important it is and how hard it is to build. For global teams trust is vital. Trust enables your team to bridge the challenges of physical and cultural distance. Specifically, it drives six enablers of team performance:

▶ Delegation

▶ Accountability

▶ Decision making

▶ Constructive conflict

▶ Team support

▶ Motivation.

Building trust in a global team is a challenge for three reasons:

▶ Physical distance makes it far harder to know other team members.

▶ Cultural distance makes misunderstanding far easier.

▶ Global teams deal with high stakes challenges which require higher levels of trust.

Given this, it is no surprise that global team members see trust as one of the biggest determinants of success or failure. Seventy-two per cent rated trust as one of the top five factors for their team. But the nature of trust is asymmetric: it means different things to team members and team leaders. The team leader is mainly concerned about whether team members have the capability and capacity to deliver. Team members are more concerned about whether they can trust management to look after their interests.

One type of trust is about credibility, the other is about values alignment. Both types of trust are essential in a high-performing team. Focusing on just one type of trust is like running on one leg: you can make progress, but not very well.

This chapter will show:

▶ the nature of trust in global teams

▶ how trust drives performance

▶ how teams can build and sustain trust.

The power of trust

To discover the power of trust, pick up a dollar bill.

On one side it will have a portrait of George Washington. On the other side it will proudly proclaim 'In God We Trust'. Regardless of your religious beliefs, the real trust is in the piece of paper you are holding. It is worth one dollar because you believe it is worth one dollar, and so does everyone else. It is not like a cow, or a gold coin, which has intrinsic although debatable value. It is a piece of greenish paper. But you can convert these pieces of paper into cows, gold or whatever you want if you have enough pieces of paper.

What would happen if everyone looked at the paper and decided that it was worth as much as any other bit of small, dirty, second-hand paper? Chaos would ensue as we resorted to barter. If I went to a coffee shop I would have to barter a chapter or two of my book for a coffee, or twelve minutes of a motivational speech for a coffee, and a slice of cake would be another problematic negotiation.

Trust affects everything we do. We may worry about crime, but we normally assume we can walk to the shops without getting mugged or murdered; we trust that contracts will be honoured; we trust that food and water is safe. When trust is abused, we are rightly shocked.

Without trust, nothing works. Without trust, nothing works. Trust is a fundamental building block of making society and global teams work.

The nature of trust in global teams

Trust is a small word with a big but elusive meaning. We all know what trust feels like when we experience it, and when we lose it. But defining it is hard. It is like leadership: we know it when we encounter it but everyone has a different way of defining it.

Before leaping into a trust discussion, we will define what it means here. Over many years I have found one tool to be the most useful for explaining trust: the trust equation.[64] Here it is:

$$t = \frac{i \times c}{s \times r}$$

Here is how it breaks down:

t = trust

i = intimacy

c = credibility

s = self-orientation (or selfishness)

r = risk

To put it simply, credibility and intimacy build trust. Intimacy is sometimes referred to as affective or personal trust. It comes from shared values, shared experiences, shared social, educational and cultural backgrounds. None of this comes pre-packed on a global team: affective trust does not come naturally. Credibility comes from a track record of consistently delivering on expectations. On a global team, your track record is unknown, so you have to earn trust all over again.

Self-orientation and risk work against intimacy and credibility, for different reasons. Someone who is highly self-oriented, or plain selfish, finds it hard to build trust. They are clearly in it for themselves, not for the team. Team members will find it hard to trust such a person. Risk is important because the higher the risk of a situation, the more trust is required. Since global teams are often working for high stakes, that implies they require high levels of trust. As we shall see, building credibility and intimacy on a global team is far harder than on a domestic team where people are likely to know each other.

It is no surprise that trust figures so highly as an issue for global teams. Compared to domestic teams, the need for trust is far higher but the ability to build trust is far lower. It is a perfect mismatch.

We will briefly explore each element of the trust equation and show how it can build or erode trust on global teams.

Intimacy: personal or affective trust

Personal trust comes from having shared values and backgrounds. Friendship is based on personal trust. This matters in business because we instinctively prefer to work with people like ourselves. That creates a huge bias in recruitment and promotion decisions. This unconscious bias creates a homogeneous culture, especially at the top of the firm. While diversity is valued and promoted in many cultures, conformity is valued more in others.

We are the ones with exotic values and beliefs. The desire for personal trust is a challenge for global teams. Any global team will be full of people 'not like us'. They will have different values, beliefs and perspectives. The problem is not just that they are not like us: the problem is that we are not like them. If our starting point is that they are the people with exotic values and beliefs, we will find it hard to bridge the gap. Our starting point should be to see that we are the ones with exotic values and beliefs: see how our behaviour looks odd to others. Then we can start to understand each other and respect each other.

Personal trust and relationships are seen as a nice to have extra in the Anglo and Germanic worlds. In many cultures, personal trust is a must-have, not a nice-to-have. There is a reason that many business conversations in the Middle East start with personal chit chat. It is not wasting time; it is a way of finding personal trust: why would you do business with someone you do not trust?

Of course, personal trust is not enough. We all have friends who we like and trust personally, but we would never hire them as colleagues. Trust in colleagues needs the professional trust which comes from deep credibility.

Credibility: professional trust

Credibility is about professional trust. Credibility comes from doing as you say, consistently. The obvious challenge is doing. The less obvious challenge is not what you do, but what you say: setting expectations clearly. People tend to hear what they want to hear. When you say that you 'will try' or you will 'do your best', the listener hears that you 'will'. One month later you can honestly say that you 'tried' and 'did your best', only to be met with silent anger that you did not deliver. Credibility will have been lost not because of what you did, but because of what you said. It is better to have a difficult conversation early about expectations than to have an even more difficult conversation later about results.

On global teams it can be hard for both linguistic and cul- **'Getting to yes' is** tural reasons to have difficult conversations. At a simple **not enough.** level, what is said clearly at one end may not be understood at the other end for linguistic reasons. But communication may also fail for cultural reasons. Difficult conversations are even more difficult where there is a culture of conflict aversion, respect and a desire to please. This is where you discover that 'getting to yes' is not enough because 'yes' means different things in different cultures. For instance, here is one experience working with colleagues in India where economic necessity clashed with cultural reality:

'I was based in America and we were under pressure to outsource work to India over- night. If I said to India will you do A and B and C they would say: "yes I understand. It is doable and we have the resources". But then the deliverables would always fall short. I was being charged out at $350 an hour but India was at $15 an hour so there was huge pressure to farm out stuff to India. We never sat down with them and we never saw them. It was all email communication. In many cases you got back in the morning and found that you had to fix all the work that had been sent from India.'[65]

If you want something done, you have to explore what lies behind the yes: what are the obstacles to success, what resources are required and what tim- ing is possible? Getting to *si, ja, oui, hai* and *da* is not enough, despite the protestations of the *Harvard Business Review*.[66] On a global team credibility is occasionally lost through poor work; more often it is lost by failing to set expectations clearly from the outset. If you are in a position of power, then you will find that more conflict averse and hierarchical cultures will not push back when they need to. They will say 'yes' to please you, and the 'yes' will be a statement that they intend to do their best.

Two further examples will make the point that 'yes' is not enough in any language:

▶ 'My German colleagues spoke idiomatic English, but that did not mean that they agreed. After each meeting where they had agreed I would get a long email explaining why they disagreed.'[67]

▶ In Japan *'hai'* often implies understanding, not agreement or commitment. Depending on context, *'hai'* can mean:

▶ yes

▶ I'm here

▶ I understand

▶ I am about to speak

▶ what?

Your task is to understand the nature of the 'yes' and explore what is required to convert the 'yes' from a statement of goodwill into a firm commitment to outcomes.

Equally, if you are the one making the promises, be careful what you promise. If there are any assumptions, conditions, support required, potential obstacles, risks or concerns, make sure that these are fully understood before you commit. Your credibility hinges on what you say as much as what you do. But ultimately, you have to deliver and you have to deliver consistently. Consistency is essential because that makes you predictable and reliable: 'We build trust through consistency. This means we know how each person is going to act because they should be consistent and predictable. That means when they act in an unexpected way I start to lose trust in them'.[68]

Risk

Risk is like kryptonite to trust. The higher the risk, the greater the trust required. You may trust a stranger in the street to give you directions to the post office. You would be unwise to trust the stranger with your life savings. On global teams, risk is high. Global teams are not created for trivial reasons. They tend to work on high-profile and high-impact challenges. Global team members depend on relative strangers to help them deliver outcomes and to perform. That makes them high profile and high risk for each team member. Trust is at a premium on global teams. But building trust is particularly hard. Trust and global teams form the perfect storm.

Risk is like kryptonite to trust.

When managers think about risk, they normally think about rational risk. This is the sort of risk which will appear in risk logs, with heat scores and mitigating actions. This sort of risk is worth understanding, and most firms do a reasonable job of understanding it. But there is a far greater sort of risk which affects managers, and is rarely spoken about and rarely managed: personal and emotional risk.[69]

On a global team there will be plenty of logical risks: maybe deadlines will not be met, or deliverables will not be up to standard. The team will know how to manage that. But for team members, risk is personal:

▶ Can I trust colleagues who I do not know or see, to deliver?

▶ If the project works well, will I be recognised for my efforts? What if things go awry?

▶ How can I manage expectations and avoid over-commitment?

▶ How can I influence decisions which will affect me when I don't know the decision makers?

▶ Am I really in control of my destiny?

These are real and natural risks which team members face. If the team leader wants full commitment, then these concerns have to be addressed as much as the rational risks associated with the project plan. Managing personal risks remotely with people you rarely see is not easy.

Self-orientation

The final element of trust is self-orientation. It is human nature that we all believe that we are at the centre of our own universe. But team work requires that we put the needs of the team ahead of our personal needs occasionally. We have all worked on teams where one or two people are pursuing their own agendas. The effect on the rest of the team is toxic. The team is only as strong as its weakest link. A selfish person is a weak team player. This is universal; put simply, 'self-orientation destroys trust'.[70]

In a domestic team it is fairly easy to know who is playing for the team and who is playing for themselves. You can see who is doing what day to day. Even if you cannot see them directly, the office grapevine offers plenty of intelligence about how people are doing. On a global team there is no way of knowing how people are behaving. You can make a request, and it is hard to judge how much time and effort it takes. For instance, if you ask for some local market data, one country might be able to find it in an hour from published sources. Another country might spend a week working intensely to generate equivalent data which is not as good. All you see is the outcome, and where outcomes are weak it is easy to draw negative conclusions around competence, effort or priorities.

The trust equation shows that building trust is both important and hard in any team, and that it is even more important and even harder in a global team. Fortunately, the trust equation not only diagnoses the problem, but also prescribes the solution. By working on building intimacy and credibility while managing risk and self-orientation, you can build a high-trust and high-performance team.

The next section of this chapter shows how trust builds performance. The final section shows how you can use the trust equation to build trust in a global team.

How trust drives performance

Trust is essential to a global team because it enables five habits which all effective teams need:

- Constructive conflict
- Delegation
- Accountability
- Teamwork
- Effective communication.

Each of these themes is explored briefly below.

Trust and constructive conflict

Surprisingly, conflict powers strong organisations and strong teams. This not about conflict with external competition. It is about internal conflict within the team and within the organisation. Some of the best team-based organisations make conflict a core value. McKinsey regard an obligation to dissent as essential: 'everyone is supposed to have an equal voice and is expected to contribute to discussions — voicing your dissent is not optional, it is required.'[71] This sort of challenge does not weaken the team; it strengthens the team.

Conflict powers strong organisations and strong teams.

If a global team, or any team, is to achieve a high-impact goal it needs to be sure it is going about it the right way. It also needs each team member to be committed fully to both the ends and the means. Any doubt about either leads to uncertainty, doubt and low commitment. It is not enough to have passive compliance from global team members: you need active commitment. Active commitment only comes about when each team member completely understands and buys into the goals and methods of the team: that requires a culture where doubts can be aired, not hidden. Speaking out appropriately leads to constructive conflict and strengthens the team and its approach. But speaking out can only happen in a high-trust environment where speaking out is encouraged, not sanctioned.

In the past, leaders were expected to be like old-fashioned bosses: they had the brains and set the direction for the team. But no one on a global team has a monopoly on wisdom. The knowledge and judgement of the group is nearly always greater than that of any one team member. Team exercises like desert survival or moon survival[72] ask individuals to select from a list the most important pieces of survival equipment. Routinely, the final group decision is better than the best individual decision. That means you need healthy debate and disagreement before you find the optimal solution.

The natural instinct in many teams is to compromise in order to avoid causing offence and to maintain team harmony. But this leads to sub-optimal solutions to which no one is fully committed. It means deeper challenges remain unresolved. But the conflict has to be constructive. As one team member from Serbia put it:

'I have a really high level of trust that I can speak up and disagree and say what I believe and my views will be respected. I trust that even if I disagree we will come to a conclusion and then work together to make it happen. In previous jobs I put up mental walls which meant that I should not say this or that. Those walls do not exist here.'[73]

High-performance teams need a culture where it is safe and there is encouragement to speak up. It needs to be safe for people to speak out: 'you want a high performance team where you have adversarial conflict in a safe environment so you can push the boundaries without being thrown under the bus. To be competitive you need to change all the time, so that means you need conflicts.'[74] Encouraging team members to have their say leads to better decisions and higher commitment.

Culturally, many societies avoid any sort of conflict, healthy or otherwise; loss of face and criticism of bosses are not acceptable:

▶ 'Thai teams take a long time to build trust with foreigners because initially they feel insecure with foreigners. It may take 3 to 6 months to create trust. You do not get a completely open dialogue and it does not happen in a week.'[75]

▶ 'When I say something to my team in India they will question me more but if a Brit says something they will blindly do it until the trust has built enough to stabilise the team and to encourage them to challenge where they need to go, and that may take six or 12 months.'[76]

There are no short cuts to building the sort of trust where everyone feels confident enough to express themselves. You have to invest the time to build the relationship and track record. This is a challenge to leaders from the Anglo sphere who expect to hit the ground running and find out what is happening immediately. Getting to the truth takes time and patience.

Trust and delegation

There are plenty of reasons for not delegating:

▶ I can do it better myself.

▶ I can do it faster myself.

▶ I need to take personal responsibility for this.

▶ The team don't have the skills for this.

▶ This is too important to delegate.

These reasons require a little translation, which all team members intuitively understand:

▶ I can do it better myself: I don't trust my team to do it well.

▶ I can do it faster myself: I don't trust my team to do it promptly.

▶ I need to take personal responsibility for this: I don't trust my team at all.

▶ The team don't have the skills for this: I still don't trust my team.

▶ This is too important to delegate: I will never trust my team on anything worthwhile.

Essentially, every reason is the same reason: I don't trust my team. Lack of delegation leads to stress and overload for the leader, and to loss of morale and commitment from the team. It is discouraging to find that you are not trusted with significant tasks.

In global teams the trust to delegate can be elusive, because there are often unspoken fears about the capabilities of other team members around the world:

▶ 'We had run down our local expertise but kept it in headquarters: so the HQ team did not trust the local people very much because they had not got the same level of skills.'[77]

▶ 'We either attract someone who wants to be a big fish in a small pond or someone who wants a lifestyle change. But the really A* people want to be a big fish in a big pond and it is hard to attract them. So it is hard to trust these people completely when the stakes are high.'[78]

These fears may be unspoken, but they are well understood by team members. When they are delegated no meaningful tasks, it is natural for them to disengage, which leads to a vicious circle. As team members disengage, performance slips, which confirms to the team leader that delegation does not work. Here's how one COO of a global team describes the problem: 'poor performance creates a negative feedback loop of tighter controls and lower trust leading to poorer performance'.[79] The challenges of physical, cultural and linguistic distance make it hard to break the circle of declining trust on both sides. Misunderstanding breeds mistrust.

In place of the vicious circle of declining trust and delegation, it is possible to create a virtuous spiral of increasing trust and delegation. Effective delegation not only eases the burden on the team leaders, but also empowers and motivates the team, which results in better performance and more delegation.

Trust and accountability

Accountability is essential for performance management. Without accountability it is hard to measure or manage performance. Accountability marches hand in hand with delegation.

In a global team, accountability requires higher levels of trust than for a domestic team.

In a global team, accountability requires higher levels of trust than for a domestic team.

In a domestic team, it is easier to correct mistakes in real time because the team and its management and all the corporate support systems are working at the same time. In a global team, you have to trust that other parts of the team will make the right decisions on your behalf while you are asleep. They may be making high stakes decisions which you cannot reverse.

For instance, a hedge fund operates globally. Its control systems can prevent non-compliant trades but cannot prevent dumb trades. These trades will happen across time zones when one or more centres will be closed. Unwinding a poor trade can be very costly. New York can only delegate to London and vice versa if they have complete confidence in each other.

Trust is also vital for corporate communication. Paul Abrahams is accountable for corporate communications at RELX, a London-based international information and analytics group with $9 billion annual revenues. His boss, the CEO, is on the road for 180 days a year. It is simply not practical to clear every routine communication with him, and the pressures of 24-hour news mean fast responses may be required on occasion. Effective working requires clear accountability and delegation, which in turn depends on trust.

Trust and teamwork

Trust is vital between team members. In the words of Mike Jedraszak:[80] 'You have to trust that you are pulling in the same direction and you will look after each other especially when there are mistakes.' Trust is particularly important in times of stress and when things go awry: 'Working in a global organisation you realise that people see the world in a completely different way. Therefore when something unexpected happens you have to recognise that what they are saying and doing isn't their way of challenging you.'[81] In times of stress trust helps the team pull together, not pull apart.

Within a local team this mutual support is relatively easy to achieve. You can see when someone is struggling or staying late. And it is easy for team members to ask for help from someone sitting nearby. Supportive relationships grow naturally. Building supportive relationships remotely is not at all natural. It is hard to ask for help from people you don't know in a distant time zone and it is hard to offer help when you cannot see and do not know who needs help. Relationships across the team become reduced to a series of arms'-length transactions. Any high-performing team is based on strong relationships, not on transactions.

Trust and communication

Trust and communication is a two-way street. Better communication builds trust and more trust enables better communication. Trust-building communication is not about effective broadcasting. Elements of trust-building communication include:

Trust and communication is a two-way street.

▶ Listening
▶ Transparency
▶ Brave honesty.

Listening

It is normal for team members not to understand each other on global teams. It is also normal for central management not to understand each region and vice versa. When we are not being understood, it is human nature to repeat ourselves and explain things more clearly so that we can be understood better.

But the problem is not that other people do not understand us. The problem is that we do not understand other team members properly. Speaking more may make us feel better but it does not solve the problem of understanding. To be understood, first we have to understand.

Effective team members have the characteristics of effective leaders and sales people: they have two ears and one mouth. And they use them in that proportion. Listen twice as much as you speak.

Effective team members they have two ears and one mouth. And they use them in that proportion.

Listening helps you in three ways.

First, it helps understanding: 'Leaders have to put themselves in other people's shoes. They have to understand why things matter to other people and understand not just what they are saying but why they are saying it.'[82] When we understand what the other person thinks, want and needs, we can present our thoughts in a way that makes sense to them. We can tailor our message so that it is heard and understood.

Second, listening is a good way of making the other person shut up. If someone thinks they have not been heard, they will remain in transmit mode: they will keep talking until they are satisfied that you have heard them. They will only go into receive mode once they have completed their transmission. So let them know they have been heard and understood through active listening: paraphrase back to them what they are saying. Your summary will assure them that they have been heard, and will keep their transmission short.

The third reason listening helps is because it is flattering. Research show that there is no point at which flattery becomes counter-productive, in any culture.[83] Listening flatters because it shows you are interested in what the other person has to say. In a time-short world where we feel under-recognised, it is flattering when someone invests scarce time listening to us, and apparently valuing what we have to say. Listening shows selflessness, the opposite of self-orientation. It is a short cut to building relationships across borders.

As a leader, you have four levels of listening and communicating:

▶ Talking, not listening. This is the old-fashioned leader's form of communication. It looks strong but is ineffective: the leader has no way of knowing what has been heard, understood or accepted.

▶ Passive listening. This where listening is defined as not talking, or more precisely as waiting for the other person to shut up so you can make your point. At least it lets the other person talk, but it leads to no understanding or meeting of minds.

▶ Active listening. This involves paraphrasing back to the speaker, in your own words, what you have heard them say. This flatters them, avoids misunderstandings and enables you to tailor your message so that it is understood and accepted.

▶ Active listening and positive regard. This trusts that the other person is acting and speaking with goodwill and avoids jumping to negative conclusions: it builds trust and makes it easier to have difficult conversations around disagreements and expectations.

Global teams require high trust and that requires high listening skills: active listening with positive regard.

Transparency

Transparency builds trust for three reasons. Transparency enables:

▶ Better control and support

▶ Better context and understanding for team members

▶ Better ways of raising and dealing with bad news

Better control and support

Some of the most innovative work on making global teams work is being done by some of the smallest global organisations. Both The House Media and Modern Tribe[84] are web design agencies which work globally and have fewer than 60 staff or contractors. One is based in San Francisco, the other is in London. They both take transparency to an extreme (see text box). **High transparency can work either as a tool of coercive control, or as a way of enabling autonomy based on high trust.** This level of transparency demands high trust but also gives high trust. High transparency can work either as a tool of coercive control, or as a way of enabling autonomy based on high trust. The House Media and Modern Tribe clearly use transparency to enable highly dispersed team members to work autonomously around a lifestyle which works for each individual. Transparency is about support and trust, not coercion and control.

Extreme transparency

The House Media and Modern Tribe are web design agencies which face the same challenge of co-ordinating the work of highly talented, highly dispersed talent around the world to meet tight deadlines from demanding clients. Both have, independently, created similar solutions to the challenges of global working, based on extreme transparency.

Shane Pearlman, CEO of Modern Tribe, describes how he works: 'We manage the queue of work tightly with Scrum.[85] We also have a daily stand-up meeting where every team member meets every day and goes through everything on

▶

their docket using the YTB format: Yesterday, Today and Blockers, and we also ask if they really need a meeting. Everything must have a single owner: you can always ask for help, but you are still accountable.'

Michael Murdoch, CEO of The House Media, also uses technology to create total transparency: 'Slack.com can keep you up-to-date on the whole chat very fast. You never miss anything. Trello.com is a project management tool which connects us to the client and to developers. It keeps a full record of all the conversations. It avoids confusion and it is easy to follow and to catch up. Internally we used to have 100 emails a day, but now it's down to 25 a day and all are from clients, because all our team conversations are in Slack or Trello.'

The aim is always to help people complete their task quickly and creatively. So let people know what the goal is. Dropbox helps with this, because it is all stored in the cloud and everyone can see what is there without me having to be the gatekeeper. But I can still see what is going on.'

The technology solutions may differ, but the intent is the same: everyone has total visibility of progress; they also have high autonomy and can write their own work tickets and decide when to progress their ticket through the system to show progress. This avoids surprises and enables support to be brought in promptly, where and when required.

This level of transparency could be abused to create a coercive culture of tight control, but that is the opposite of what Murdoch and Pearlman intend. In Pearlman's words: 'We want to create a space to help people work together as a lifestyle.' But this is also a high-performance lifestyle: 'Regardless of where you live, it could be San Francisco or Bolivia, or you can live on the beach in California, or you can have four kids or none, I don't care: I will pay you the same because work is work regardless of your background.'

Transparency requires trust and builds trust.

Context and understanding for team members

Transparency is about full disclosure, which should answer all the questions which all journalists are trained to answer for every story: what, who, when, where, how and why. Managers often focus on the obvious questions of what, who, when, where and how. But the most interesting question is often why. In the words of mad media mogul Elliot Carver in James Bond: 'When I was sixteen, I went to work for a newspaper in Hong Kong. It was a rag, but the editor taught me one important lesson. The key to a great story is not who, or what, or when, but why.'[86]

The key to a great story is not who, or what, or when, but why.

Asking why may not lead you to the brink of global domination, but it will help your global team work better. Investing time to communicate the context of how and why, in addition to who, what, when and where, is not just good communication: it builds trust.

The 'why' and 'how' questions matter. Two examples make the point:

▶ The Financial Times has a goal of having one million subscribers. There are good ways and bad ways of achieving that goal. Discounting and attracting price sensitive, disloyal customers would reach the one million target fast. But the Financial Times wants sticky customers who are actively engaged with the paper. That leads to a deep discussion about how. In the words of CEO John Ridding: 'we have to work out how we build engagement with our readers and how we build habit. We can measure engagement. And we are building a new access model to encourage greater engagement'.

▶ A Japanese insurer in London was required to serve the parent firm's[87] global clients' local needs in London, and be profitable. That raised a contradiction: many clients were unprofitable to serve outside Japan. So there had to be deep discussion about how to manage this trade-off. Should you drop clients, and if so how? How do you balance the need for local profitability while serving the global clients' needs?

There are always good and bad ways of reaching a target. In a global team, understanding this context is vital to making the right decisions and achieving the goal the right way.

Transparency and dealing with bad news

One CEO of a global bank was famous for his 'solutions' speech. It sounded great. The essence of it was: 'are you a solutions person or a problems person? I need solutions, not problems! So don't come to me with problems, come to me with solutions!' This sounds great as a platform speech. It was a terrible way of dealing with bad news. As the bank's loan book turned sour during 2006–7, management did what was natural: they avoided bringing the bad news to the table, because that would mark them out as problem people, not solutions people. By 2008 the bank had gone bust at a cost to the taxpayer of many billions of dollars, pounds or euros.

Transparency is very important for trust. Effective global leaders create an atmosphere of trust where bad news can come to the surface fast. Transparency is very important for trust. 'It is important to know what is going on. There has to be transparency, clarity and commitment to deliver what they say: it cannot just be lip service. I am always transparent and I will deliver bad news and watch the reaction.'[88]

In global teams, this level of trust is important because the team leader cannot micro-manage: you cannot look over someone's shoulder and see what is happening. You are remote from the work, so you have to trust the team to tell you what is really happening:

▶ 'In a global team top management are so far removed from the day to day that they can get it very wrong very fast so they must not micro-manage; instead they have to delegate.'[89]

▶ 'You cannot micro-manage people because you will always be behind when you are working across borders.'[90]

▶ 'Michael needed to micro-manage because we were new and we did not have the trust from him. But now we see why we both work the way we do. So now we have less micro-managing and more flow.'[91]

Leaders do not like surprises, not least of all because they are rarely good. In a global context, there is plenty of scope for misunderstanding, which leads to surprises. This means that you have to over-communicate, and communicate early to avoid or minimise surprise. Avoiding surprises is a consistent theme for global teams:

▶ 'If people are surprised by anything then they also become suspicious.'[92]

▶ 'One of our mantras is no surprises.'[93]

▶ 'You have to communicate risks early to avoid surprises.'[94]

Avoiding surprises requires brave honesty and open communication, which is not natural in many cultures, as we shall see in the next section.

Brave honesty

Politicians believe that they are honest if they have not been proven guilty in a court of law, and even then they will claim that they were misunderstood. Then

Telling the truth takes courage

they complain that no one trusts them. Politicians are the least trusted profession to tell the truth: 21 per cent of the population trust politicians, while 89 per cent trust doctors. They are even less trusted than estate agents (25 per cent), journalists (25 per cent) and bankers (37 per cent).[95] But before we mock these professions, some humility is required. Only 25 per cent trust business leaders to tell the truth. Telling the truth takes courage, and we all know when someone is shading the truth.

Trust-building communication requires a higher level of honesty, of the sort which courts expect of witnesses: the whole truth and nothing but the truth. The difficult bit is telling the whole truth, especially in societies which are hierarchical, respect based and conflict averse. Brave honesty is important in three areas:

▶ Setting expectations. Expectations are mutual. The team leader needs to be clear about what is expected, and team members need to be clear about what is possible. Unclear expectations on either side lead to unwelcome surprises and loss of trust.

▶ Project management. As with expectations and performance management, it is important to avoid surprises. Surprises are evidence of withheld information. You need brave honesty to raise unwelcome news. But if this is done early and constructively (with suggested solutions, not just problems), you will build trust.

▶ Performance management. In every culture managers dislike giving negative news to team members. Avoiding bad news until the formal annual appraisal destroys trust fast, because the bad news comes as a surprise. It shows that the manager has been withholding the truth from a team member. Having the difficult conversation early but constructively enables the team member to adjust course. Done well, the difficult conversation shows that you are committed to the success of your team member and it builds trust.

'Brave honesty' is culturally difficult in countries where there is focus on hierarchy and saving face. The Dutch are normally at one extreme in terms of brave honesty: they are likely to talk straight from the start. Indians, Thais and other Asians are often at the other extreme. Building a culture of brave honesty across a team takes time and finesse. If the Dutch are let loose on a Thai team from day one, there is likely to be a rapid breakdown of relations: the Thais will be offended by the straight talk, and the Dutch will be frustrated that they cannot find out what is going on.

How to build trust in global teams

Just as the change equation describes the nature of trust, so it provides a guide to how you can build trust. The two essential components of trust building are shared values and credibility. We will look at each in turn, from the perspective of team members. We will then look briefly at how the organisation can build a framework in which high-trust teams can be formed globally.

Creating shared values across a global team

Shared values encompass both a shared purpose and shared beliefs.

A high-trust global team starts with a shared purpose, or common goal. Everyone has to be pulling in the same direction. In the case of Mandarin Capital they hard-wire this in through the performance and compensation systems: everyone's compensation depends closely on everyone else, so teamwork is at a premium. In the words of Jenny Gao, managing partner at Mandarin Capital Partners: 'We decided to have the same evaluation, same carry interest, so we have shared purpose. That means you have to trust your team members to deliver for you because your compensation depends on their performance as well as yours.'[96]

In contrast, we noted another professional services firm where just 40 per cent of partner compensation was tied to global performance. With over 300 partners, each partner made the logical decision to focus on the 60 per cent of compensation they could control: their own performance. They paid only lip service to the idea of global working.

Shared values is often shorthand for: 'I wish everyone would share my values and beliefs.'

Shared values is often shorthand for: 'I wish everyone would share my values and beliefs.' To share values, first you have to understand each other's values. Values do not come from a carefully crafted values statement.

They are the product of daily behaviours which reflect daily beliefs. These beliefs will often reveal assumptions which are so deep that we do not even realise that they are assumptions.

A simple example makes the point: when should you speak up? It is standard practice to find that in any global meeting share of voice is very unevenly distributed across nationalities. Americans speak up and have the highest share of voice, followed by other English speakers and then other Europeans. Finally, it takes real effort to get the Japanese participants to say anything. And the reactions from each nationality are quite different: the Americans wonder whether the Japanese have anything worth saying, and the Japanese wonder why the Americans talk so much. The reactions of Japanese to Anglo culture shows there are things we take for granted:

- ▶ 'I was surprised by so many things, like taking holiday!'[97]
- ▶ 'In this country you are unlikely to say sorry or feel guilty.'[98]
- ▶ 'In Japan you can only talk when you are asked to talk. So IESE[99] was a total shock: I had to speak up because there were marks for class participation.'[100]
- ▶ 'Japanese people do not listen to other guys at the same level: they only listen to high level people. So I have to control them through their boss or an even higher guy.'[101]

And the Chinese are also different:

- ▶ 'The Chinese worry about different things. Italians worry about the downside, the Chinese don't understand why you worry about downside. Do you think you are going to fail? They only think about success.'[102]
- ▶ 'One challenge was to get the Chinese to think analytically. We try to create our own culture at CRU. Our Chinese are naturally good at telling facts and reporting government policy but they will not give their own views and they will not be open, unless pushed, so there are limits.'[103]
- ▶ 'Chinese companies have a much more formal hierarchy; in China they want a clear indication before a junior person is allowed to talk. In Europe anyone can talk, so we have to design each meeting carefully: who attends and who can talk and when they can talk.'[104]

Clearly, these differences have the ability to cause misunderstanding and loss of trust. And the critical point is that they are differences: we cannot assume that one set of values is better than another. So the challenge for a global team is to discover what the different values are, and to arrive at a common understanding about how to work together.

Shared values do not come from a carefully crafted values statement. They come from daily practice. Shared values are discovered, not designed. Discovering shared values takes time, which global teams do not have. There are two ways to short cut the discovery process.

Shared values are discovered, not designed.

Method one: spend time together socially

The most effective way to discover shared values and to build trust is to spend time together. Find an excuse for the team to meet in person. The formal agenda should have some value, be it around training, project planning, strategy development or understanding the customer. Of equal value is the informal agenda where team members spend time together and get to know each other. Time and again, global teams found these informal moments built trust and enhanced communication:

▶ 'We trekked around Iceland for a few days so after that those people have a very strong bond, they have a common experience which is difficult to recreate in any other way.'[105]

▶ 'Face-to-face is where you really get to know people and know how people feel and if they are burning out. One of the best things I did was to take the train from Paris to London with my Euro lead and I just found out so much more as result.'[106]

▶ 'We rented a 12th or 13th century mansion in Kent near London and went down there. It was a self-catering place which is very un-corporate. So we all had to do the cooking and cleaning together and planning meals. And that worked really well.'[107]

▶ 'We did a workshop on trust and then we did a mini Olympics such as throwing a paper plate in a straight line. We just had fun and it helped build trust a lot.'[108]

▶ 'At least once a year you need to sit down and get drunk with them so that when things get tough later in the year people default to goodwill rather than to frustration. I spend more money on our annual gatherings than I ever could on an office. Distributed working is not a cost saving. We put people in a socially cohesive context, such as kayaking for two days. It builds relationships which last for the rest of the year.'[109]

What most of these experiences have in common is that there was time invested in non-work activity. Having fun at the firm's expense may be seen as a waste of money, but it is not a waste: it is a critical investment in building trust as well as mutual understanding and respect. Once you have the personal trust, you can build the professional trust. The Anglo world tends to start with the professional relationship and only rarely works back to a personal relationship. Most Asian and Middle Eastern cultures start the other way around: they want to build the personal relationship first and then move to the professional relationship. This can be hugely frustrating to both sides when they first meet: the Anglo world will be annoyed by apparently having to waste time on small talk. The other side will be frustrated that they are getting pushed into talking about business before they know whether they can trust the person.

What is noticeable is the absence of formal team-building exercises in these examples. Formal team building is a mixed blessing. Some people love abseiling and team-building games, and many such activities are culturally specific: they work better with some cultures than others. Instead, find a way in which everyone on the team can interact socially. This means that gatherings of the global team should not be scheduled tightly with workshops and other formal work-related agenda items for 16 hours a day. That has the veneer of productivity, but misses the chance to invest in the social capital of the team. Create the space for the social interaction, so that the team can get to know each other properly.

Method two: work formally on understanding each other

Social interaction helps build understanding and intimacy across the team, but it can also be a random walk of interactions. At any global conference, tribal instincts take over: nationalities and functions do not mix. Attendees seek out people from their own nationality and function. The random walk of discovery may be entertaining, but it is inefficient. It makes sense to structure and accelerate the process of discovery.

Here are three simple ways of structuring and accelerating the discovery process for the team.

▶ Use standard team-building exercises. Exercises which help team members understand and value each other's differences help: MB/TI[110] is a stock exercise for such events. It has minimal academic standing, but the academics miss the point. MB/TI is not about discovering some deep psychological truth, it is a tool to help people understand and respect each other more.

▶ Conduct a critical events exercise to reveal the hidden assumptions and beliefs of different team members. Map out the most challenging events and situations the team is likely to face, and then work out how the team will deal with each situation. This creates a practice-based version of a team charter. Team charters tend to lay out fine principles which, like any plan, rarely survive first contact with reality. By focusing on real dilemmas, decisions and differences which the team is likely to face, the team can work out what in practice they will do.

▶ Work explicitly on national stereotypes: these exist in people's minds and create biases which make it hard to build trust. By bringing them out into the open, you help team members discover their own biases and you help them see how other people may see them. Perceptions may be false, but the consequences of perceptions are real and damaging. A typical stereotypes exercise is outlined in the table below. Part one lets team members vent and describe the typical stereotype of each nationality, which is often negative. Part two pushes the team to see the positive side of each stereotype. You can add a Part three which asks how each nationality could be even better.

Many other exercises are possible. The point of each exercise is to help team members discover that other people have different styles, and to value and respect those different styles. These exercises also hold a mirror up to each team member: they show that their style is not the only style and is not a perfect style. It is simply one way of doing things. These exercises create a language and a reference point for the team in future: they offer a non-confrontational way of discussing differences and finding a way forward for the team.

National stereotypes exercise

Nationality	Typically mentioned stereotype	Alternative perspective
Any foreigner	Why don't they understand us or speak our language? Can I trust them?	Why don't we understand them or speak their language? Can they trust us?
Americans	Loud, brash, pushy	Optimistic, energetic, can-do
Brits	Euphemistic, pessimistic—what do they really mean?	Fair play, flexible and open
French	Arrogant, intellectual and argumentative	Bringers of reason and insight
South Asians	Say 'yes' but then can't deliver	Partners who will do their best to please
Germans	Literal, dull and boring	Highly practical and reliable
Japanese	Never say anything: have they got anything worth saying?	High effort, high quality, high reliability and good team players
Chinese	Pushy; money and face focused	Hard working and focused

Building credibility across the team

Credibility is a different form of trust from values and intimacy. Intimacy is about personal or affective trust. We are all likely to have friends whom we trust in the sense of shared values and intimacy. Despite trusting them personally, there are a few we would never trust professionally. Personal and professional trust are different, although personal trust is seen as the gateway to professional trust in many cultures. In Anglo culture, professional trust comes first and foremost: personal trust follows.

Credibility is hard to win and easy to lose. There are very few short cuts to credibility. Time served with consistent reliability counts. And that makes credibility very tough for global teams which come together on an ad hoc basis.

> **Credibility is hard to win and easy to lose.**

For instance, Mitsui OSK Lines are a major shipping line and rely on agents around the world to handle their ships locally. The agents manage a huge amount of logistical detail: they cannot be micro-managed. They have to be trusted to get it right. And this was especially true in the days before the internet: fax is a remarkably good tool for encouraging delegation and trust, because you cannot manage detail by fax. The relationships with their agents go back generations:

Most of our agents work with us for many years. So it is very easy working with them: it's all about performance. Half of our agents have been working with MOL[111] 45 to 60 years from father to son. They are our eyes and ears in the local market so we rely on them. They are kind of family to us, based on trust and relationship.' [112]

Mitsui OSK Lines need agents they can absolutely trust in good times and bad: a track record which stretches over decades counts for everything.

In contrast, when credibility is lost it can be exceptionally hard to recover. We were working in a chemicals plant in central Japan and occasionally we heard the management talk about some terrible work done by a global and prestigious firm of consultants. The consultants were blacklisted and it was clear that it was a raw issue for the management. The consultants had zero credibility. They had performed their work 20 years previously.

The bias of most managers is to work with people they know and trust. One new Japanese partner at a large professional services firm got over the credibility problem by bringing all of his team with him, and all his clients followed as well. So the clients got a partner they trusted, and the partner got a team he trusted. Such wholesale moves of teams and clients are not unusual in professional or financial services, and have the ability to lead to litigation.

There are three ways to build credibility. The first two take time; the third way offers some short cuts.

Method one: always deliver; always

An inscription on the James Farley Post Office in New York City reads: 'Neither snow nor rain nor heat nor gloom of night stays these couriers from the swift completion of their appointed rounds.'

Trust is like a vase: it takes time and effort to build it, but it is very easy to break.

The US Post Office understood that you must always deliver if you are to stay in business. Excuses don't work if you want credibility. The reality is that credibility has to be earned: 'you don't declare trust; you have to gain trust'.[113] Earning trust comes from consistent delivery. Occasional flashes of brilliance do not build trust if there are also occasional failures. Trust is like a vase: it takes time and effort to build it, but it is very easy to break. Once it is broken, it is even harder to repair.

Method two: set expectations

We have already noted that credibility is about alignment between what you say and what you do. What you do matters, but it is also critical that what you say is clearly understood. Setting expectations is a vital part of credibility: only commit to what you can deliver. If there is any doubt about delivery, have the difficult conversation before you start. When you finish, do not assume that you have built credibility. Check that your contribution has been noted and meets expectations. Many managers avoid negative feedback, so you have to make sure that you deliver what they expect. If anything is amiss, you have a chance to correct it.

Method three: employ some short cuts

There are some short cuts which gain temporary credibility. They enable you to walk through doors which would otherwise be shut. But once through the door, you still have to earn the credibility you have borrowed by performing reliably.

Credibility can be granted from one of three main sources: referrals, qualifications and membership.

▶ Referrals count. If someone you trust refers you to someone else, you are more likely to give that person the benefit of the doubt than someone you have never heard of before: 'If someone I know and trust introduces me to somebody else I am more likely to trust that person.'[114]

▶ Qualifications are a powerful short cut to credibility in some professions. We will more or less happily submit to the tender care of a qualified dentist, but would probably be less keen on entrusting our teeth to a mechanic armed with a pair of pliers. Unfortunately, qualifications do not count for so much in management. Saying that you have an MBA does not assure you of a leadership position: with up to one million MBAs[115] being minted every year, the qualification is rapidly becoming devalued. Saying that you have an MBA from Harvard is likely to get a very mixed reaction.

▶ Membership of a credible organisation. This is hugely powerful. Doors open readily for partners of the big four accounting firms: KPMG, PwC, Accenture and Deloitte. The same partners suddenly find doors remain shut when they decide to leave and operate on their own. They have initial credibility because of their firm, not because of who they are. This works powerfully within firms as well as across firms.

Within a firm, credibility is to some degree granted simply by being a member of that firm. If you work at Goldman Sachs or McKinsey, you can be fairly sure that your colleagues will also be bright and highly driven overachievers: they would not have survived the recruiting process otherwise.

Other firms go to great lengths to develop common standards and common values, which makes it far easier to work across borders. Team members know that other team members will have a basic level of competence and some common values. For instance, GE invests over $1 billion a year in talent development[116] through its training centre at Crotonville and other hubs globally in Munich, Shanghai, Bengaluru, Abu Dhabi and Rio de Janeiro. These centres not only impart skills, they impart values.

Even within these firms, short cuts to credibility may be short but they are not strong. At the start of any assignment, there is normally a battle between the team leader and HR. The team leader will fight tooth and nail to bring on talent that can be trusted. Essentially, any talent that is available is questionable: if they are great talent, why aren't they assigned already? So the team leader will try to recruit known talent while HR will be pushing hard to place the untried and untested, along with a few others who may need a second chance. Absence of a good track record means that even in excellent firms credibility is not taken for granted.

Conclusions

Trust matters for three reasons:

▶ Trust is the currency of global leadership. It is better to be trusted than to be liked:[117] courting popularity is weak and popularity is fickle. But trust is lasting and gives you strength with your team.

▶ Trust is also the glue that binds your team together. A high-trust environment encourages open and honest conversations, which are essen-

tial if the team is to understand each other and
work well together.

▶ Trust helps to drive performance. It is easier to delegate and create a sense of autonomy and accountability with a team you trust: you do not have to
micro-manage them.

**Trust is the
currency of global
leadership. It
is better to be
trusted than to be
liked**

There are few short cuts to building trust. However, the trust equation gives
simple guidance on how you can go about building trust with your team:

▶ Build intimacy. Get to know each team member as a person. Meeting
face to face is a huge first step to building trust. Find excuses to bring
the team together: training, planning, workshops. Behind the formal
agenda, the informal social agenda of building trust pays huge dividends. Trust goes hand in hand with mutual understanding. Invest
time in knowing your team.

▶ Build credibility. Always deliver on promises, however small they may
be. And be very careful in setting expectations: people hear what they
want to hear, which may be different from what you think you said. It is
better to have a difficult conversation early about expectations, than to
have a far harder conversation later about how expectations were not
aligned or met.

▶ Be selfless. Show that you are prepared to put the interests of your team
ahead of your own immediate interests, at least occasionally. You are
very important in your followers' lives and they need to know that you
support them.

▶ Manage risk, which is personal to each member of your team. You can
do this in two ways. You can reduce risk by cutting up a large and risky
project into small, manageable pieces for your team. Even if the whole
journey is daunting, the next step may be simple. Second, you can
show that the risk of doing nothing is greater than the risk of the way
forward.

Although trust is the magic ingredient that makes global teams work, there
is no magic in building trust. It is a form of social capital which requires
investment of time and effort, but once you have made the investment it
pays a steady return.

5

Communications

Less noise, more understanding

'Many people communicate, few people connect'[118]

We live in an age of hyper-communication. Never has it been so easy for people to communicate with each other: the cost, speed and accessibility of communications today is beyond the dreams not just of our grandparents, but even of our parents.

And yet, global teams consistently see communications as one of their greatest challenges. So how can communications be so difficult in the golden age of communication?

In practice, global teams do not see the problem as being about communicating: they see it as one of understanding. We may communicate more than ever, but we understand as little as ever. Better communications does not always lead to better understanding.

We may communicate more than ever, but we understand as little as ever.

Global teams feel the communications and understanding problem keenly. Seventy-six per cent of interviewees rated communications as one of the top five challenges facing the team. This was not about having a common language, nor was it about technology. Only 8 per cent of interviewees saw common language as a challenge for the team. Even where the interviewee spoke the language of the parent firm, over 70 per cent still saw communications as a core challenge.

Many saw technology as part of the problem, not part of the solution. Technology may help communication, but it does not help understanding. Many teams feel that hyper-communication is now becoming

Technology may help communication, but it does not help understanding.

85

destructive. Technology increases the quantity and decreases the quality of communication. It also can be a huge time sink, distracting attention from the work in hand.

At the heart of the communication challenge is noise. The way we think affects how we encode and decode information. Our unconscious biases mean that information is distorted when we send and receive information.

In this chapter we will explore how global teams can deal with noise and how to communicate effectively:

1. The signal to noise challenge for global teams
2. Linguistic noise: semantics
3. Cultural noise
4. Psychological noise
5. Technology and noise
6. Effective communications and the use of technology

1. The signal to noise challenge for global teams

When global teams worry about communications, they are worrying about understanding. Communicating has never been easier, but understanding remains elusive. We all have experience of communicating something very clearly and very simply, and then finding that the other person has completely misunderstood what we have said. This is how conflict within the office and within the team arises. There has been honest speaking and honest listening, but the outcome is complete misunderstanding.

Misunderstanding arises because of the noise. Between the speaker and the listener there is a huge noise barrier which confuses the message. Neither party is aware of the noise, so they think they have understood each other. We may believe our signal has been clear, but the noise has distorted it. Noise scrambles the signal at both ends of the message: the sender does not always encode their intended message accurately and clearly; the receiver of the message scrambles

Noise scrambles the signal at both ends of the message the message by listening imperfectly and interpreting the message with their own personal and cultural assumptions. Both sender and receiver may act with the best of intentions and still fail to understand each other.

Communications theory holds that noise comes in four forms. Each form of noise is worse on a global team, which arguably has to contend with a fifth form of noise as well. The four standard forms of noise are:

1   Physical. Distractions such as noise, light, pop-up ads, excess heat or cold can all affect our attention.

2   Physiological. When we are tired, ill, on medication, hungry or thirsty, we all struggle with our concentration.

3   Psychological. We all have different ways of thinking and of processing information.

4   Semantic. Language can be a barrier to understanding, even for native speakers. Jargon, over-complex language, euphemisms and management-speak all hide the truth rather than illuminate it.

The fifth challenge is perhaps the greatest: cultural noise. What we say and how we hear things is determined by a set of invisible rules and assumptions which are so deep we do not even realise that we are making them. We could label this cultural noise as 'psychological' because it is about the way we think. But psychological noise in global teams can be driven as much by cultural assumptions as by individual choices. So it pays to separate out the two sources of noise:

▶   Psychological noise is driven mainly by individuals' choices about how they process information: these choices appear across many different cultures.

▶   Cultural noise is driven by the way different cultures process information: these are consistent patterns within a culture. They are commonly adopted by team members from those cultures.

All these sources of noise are a greater challenge for global teams. If we share an office, we know whether there are physical problems and we can deal with them: we can change the layout of the room, fix the air conditioning or find a quieter space as required. We cannot do that with a global team dispersed around the world. Time zones may require some team members to be attending from home, or from an airport or public transport where conditions are less than ideal.

Within an office we can also see if someone is not well, tired or hungry. We can see if they are not paying attention or if they are playing with their smartphone. We cannot see that remotely; even on Skype it can be hard to pick up the cues. Given the nature of global working, many global conference calls are arranged so people in East Asia are dialling in late at night and team members on the West Coast are joining early in the morning before they go to work. Not everyone is at their best late at night or early in the morning; and if they have been entertaining a client during the evening, then the last thing they need is the late-night conference call. Europeans are often the lucky ones on global calls: because Europe bridges the time zones between Asia and North America, Europeans often manage global calls during working hours. This makes them only dimly aware of the challenges their global colleagues face in terms of time zones and the physiological noise that creates.

However, these problems pale into comparison to the big three sources of noise: psychological, semantic and cultural. We will explore each of these in turn. At this stage, we simply need to note that these sources of noise scramble and distort communications.

When managers are faced with the challenge of making themselves understood, they normally focus on their signal. They will use two tactics:

▶ Amplify the signal: make sure the message is sent louder and clearer than before; repeat the message; use multiple platforms and channels to reinforce the message.

▶ Vary the signal: find different ways of expressing and explaining the signal so that it has more chance of being understood.

In a global team, both methods will fail:

▶ Amplifying the signal does not improve understanding. The noise is still distorting the signal, so the misunderstanding still remains. The result is increasing frustration from both speaker and listener.

▶ Varying the signal leads to further confusion: the more variations there are around a message, the more opportunities there are for misunderstanding as the noise distorts the signal.

Volume does not improve quality in communication, unless you are part of a heavy metal band.

For the same reason, technology does not help. It allows for far more communication, but it does not remove the sources of noise. As long as the noise remains, the message will be distorted and the misunderstanding will continue. Volume does not improve quality in communication, unless you are part of a heavy metal band.

In the following sections we will explore the big three sources of noise and how to deal with them:

▶ Semantic

▶ Psychological

▶ Cultural.

2. Linguistic noise: semantics

In the last chapter we saw that in Japan '*hai*' can mean:

▶ Yes – I agree.

▶ I am about to speak.

▶ What?

▶ I understand (but might not agree).

It is tempting to think this proves that Japan is a completely impenetrable culture for foreigners. But before we dismiss Japan so easily, let us see what 'yes' can mean in English:

▶ Yes – I agree.

▶ I understand and fundamentally disagree (think of a long drawn out 'yes' said thoughtfully and doubtfully).

▶ Success! (think of someone watching their team score a goal and giving a mini fist pump while exclaiming 'yes!').

▶ Can I help you?

So now the Anglo world appears to have a completely impenetrable language and culture where the simplest of words can mean fundamentally different things. For the Japanese, Americans and British, it is totally obvious what they mean when they say '*hai*' or 'yes', but foreigners who do not have the cultural context will not have the understanding. There are plenty of stories of western people thinking they have gained agreement when they hear '*hai*', only to be frustrated later when they find they are nowhere near agreement.

Context gives far more meaning to words. On a crowded tube in London, 'excuse me' has an extreme range of meanings depending on the tone of voice:

▶ Very polite: 'I am very sorry for troubling you, but would you mind if I squeeze past you?'

▶ Very rude: 'Stop being so selfish and just move out of my way!'

On a global team, context is elusive. On a video call, few will understand the cultural context; on a phone call there will be no visual context; on email there is no aural, visual or cultural context to clarify the message. Not surprisingly, many global team members dislike email intensely, as we shall see in the section on technology.

If simple language is easily garbled by noise, management language is far worse. Management language is already noisy: it distorts simple language in three ways:

▶ Management jargon

▶ Insider jargon

▶ Colloquialisms.

Management jargon

Management jargon is a plague, at least in the English language. Management jargon abuses the language in two main ways. First, it is used to give the speaker a veneer of sophistication, power or importance. Second, it is used to avoid saying awkward things: it can be a language of euphemism. Both sophistication and euphemism create noise around the message: native speakers will normally see their way through the noise, but that is much harder for non-native speakers.

Here are a few examples of management speak being used to project sophistication which does not exist:

▶ Strategic intent: anything we think is important today

▶ Core competence: something we think we might be good at

▶ Transformation: we are going to change something

▶ Paradigm shift: something is changing

▶ Value proposition: what our customers want

▶ Empower: get a colleague or customer to do your work.

You can add: core values, best practice, next practice, leverage, co-opetition and many more. You can create your own dictionary of shame by reading company reports, listening to business speakers or going to any business meeting. These grand words hide simple meanings. In the case of strategic intent and core competence, they represent a complete distortion of the original meanings of the two ideas.[119]

In contrast to these power words, management speak is full of euphemisms designed to avoid the awkward truth. Nowadays, virtually no one is laid off or fired. They are rightsized, offshored, best shored, delayered or occasionally even downsized or let go. And performance reviews are never negative. Typically, 90 per cent or more of staff will be rated above average. This is statistically impossible but emotionally inevitable, because anyone who is rated below average is a prime candidate for being rightsized. Performance weaknesses are described as development opportunities; crushing weaknesses might be described as a development challenge. All these euphemisms create noise which hide the awkward truth. Layering on cultural noise as well results in meaning being lost completely.

90 per cent or more of staff will be rated above average. This is statistically impossible but emotionally inevitable.

Insider jargon

Insider jargon serves two functions.

The positive function is that it serves as a shorthand which everyone in the organisation can understand. The negative function is that it is a good way of excluding and confusing outsiders. For instance, one restaurant chain manager mentioned '1326 P12MA is at 93 MSU'. That is completely meaningless to an outsider. It referred to one of their restaurant formats (13) and to its geographic location (26); P12MA referred to the previous 12 months' average performance on a unit adjusted basis (MSU); 93 showed that its performance was down against the index of 100. Explaining that in plain English is possible, but the jargon is quicker for the insider.

Within a global team you need a common language to ease communication: to outsiders this may seem like jargon. But consistent use of a common language helps everyone understand each other better, especially where many team members may be communicating in their second or third language. But creating this common language takes time and discipline. Here is how Laird, the specialist technology company, regard the language challenge:

Lack of consistency in language drives confusion. *'New leaders coming into the firm often like to bring in their own language, but we are very disciplined about language. For instance do we talk about employees or staff or associates? Should we talk about customers, clients or accounts? You have to be consistent especially for people who have English as a second language and 75% of our audience have English as a second or third language. Lack of consistency in language drives confusion. If you use a different word people will think you have a different meaning.'*[120]

It is not just language which needs to have a common basis. All communications need to work from a common basis. For instance, try saying these numbers, fast:

- ▶ 20,00,00,000
- ▶ 3,00,000

If you immediately answered '20 crores' and '3 lakh' you may well have a South Asian background. If you were confused, then you will have shared the experience of the STIR Education finance committee after it moved its global accounting function to India. They were surprised to find all the reports used lakhs and crores, which meant all the commas were in the 'wrong' places. A lakh is 100,000 or 1,00,000 in Indian notation; a crore is 10,000,000 or 1,00,00,000 in Indian notation. To Indian eyes, it was obvious what the numbers meant. Everyone else was plain confused. Standard forms of communication help everyone.

Colloquialisms

Perhaps the worst speakers of global English are the British and the North Americans. Perhaps the worst speakers of global English are the British and the North Americans: they use idiomatic English which is culturally rich and colourful. Idiomatic English enriches communication between native speakers and creates confusing noise for non-native speakers. Native speakers also tend to use longer words, longer sentences and more complex grammar, and they speak faster. Then they wonder why no one understands them at global meetings, where non-native English speakers understand each other perfectly.

Native speakers use colloquialisms without even realising it. One senior Nokia executive made a motivational speech about the future of the company where he said that Nokia would make a big bet on a new technology. The intended meaning was that Nokia was making a bold investment in the future. What was heard by the sales team was that the leadership was desperate and had resorted to gambling.[121] As it turned out, the sales team's interpretation was correct: Nokia did gamble and they lost, leading to their takeover by Microsoft.

Two forms of colloquialism that nearly always fail are jokes and sporting references. Jokes rarely translate well and sports are often culturally specific. Not everyone plays cricket, ice hockey, baseball, American football or even rugby. And even in countries where these sports are played, not everyone is keen on them. One health-care insurer made the obvious discovery that it needed gender balance: male sales reps with sporting small talk were not getting very far with female physicians and buyers in the United States. Common language is about a common culture, not just a common dictionary.

Common language is about a common culture, not just a common dictionary.

If jokes and sporting analogies are dangerous, then religious and political small talk is completely off limits: it is bound to cause offence to at least some people, and may also be illegal in many countries where freedom of speech broadly means that you are free to support the authorities as much as possible.

The one consolation for non-native speakers is that the British and North Americans are more than capable of misunderstanding each other. As Irish writer George Bernard Shaw put it: 'The United States and Britain are two nations divided by a common language.'[122] The power of television and the internet means that most of the semantic differences between the two countries are, more or less, understood. But it can still cause some confusion. Admitting that I was responsible for a detergent brand called Fairy Liquid in the UK was the source of amusement and embarrassment in America where a fairy was a derogatory way of referring to a gay person: managing gay liquid?

The bigger cause of confusion between Britain and North America, and across all global teams, is cultural noise. Even if the language is understood, cultural noise will distort the meaning. Cultural noise is the focus of the next section.

3. Cultural noise

When we travel to an exotic country we know we are in a different culture and make the effort to adjust. But cultural differences exist much closer to home, and are at least as dangerous because we do not see that they exist and so do not make the effort to adjust: confusion and misunderstanding is the outcome.

A study of Anglo-French leadership[123] showed just how much cultural noise can confuse relationships. To outsiders, France and England are close neighbours and look similar. But the study shows that when you travel by train 30 kilometres (or 20 miles, if you are British) through under the channel tunnel, suddenly everything changes. As one *chef de cabinet*[124] explained: 'You Brits are very pragmatic'. Most people would take this as a compliment: I had learned enough to know that from a French person, this was probably an insult. I asked for an explanation. The *chef de cabinet* continued: 'In France we are intellectually rigorous, so we work decisions from first principles. That means when we make a decision we can stick to it. But you Brits make a decision which is pragmatic today, but that means you might change your mind tomorrow. And because you have no body language, we don't know what you are really thinking. So we don't know what you are thinking, but we do know that you will change your mind.' To comfort me, he added: 'But don't worry, the Germans are worse.'

If culture can cause so much confusion over just 30km, over 15,000km the challenges are even greater.

Cultural noise changes everything. It changes:

▶ How people say things
▶ How people hear things
▶ What people will and will not say.

Cultural noise comes in more or less endless varieties.[125] Here, it is sufficient to highlight three of the differences which challenge global teams:

▶ Hierarchy versus democracy
▶ Task versus people
▶ Optimistic versus pragmatic.

Hierarchy versus democracy

Hierarchy, or its absence, dictates patterns of communication within a firm and within a team. The more hierarchy there is, the less direct communication there will be between the most junior and the most senior people. The more junior team members will be very uncomfortable challenging the boss, whereas in the more democratic languages challenge will absolutely be expected. Google, for instance, expects people to speak out regardless of the formal hierarchy:

'I was trying to hire for a hard to find European role: I was at the point of interview fatigue when I found someone who was very smart and I felt we could coach him on his style. Then someone two levels below me came and said: 'two months ago you talked about representing Google, do you really mean it?' I could not say no: so we decided not to go ahead with the hire. So that is about Google values: you have to be open to challenge and you have to hire to the right standard. You have communication channels where people can speak up. This meant that the next time I have my team together they realise they really can speak out.'[126]

In democratic cultures, the absence of challenge will be taken as assent and agreement. In the more hierarchical countries, the real challenge may start once the boss has left the room. This causes confusion where the leader is working on the basis of democracy (the team has agreed and committed) but the team is working on the basis of hierarchy (the leader has given guidance only). It is not unusual for Japanese leaders to give ambiguous guidance to their team: this enables the team to make decisions without having to defer to the hierarchy.

Hierarchy can also mean that much is left unsaid. Even in democratic cultures, the boss often does not get feedback: they are the last to know that their team does not value them. It is even harder in deferential cultures for the boss to hear what the team really thinks. In the words of a Singapore-based leader:[127] 'I don't think people understand how much leaders value feedback. There is very little feedback, and that is a cultural issue in Asia where people are very deferential in expressing their views, even if they are strongly held.'

Hierarchy is baked into some languages. China attempted to remove the hierarchy from language in the Cultural Revolution. Everyone was meant to be called 'comrade'. But language has a way of striking back, at work and at home. At work, bosses are referred to by name and title. The founder of Alibaba may be an informal sounding Jack Ma to the West; internally, people refer to him as Ma Zong: Boss Ma Even within the family, names remain hierarchical: the first born was *laoda* ('the big one'); the second child *laoer* or, literally, 'number two'. Vanke, a Chinese property developer, has resorted to fining team members Rmb100 if they use '*zong*' or 'boss' to address bosses.[128] It

Language creates and reinforces different ways of thinking.

would sound weird in English to address someone as 'Senior Vice President Smith' or 'Facilities Manager Jones'. Language creates and reinforces different ways of thinking.

Japan is, arguably, a respect based language. When you speak, you are not just conveying meaning: you are conveying different levels of respect depending on your status relative to the person you are speaking to. Even simple things like a greeting are said differently depending on the status of the two people speaking. If you see two Japanese meet for the first time, they will both bow and immediately reach for their *meishi* (business cards) which will be politely exchanged with both hands outstretched. Western people would immediately check the name and greet the person by name. The Japanese will read the person's title and position and the company they work for to understand their relative status. In

***Meishi* are guides to who should bow first, deepest and longest.**

effect, *Meishi* are guides to who should bow first, deepest and longest. As the two business people read the cards, the higher-status person will draw up slightly from the bow; the other person will bow more deeply and energetically.

Even French has the use of *tu* to address friends and family and *vous* to address colleagues; both Italy and Germany will use people's titles (doctor, professor, engineer) widely. In contrast, English is an extraordinarily democratic language. The veneer of equality minimises the linguistic and cultural obstacles to having open discussions between leadership and team members. Some team leaders encourage such open discussion, others do not.

Although hierarchy does not exist in the English language, it exists strongly in accents: 'It is impossible for an Englishman to open his mouth without making some other Englishman hate or despise him.'[129] Accents in England define both the geography and status of the speaker. Fortunately, non-native speakers are exempted from this ruthless caste system.

In summary, hierarchy creates two main types of noise relative to more democratic cultures:

▶ Team leaders do not receive open feedback.
▶ Decisions are not easily challenged or discussed.

A global team with little open discussion and little feedback to the leader will struggle to be its best.

Task versus people focus

In the chapter on trust we explored the difference between two types of trust:

▶ Affective or personal trust, based on shared values, experiences and beliefs
▶ Credibility, or professional trust, based on skills and track record.

Cultures which lead with affective trust are people focused; cultures which lead with credibility are task focused. This changes what they talk about and how they talk: it is a source of confusing noise. At a simple level, team members will expect to talk about different things when they first meet. Affective cultures will make extensive small talk so they can get to know each other; task-focused cultures will want to get straight down to business. And when the cultures collide, both sides will be frustrated. The affective culture will be frustrated that they can build no personal trust before starting on business talk; the task culture will be frustrated by the waste of time on small talk.

Task- versus people-focused cultures also differ in how they deal with conflict. Task-focused cultures will be direct when there is a problem. They will see that they are dealing with the problem in a professional manner. The people-focused culture will take offence: they will believe that the person, not the problem, is being attacked. More people-focused cultures will be more indirect in raising issues and concerns, with the result that the task-focused culture may not even realise that a problem or concern has been raised.

Being indirect is a way of being polite and avoiding conflict, but it can also result in a lack of understanding. Here is a typical example of where an indirect culture meets a direct culture:

'I said something like: "that is a really interesting idea, it is very bold. Perhaps we can look at it in a different way?" And then an American said to me: "Why don't you just say you hate it?"'[130]

In this case, the good news was that the American had enough cultural capability to know that when a Brit says 'interesting' or 'bold', they are politely saying 'rubbish'.

Direct cultures can be seen to be offensive; indirect cultures can be seen as untrustworthy:

▶ 'Italians are too direct and offensive; the Chinese do not want to offend you so they will not tell you the truth.'[131]

▶ 'In Thailand the team will never give the leader bad medicine or bad news.'[132]

▶ 'Americans can be too direct and brash, whereas the British are so diplomatic they can come across as two faced.'[133]

▶ 'We had a big position in a French company and the 65-year-old chairman of the French company visited us. And these two young MBAs from America berated him for having the wrong capital structure and told him that he should leverage up and pay out a special dividend. They told him he was an idiot. But they did not understand that the chairman thought that they were idiots.'[134]

There is no right or wrong approach: there are simply different approaches which you have to recognise and deal with. The people-focused culture will avoid conflict, which means that you have to spend more time finding out what is really going on, and you have to invest more time in building sufficient trust so that communication becomes more open and honest. It is much easier to find out what is going on in a task-based culture, because people will tell you. But they can also cause real offence within the team, so you have to work harder at maintaining team trust. This offence is usually quite unintentional:

'We sent Italian engineers to train the Chinese engineers. The Chinese repeatedly made mistakes in assembling a machine. So when the Italian engineer left, he stuck

a photo of himself on the part where they made the mistake, with a message remind-ing them what to do. This was a mistake, because it was seen as very humiliating to the Chinese.' [135]

The task- versus people-focused cultures raise challenges for the global leader around:

▶ Building trust in different ways

▶ Creating open communication and finding out what is going on

▶ Dealing with conflict differently, or not at all

▶ Creating offence unintentionally.

On global teams, cultural noise wrecks the best of intentions by distorting communication.

Optimistic versus pragmatic

Different cultures have different world views, and that infects how they think about things. China has had 30 years of breakneck growth. From 1986 to 2015, GDP per capita rose from $280 to $7,800: an astonishing transformation. [136] Most people of working age are only used to one thing: breakneck growth. They assume success will happen, because it has always happened in their past. It is an optimistic world view.

Like the Chinese, albeit for different reasons, Americans tend to be optimis-tic. The American dream is based on working hard and coming good; there is a 250-year history of nation building behind them.

In contrast, Europeans are surrounded by a deep historical and cultural legacy which they cherish. Although they have growth (and many of the planet's richest societies are European), growth has been slower overall and they have seen some industries decline and disappear. They have also seen their empires evaporate and their global domination decline, at least in rel-ative terms. Success is not assumed, and breakneck growth at all costs is not seen as the only goal. They tend to have a more cautious world view, which they would also see as more pragmatic and more focused on quality of life.

The difference between the optimists and pragmatists comes through in two ways.

First, optimistic cultures tend to use more enthusiastic language. Here is how the same project was described by different team members:

▶ American: 'Outstanding team effort' – showing infectious enthusiasm

▶ British: 'Quite good' – from the euphemistic British person, this was high praise

▶ German: 'We are 5 per cent ahead of plan' – showing commitment to detail and accuracy

▶ French: 'We need to improve our communications' – showing a commitment to do better

▶ Japanese: *'chotto ... '* and did not want to be drawn into an evaluation lest it cause offence.

Each team member was projecting very different views of the same performance: the opportunities for misunderstanding are clear. These differences run deep, as became clear when I watched two parents playing with their children in the park. An American father was teaching his son how to play baseball; a British father was playing catch with his daughter. Below is a table which shows how they interacted with their children:

	British dad	American dad
Child misses completely	Don't watch daddy, watch the ball	Good effort!
Child misses again	Remember, watch the ball, not daddy	Great try!
Child connects with ball, just	Well done! Now let's do it again: watch the ball, not daddy.	Outstanding! (Parent high fives child)

The parents were not only transmitting a skill to their child; they were also transmitting a different way of thinking.

The second way in which the optimistic and pragmatic cultures miscommunicate is over what they talk about. The optimistic cultures are very success focused and always look at opportunities; pragmatic cultures more readily look at the obstacles to success and how to overcome them. In theory, that makes the two cultures a good combination. The success cultures create energy, see the opportunity and drive forwards. The pragmatic cultures make sure that road blocks are removed and that unnecessary risk is not taken. In practice, these two world views lead to frustration on both sides.

4. Psychological noise

Cultural stereotypes are just that: they are stereotypes. Within any culture, there will be plenty of people who deviate significantly from the standard stereotype. Different people have different styles. These different styles are the source of psychological noise. We all encode and decode information differently. There are as many different styles as there are human beings, so we need a shorthand to identify and deal with some of the most important and common style differences. This is what the venerable MB/TI[137] method attempts to do. In the spirit of MB/TI, here are some of the most common sources of psychological noise:

▶ Big picture versus Detail

▶ Thoughtful versus Expressive

▶ Logical versus Creative

▶ Spontaneous versus Systematic.

You can create many more trade-offs between different ways of thinking which you observe. The goal here is not to complete a psychological study of all humanity. The goal is to show that there are different ways of **Differences should be a source of strength, not weakness.** thinking. These differences should be a source of strength, not weakness. A strong global team will have a balance of styles. If you have a team of deeply thoughtful people only, team meetings will echo to the sound of silence. If everyone is expressive, it will sound like a chimpanzees' tea party, where the chimpanzees are drinking whisky, not tea. If everyone is big picture, then nothing practical may emerge; if everyone is focused on the detail, they may land up doing precisely the wrong thing, but they will do it very well.

Although a balanced team is very strong, it is also very hard to manage because of all the noise and potential for misunderstanding within it. Taking just the four trade-offs listed above we can see how each one can be a source of strength and of misunderstanding. We will naturally believe that our way of thinking is the 'best' way of thinking. But we need enough self-awareness to realise that it is not the best: it is simply different. We need to recognise that other people may not appreciate or understand the way we communicate, and that we should value and harness the different approaches of our colleagues.

Big picture versus detail	**Big picture**	**Detail**
	Self-perception: conceptual, theoretical, imaginative	*Self-perception:* concrete, practical, realistic
	Seen as: flighty, impractical, aloof	*Seen as:* dull, traditional, slow moving
Thoughtful versus expressive	**Thoughtful**	**Expressive**
	Self-perception: logical, critical, reasonable	*Self-perception:* open-minded, energetic, spontaneous
	Seen as: negative, can't do	*Seen as:* domineering and chaotic
Logical versus creative	**Logical**	**Creative**
	Self-perception: ordered, methodical, rational	*Self-perception:* source of ideas, creating possibilities
	Seen as: rule bound and inflexible	*Seen as:* disordered, messy, impractical
Task focus versus people focus	**Task focus**	**People focus**
	Self-perception: makes things happen; achiever and striver	*Self-perception:* empathetic, team builder, supportive
	Seen as: insensitive, trampling over others	*Seen as:* bleeding heart who does not get things done

These styles create noise. Big picture people become very frustrated when detail people hold them back: they hate being 'caught in the weeds'. The detail people become frustrated that the big picture people have no idea about how to convert ideas into action. Likewise, task-focused and people-focused people simply talk about different things: task or people. They don't disagree: they simply don't connect.

You can no more mandate that people change their style than you can ask a leopard to change its spots. These different styles are embedded in how we think and how we communicate. Instead of trying to enforce a uniform style of communication, the global team has to learn to adapt to a variety of different styles. The lesson from MB/TI training events is that the process counts as much as the substance. Training in different styles enables team members to:

▶ understand different communication styles exist within the team

▶ respect and value the different styles as opposed to judging them

▶ encourage team members to adapt how they talk and listen to colleagues with different styles

▶ legitimise discussion about styles

▶ help team members discuss misunderstandings positively: realise that they may be the result of different styles, not because of any ulterior motives.

In practice, these different styles continue to be a source of friction on all teams. It takes time for teams to understand each other properly. Long-standing teams can achieve a level of cohesiveness which makes communication both natural and easy.

5. Technology and noise

Technology enables communication, but not understanding. Technology does nothing to remove the noise of communications: cultural, psychological and semantic noise still lead to misunderstandings.

Good use of technology is about how you use it: more technology is not always good. Technology has to be the servant, not the master, of communications.

In this section we will explore the perils of technology:

▶ Technology and trust

▶ Technology and communications overload

▶ Distractions of technology

▶ Proliferation of platforms

▶ The plague of email.

Technology and trust

Communication and trust support each other. But technology can undermine trust and communication rather than enhance it.

Technology can undermine trust and communication rather than enhance it.

To understand why technology can undermine trust, step briefly into a time machine and travel back to the days of the Roman or Ottoman empires. These were vast empires. When an official was despatched from Rome to some far-flung province such as Judea, the official had to be trusted. The governor of Judea could not get onto a conference call every day to discuss variations in the salt tax, or debate what to do about some local trouble makers. The governor had to be relied on to make the right decisions: if he happened to crucify the wrong person, well that was a risk you took.

The empires of old teach us that in the absence of strong communication, you need strong trust.

The empires of old teach us that in the absence of strong communication, you need strong trust. Trust enables greater delegation, autonomy and accountability. As the frequency and volume of communications has increased, so the required levels of trust have declined. It becomes easier to measure, monitor and control from the centre, and less delegation and autonomy is required or expected. Team members are well aware that when they are being micro-managed remotely; that is in effect a vote of no-confidence in them. More trust means less micro-management and the need for less communication. This trade-off exists to this day in global teams, as Rob Watson of Rolls-Royce noted: 'over time trust takes over and you can reduce the formal systems'.[138] Just because technology gives us the ability to micro-manage, it does not mean we should micro-manage.

Technology and communication overload

Global teams express mixed feelings about how much they should communicate. In principle, they see that more communication is good. In practice, they often feel overwhelmed by the sheer volume of communication.

More technology and more communication is not always good. Network theory shows that when you add more nodes (team members), the number of edges (connections) grows very rapidly. The number of connections is given by a simple formula:[139] $c = n*(n-1)$, where c is the number of connections (or edges) and n is the number of nodes. So that means a team of four people will have just twelve ways of connecting with each other individually. A team of ten people will have ninety different connections between individuals.

If you include all the possible communications within a team, you land up with a factorial function. So four team members will have twenty-four ways of communicating with each other individually, or with sub-groups of the team. A team of ten has 3,628,800 potential communication combinations between individuals and sub-groups of the team.

Within and beyond the global team, there is an insatiable appetite for more communication. Team members want to know what is going on; they want to be involved in decisions; they require support and help. Beyond the team there is the constant pressure of reporting requirements, plus the need for a never-ending variety of ad hoc reports and presentations to a wide variety of stakeholders. Because technology enables so much communication, people expect to have it all. Thirty years ago rock singer Freddie Mercury sang: 'I want it all and I want it now'.[140] That pretty much sums up what everyone wants in terms of communication. The result of this overload is:

▶ Loss of productivity by focusing on reporting, presenting, reviewing, responding and communicating rather than doing

▶ Loss of focus: too much information means that the really important messages can get lost in the mountain of less important information.

Effective global teams have to establish clear communication protocols and patterns, based on understanding what they need to communicate and why they need to communicate.

Distractions of technology

The media often carries articles showing how much time is wasted in the office. Some estimate that as much as 40 per cent of time in the office is not productive.[141] In 2012, the McKinsey Global Institute found that the average worker who handles information spends more than half their time communicating about their work and just one-third of their time actually doing their work. Email interruptions mean that tasks take up to three times as long as they did before email:[142] so much for the productivity revolution.

The reliability of each survey can be questioned, but the overall conclusions will strike a chord with anyone who works in an office: there is a vast amount of unproductive time. Some of this comes from pointless meetings and office gossip. But increasingly, the finger is being pointed at technology. Social media, surfing the web and endless emails are all good alternatives to actually working. Technology can enable communication; it does not ensure productive communication.

Technology can enable communication; it does not ensure productive communication.

Technology also hampers productivity in two more ways. First, it simply raises expectations. Because we can answer emails at any time of the day or night, we are expected to answer at any time of the day or night. For a global team, this can be devastating: there is no escape from the 24-hour cycle of communication. In the words of one globe-trotting leader: 'global teams are 24/7. It never ends so at some point you need to say "stop"'.[143] Teams need clear protocols about when emails are expected to be dealt with, and when there should be downtime.

Technology also means that we are expected to produce more. Before Power-Point, a 12-page presentation would take time and effort, with the involvement of a graphic designer. It would be short, but to the point. With PowerPoint, there is always another slide we can produce, and we do it ourselves. So expectations have risen in volume terms, and, instead of delegating production out, managers do it themselves. They are rarely very good or fast at producing PowerPoint, and they are a very expensive production resource. Technology may not raise quality, but it raises expectations about what managers are meant to do.

Proliferation of platforms

There is a seemingly endless variety of technology platforms which can be used for communication. Each one has its advocates. The problem arises when everyone has a different preference. When there are too many platforms, it becomes hard to know how to reach people:

There is a proliferation of platforms which means that you never know what is the most effective way to communicate with different people' [144]

WhatsApp, Facebook, Google Hangouts, Skype, Facetime, email, SMS, Slack and even the phone all have their place. But each global team needs clear protocols about which platforms will be used and when. More focus is better than more choice when it comes to communicating.

The plague of email

Most global team members express a strong dislike of email, for three reasons.

First, there is simply too much email. 'Reply all' ensures that too many people receive too much email. Some estimates indicate that over 100 billion business email messages are sent each day, with busier managers receiving over 100 email messages a day.[145] Whatever the precise number is, all managers are familiar with email overload where it is hard to keep track of the truly important conversations. The trivial drowns out the important. The volume of emails is also a soak of time, with email distracting attention.[146]

Second, email is abused. It is often used not to communicate, but to leave a record which can be used to prove that the sender was doing the right thing. Inevitably, this requires a response from the other side to show that they are doing the right thing. This use of email is a good way of telling colleagues that you do not trust them, so you want a record of all your interactions with them.

Third, email is easy to misinterpret. Face to face, you can pick up plenty of visual cues about what the other team member is thinking and feeling. And because face to face is a live conversation, it is easy to adjust when there is a misunderstanding. Phone calls miss the visual cues, but at least you can hear the voice and adjust in real time to misunderstandings. With email there are no visual or aural cues to guide you, and there is no chance of adjusting to any misunderstandings.

Email: the technology that people love to hate

▶ 'We used to use email and that led to people getting annoyed and confused. Email is not part of the revolution. It is old fashioned and private.'[147]

▶ 'Communication is easier when you can see their body language. Email dilutes the message; you lose the context. Email "reply all" is a plague.'[148]

▶ 'Email does not help. Phone is the forgotten technology: we should use it more.'[149]

▶ 'We do not just use email because you do not get the interaction and you cannot build trust.'[150]

▶ 'I have to tell young people in the office: don't send me an email in the office – come and talk to me. When someone talks then I can see what they are thinking and see if they are time pressured.'[151]

▶ 'The same conversation goes well if it is in person but with email lands up with people hating each other.'[152]

▶ 'Emails are dangerous in a global world. Emails are important for proof, but they do not help.'[153]

▶ 'As a global team we need to understand each other. Email does not give you the tone of what people are saying.'[154]

> 'It has prevented us getting things done, fried our brains and . . . made us all passive aggressive.'[155]

> 'People often use email for the sake of it and just to prove that they have read the incoming email. Email is a wonderful tool but it is sometimes abused. As a company, we are currently embarking on a real drive to reduce email traffic.'[156]

Email is destroying business efficiency and it destroys people. It is the scourge of modern business.

> 'Email is too formal and is destroying business efficiency and it destroys people. It is the scourge of modern business.'[157]

In between the deluge of hatred for email, there are a few voices who speak up for it – or at least for some form of asynchronous communication. The benefit of asynchronous communication is that it allows for more considered responses than a real-time conversation, and it is easier for non-native speakers of English. The IT manager who described email as the 'scourge of modern business' (above) also recognised that 'working with India it helps to have a lot of written communication because it gets past the problem of accents and gets over the language problem. It also lets people structure their ideas and their responses.'

Used well, asynchronous communication helps. But firms are looking at more flexible alternatives to email which are more open and enable more group discussion. Slack is becoming widespread. In the words of one user: 'I've gone from receiving around 180 emails a day down to about 30 since we started using Slack. That alone has radically improved productivity.'[158] The trend is towards using more informal and open communication platforms. In time, these will also become abused.

The problem is not the technology: the problem is how we use it. Any substitute for email will not provide a magical fix unless behaviours change. We are all learning how to cope with an age when we have flipped from a communications deficit (imagine doing everything by fax) to an age of communications overload.

6. Effective communications and use of technology

At the heart of effective communication is the need to reduce the noise between the sender who is encoding information and the receiver who is decoding it. That means that communication starts with people, not technology.

Effective communication starts with understanding the three Ps of communication:

▶ Purpose

▶ Process

▶ People.

Purpose

Asking 'why communicate?' may seem as pointless as asking 'why breathe?' But step back for a moment and look at all the communications you receive: not just emails and phone calls, but also all the meetings you have to attend. Every meeting is about communicating. Most managers find that a large amount of their time spent on the phone, email or in meetings is wasted. Which comes back to the obvious question: what was the point of all that communication? Lack of clarity and lack of purpose lead to wasted time and effort. Given that communication across a global team is harder than in a domestic team, it is vital to minimise waste.

If a team is clear about why it is communicating, then it can create the right processes and protocols. We have seen how some smaller and more innovative global web design agencies have thought through the purpose question closely, and have come up with solutions which are efficient and focused. Clear purpose drives clear process, which drives appropriate use of technology. In summary they identified four needs, and use technology which is fit for each purpose:

1 Keep track of progress. Everyone updates progress in real time using Trello or similar project management software. And everyone has access to and visibility of each update. This minimises the need for formal updates, and gives each team member the autonomy and accountability to manage their own work.

2 Identify and deal with blockages early. Every day, have a virtual YTB meeting by video conference using Skype, Google Hangouts or similar. Each team member will summarise in less than one minute:

   ▶ Y: what they did Yesterday,

▶ T: what they will do Today

▶ B: any Blockers they face, and any help they may require.

3   Re-create the office banter around the water cooler: use Slack.

4   Build a sense of trust across the team. Once a year invest in a global offsite meeting where everyone can get together, not just for business and for training but to develop social and personal bonds of trust. Once a year, high tech has to be supported by high touch.

By being clear about why the team needs to communicate, the team cuts the time spent on communication dramatically, while increasing levels of transparency, trust, control and support. As one team leader put it: 'I used to deal with hundreds of emails a week. Now I get maybe just five a week. And they are all from clients.'[159]

Process

Too much choice is not good. Global teams work across too many time zones, cultures and communication platforms. Too much choice is not good. Every team needs to establish a pattern of communication which is predictable and reliable. This means making choices:

▶ How often to communicate

▶ When to communicate: what time in which time zones

▶ Which platforms to use (email, video conference, phone, etc.)

▶ Why they will communicate: each meeting and message needs a clear purpose.

Given the proliferation of communication platforms, clear technology choices have to be made: the whole team needs to settle on the same technology if they are to communicate at all. This means making choices around:

▶ Synchronous versus asynchronous communication. Video and phone allow for real-time interaction, but email and other asynchronous technologies allow people to sleep and catch up on messages the next day.

▶ Public versus private platforms, which also gives a cultural message about how much transparency and trust is expected across the team. For instance: email is private, Slack provides the water cooler forum for the team.

▶ Formal versus informal communications. Teams are not just about tasks: they are about people. Create an informal space where the team can re-create the water cooler experience: share gossip, stories, jokes and ideas. This builds trust and can lead to good ideas.

▶ Face to face versus impersonal communications: up to 85 per cent of managers value face-to-face meetings over virtual; only 3 per cent think virtual is more effective, at least in a sales situation.[160] Technology enables transactions, not trust.

Within each technology, team members need training on how to use the technology well. At a simple level, there needs to be a common email etiquette, for instance:

▶ Don't use email when you can phone or talk.

▶ Don't use email to build an evidence trail.

▶ Avoid 'reply all'.

▶ Avoid email where possible, given most global teams' dislike of the medium.

With the proliferation of platforms, it is easy but dangerous to assume that everyone else is on the same platform, or even knows how to use it. Just because everyone else in your local office is using the latest and most fashionable tech tool, it does not mean that the rest of the world is equally excited about it.

Agreeing the processes and protocols of communication may be dull, but it is vital.

Creating an effective pattern of global team communication

This how Alex Turnbull, CEO of the Groove,[161] describes developing effective communications for his team. As with all global teams, it was a voyage of discovery to create a solution which works for them:

'Without consistent, effective communication, everything else begins to fall apart. People don't feel like they're a "real" part of a team; they simply feel like a mercenary working in a silo. Tasks begin to slip through the cracks when there isn't clear communication around who owns them and when they'll be completed. Operating without great communication is neither productive nor fun.

▶

This is something that we've actually struggled with in the past and learned the hard way. When we started, I was determined to do things *our* way, "not like those big, slow companies". We were going to hire hungry, talented, scrappy people, and then let them work without interrupting them with burdens like meetings.

As it turned out, that didn't get us very far. We lacked alignment and anything resembling a company culture. We began a year-long experiment with finding an effective meeting rhythm, and now that we've settled on one that the entire team is happy with, we've never been running smoother.'

Here's how our rhythm looks:

Every Monday: 20-minute team call to "chat" (about weekends, personal life, etc . . . discuss the previous week's performance and priorities for the coming week).

Tuesday–Thursday: 10-minute team call to discuss what each member accomplished the day before, what they plan to accomplish that day and any blockers that stand in their way.

Friday: 20-minute team call to discuss the week's feedback from customers and employees.

Bi-weekly: One-on-one meetings between myself and every single employee.

Monthly: A monthly recap call to discuss the previous month's performance and goals for the month ahead.

Quarterly: A quarterly strategy session to discuss the previous quarter's performance and to set goals and strategy for the next three months.

We also communicate throughout the day in Slack, where everything from collaboration to "water cooler conversation" happens.'

People

Noise comes from people and how they encode and decode information.

Clear purpose and processes minimise wasted communications; good technology makes it easier to connect people. But purpose, processes and technology will not eliminate noise. Noise comes from people and how they encode and decode information.

Where there are people, there will always be noise and there will always be the potential for misunderstanding. Here are five ways to minimise the noise within global teams:

▶ Listening

▶ Simple language

▶ Common language

▶ Positive regard

▶ Cultural competence.

Listening

We have already noted that good communication needs good listening even more than good talking: decoding well matters as much as encoding well. Repeating messages simply repeats the noise and causes frustration. Active listening and paraphrasing builds understanding and trust, and quietly flatters the speaker.

Simple language

English is spoken as a first, native language by just 5 per cent of the world's population.[162] Idiomatic English is a barrier to understanding. This presents a challenge for native English speakers. Native English speakers have to learn to speak like non-native speakers. That means they have to unlearn cultural habits and avoid colloquialisms, jokes, jargon, or sporting, cultural, political and religious references. Native speakers also have to use short words and short sentences: they should not assume that everyone can speak their own language fluently. Ideally, they would learn globish[163] ('global English') which is a reduced form of English based on just 1,500 words. Other versions of English have reduced it to just 750 key words.[164]

Common language

Common language is about having common values and beliefs. In the words of John Ridding, CEO of the Financial Times (owned by the Nikkei): 'The Nikkei speak Japanese and we speak English. But we speak the same language of quality journalism and integrity. Most important is the language of values

When teams share the same values and mission, the noise of miscommunication reduces dramatically.

and mission.' When teams share the same values and mission, the noise of miscommunication reduces dramatically.

Positive regard

Global team members need to trust and respect each other. This is vital in dealing with noise when it arises. Presume innocence, not guilt, when there is a misunderstanding: this is the basis of positive regard within the team. With positive regard, the team works towards a positive outcome instead of trying to protect their positions. Building trust comes from a combination of credibility, which takes time, and shared values. Shared values come in part from a common goal and common background (working for the same firm), but also from meeting each other and having shared experiences. Teams need to meet in person where they can.

Cultural competence

Cultural competence is not about knowing how to exchange *meishi* (business cards) in Japan, or not using your left hand in the Middle East. These are social niceties which are easy to pick up. Cultural competence is about mindset: it is about being open, inquisitive, curious and respectful about different cultures. At a simple level, at least try the local food before deciding you dislike it:

'Respect other cultures and customs. For example, younger staff love Japanese food and they are flexible and they try things out. But an older guy has never even tried it, so that is not open-minded and it shows no respect. At least I have tried Marmite,[165] but I don't like it. So at least try: don't say no before you start.'[166]

If you show respect for other cultures, you will earn respect in return. That builds trust and makes communication far easier.

Creating good communication habits is hard work. Even domestic teams struggle to communicate well; global teams have to work harder at building a common language, shared values, positive regard and real cultural competence. These habits do not arise naturally: the team has to develop these habits consciously. Team meetings' conference calls should not just cover substance in terms of updates and problem solving. At least some calls should finish with a short reflection on process, based on two simple questions:

▶ WWW: What Went Well in terms of process? What should we do more of in future?

▶ EBI: Even Better If ... how can we improve our communication next time?

This simple discipline enables the team to grow into good habits. Noise will always exist: good habits reduce the noise and make it easier to deal with noise when it arises.

Conclusions

Trust and communication support each other and are the essential oil that lubricates the work of your team: without trust and communication, your team will grind to a halt like a car without oil.

Effective communication means reducing the amount of noise that garbles messages between people.

At a personal level you can reduce noise, so:

▶ Listen actively, and listen more than you talk. Good listening is the key to mutual understanding.

▶ Use simple language. Use short words and short sentences. Avoid colloquialisms and cultural references.

▶ Use consistent and common language.

For the team as a whole, there are three priorities:

▶ Establish a consistent pattern and rhythm of communication. Ensure that everyone uses the same technology and platforms and that the routine of team-wide communication is predictable and fair: if people have to attend calls at anti-social hours, make sure that the rhythm of meetings shares the pain around the team. Communication is a beast which can devour all your time. You have to tame the beast by having a clear rhythm of communication which balances the need to communicate and the need to get work done.

▶ Build cultural competence. Recognise that different cultures communicate in different ways. What people say, when they are prepared to say it and how they will say it vary greatly. As a team leader, you have to create the context in which each team member can contribute, and you have to learn to interpret what they say and what they do not say. You have to learn to 'read the air'.

▶ Use technology well. Email is more or less universally reviled as a technology. It creates work and mistrust. Ensure everyone on the team uses the same technology platforms for communicating. Find a balance between real-time and asynchronous communication, and between open and private communication platforms. Although technology enables communication, it does not enable trust: build trust face to face.

PART THREE
Creating the firm-wide context for success

Introduction

Part three explores how the firm can set up global teams for success.

Creating the context for success looks, at first, to be the same for both domestic and global teams. Although the topics may look familiar, the nature of the challenge is different in each case, and is the subject of each chapter in Part three of the book.

Chapter 6: Goals: clear goals or shared goals?

Goal clarity is seen as a top five issue by 65 per cent of global team members. Goals which are clear at the top of the firm are rarely so clear on the front line. It is the global team which faces the daily reality of making the trade-off between the global and local needs. If the firm wants profit but the customer wants service what should the team do? Goal clarity is a challenge because it is harder for people far from the centre to understand the context and the rationale for the goals: they have not been part of the discussion which created the goals in the first place. When the context is not understood, it is easy for the team to make the **Goals which are** 'wrong' decisions, which erodes trust and erodes the **clear at the top of** willingness of the global hub to delegate effectively. **the firm are rarely** The challenge in a global context is to make sure that **so clear on the** goals are not only clear, but that they are shared, **front line.** understood and relevant to the geographic context.

Chapter 7: Systems and processes: the building blocks of success

Systems and processes may seem dull to leaders with a global vision. But they are the vital plumbing of the firm. Over 60 per cent of global team members mentioned at least one process or system as being a top five issue for them. Typically, people nearer the front line were the ones who felt the need for effective processes and systems most acutely. Making the systems and processes work is harder in a global context than a domestic context:

▶ Global teams find themselves dealing with inconsistent processes and procedures

▶ Domestic teams find it easier to adjust to any process problems

▶ There are high barriers to fixing process problems on a global team

You will never be a hero by making systems work well, but you will be the villain if they work poorly.

You will never be a hero by making systems work well, but you will be the villain if they work poorly.

Chapter 8: People and skills: global talent, global mindset

Going global raises the stakes in terms of talent:

▶ Global firms can find the best talent globally, often at lower cost than in western nations. To succeed in a global talent pool, you need exceptional skills.

▶ Global working puts new skills demands onto team members who have to be able to deal with higher levels of ambiguity, complexity and uncertainty; they also need high order influencing skills to influence remote stakeholders and decisions.

▶ Global working requires a global mindset, which involves high-level cultural intelligence: being open to new ideas and new ways of working, and learning to grow, adapt and change very fast.

Building global talent is high effort and high return.

Chapter 9: Culture: building cultural intelligence

Culture is a huge challenge and opportunity for the firm and the individual alike.

For the individual, global working is a wonderful opportunity to explore new cultures and broaden horizons. It is also a huge challenge. No one can ever acquire all the cultural knowledge required to work around the world. Instead, you have to acquire cultural intelligence, which is an ability to learn and grow fast, rather than to judge others or stick with familiar ways of working.

For the firm, culture represents a real choice. Every successful firm has a clear and cohesive culture. But should that culture be the culture of the home nation, or should the firm create a global culture which transcends borders?

Chapter 10: Structure: co-ordination and conflict

There will always be conflict between different functions, geographies and business units. Constructive conflict between these groups is how solutions are discovered and priorities are determined. In a domestic team, the rules of engagement are well established and the key stakeholders know each other. On a global team, the rules of engagement are unclear and the stakeholders do not know each other.

Making a global structure work is challenging because:

▶ There is no perfect solution
▶ The best solution changes as the market changes
▶ Any structure is a compromise and involves conflict.

Despite this, restructuring is often an effective way of refocusing the firm; sending messages about priorities; attacking entrenched power barons; and creating momentum across the firm.

6

Goals

Clear goals or shared goals?

We live in a world of key performance indicators, management by objectives and routine scrutiny of performance. Having clear goals is one of the basics of management. And yet managers in even the most sophisticated global groups were frustrated by the lack of goal clarity. This was not a minor quibble from a few managers. Sixty-five per cent of managers interviewed rated it as one of the top issues in making global teams work. How can goals be unclear in a well-run firm?

This chapter will explore the paradox that the more sophisticated an organisation becomes, the harder it is to manage goal setting effectively. We will look at the challenge of goal setting in six sections:

1. Clarity or ambiguity?
2. Coping with ambiguity
3. Why goal setting is hard in any complex environment
4. Why goal setting is harder in a global environment
5. How to set goals for global teams
6. What is the point of having a global team?

1. Clarity or ambiguity?

To any western manager, it is obvious that you need clear goals. What is obvious to the western mind may not be obvious to other minds. So we will rehearse the case for having clear goals, and then show that there is a compelling alternative. Both ways work, but not together. Where you have two ways of thinking, you pave the way for confusion and conflict within a global team.

Clear goals are required in order to:

▶ create a clear framework for decision making

▶ reduce internal conflict and confusion

▶ avoid wasted effort and duplication

▶ drive accountability and performance.

Goal setting is traditionally top down. The framework is set from the top. The high-level framework is filled with increasing detail as goals are cascaded downwards. What does not change is the framework itself, because that would lead to chaos. This is a world view which lends itself to rational, data-driven analysis and strategy much loved by consultants and reflected in tools such as the Porter Five Forces Analysis[167] and the BCG Grid.[168]

There is an alternative view of goal setting: set vague goals. This is anathema to the western mind. But if we now convert 'vague' goals into 'strategic intent', we start to see there is an alternative. When Hamel and Prahalad identified strategic intent, they focused mainly on Japanese companies, which at the time seemed to be about to rule the world. Their examples included:

▶ Komatsu: Maru-C, or encircle Caterpillar

▶ Canon: beat Xerox

▶ NEC: exploit convergence of computers and communications.

These are remarkably vague goals which require flexibility from the firm: rapid market testing, identifying loose bricks in competitors' defences, acquiring and developing core capabilities and moving rapidly – these are all required skills in support of strategic intent.

The difference in approach is driven by different starting points: 'Japanese companies start with focus on the details and a vague framework. If the details are incorrect, they assume the framework is not being built correctly and will modify the framework. Japanese have an adaptive and be-flexible approach. Meanwhile Anglo-Saxons build the framework first and ensure all the details work within that. Sometimes the details may be incorrect but the framework that was agreed at the beginning will be created.'[169]

Having vague goals is not just a Japanese fad. Some of the greatest western successes have a 'vague' or even plain outrageous goal, which might be better described as a strategic intent:

▶ Google: organise the world's information and make it universally accessible and useful[170]

▶ Coca-Cola: put Coca-Cola 'within an arm's reach of desire' [171]

▶ Apollo mission: 'This nation should commit itself to achieving the goal, before the decade is out, of landing a man on the moon and returning him safely to the earth'.[172]

These vague goals had extraordinary power: they focused the efforts of the organisation, and helped it achieve great things. In the Japanese context, the flexibility which comes from vagueness flows through the organisation. Yuki Hoashi joined NEC, but never got an employment contract and was expected to work flexibly in very different roles. This also means decision making and accountability is vague. In a Japanese context this works because there is no revolving door of employees. Everyone understands the context and can work towards a collective goal, where accountability is held collectively. In western firms there is more of a revolving door, so the top-down framework of goals, decision making and accountability has to be much clearer.

Working globally requires a global mindset. That means you have to understand that your way of thinking and working is not the only way, and may not even be the best way. Clear goals may give clarity and certainty, but they also create inflexibility, game playing and competition between silos. Vaguer goals create flexibility and encourage more collective responsibility. Neither approach is universally correct. The challenge for any global team is

> **Clear goals may give clarity and certainty, but they also create inflexibility, game playing and competition between silos.**

when you have both approaches present. The chapter on systems will show how decision making becomes a flash point when the two approaches to goal setting clash. Outsiders find it impossible to influence decisions in a context where goals are vague; accountabilities and decision making processes are vague; the decision makers live in a different time zone and speak a different language.

Global teams can have one approach or the other: they cannot have both vague and clear goals.

2. Coping with ambiguity

Clear goals are good, but they come at a price. Think of the famous phrase 'be careful what you wish for'. The downsides of goal clarity are:

▶ Focus on one priority leads to less focus on other priorities (that is the whole point of priorities), which means there is an opportunity cost that comes with any clear goal.

▶ There are good and bad ways of achieving any goal, and managers are very good at game playing: you may achieve your goal but not in ways that you wanted or expected.

▶ Clear goals which are not shared or understood lead to conflict and confusion.

▶ The desire for ever greater goal clarity can be a way for managers to focus, reduce and simplify their own accountability: it allows them to deliver their own personal goals at the expense of the wider goals and teamwork.

But global teams are the point in the firm where the trade-off between global and local or functional priorities have to be made.

For a global team, chasing total clarity is rarely worthwhile. There can be goal clarity in small businesses and at the top of global organisations. But global teams are the point in the firm where the trade-off between global and local or functional priorities have to be made. There is always going to be some level of ambiguity and uncertainty.

Global teams have to learn to cope with some level of ambiguity.

There is even a Japanese phrase for this: *kuuki o yomu*, which translates roughly as 'read the air'. Tetsuo Yanagi, a senior IT manager, explains: 'If orders from top management are not clear then American people do nothing, but the Japanese will think about what it is that management really want and how they can help. The Japanese understand the message behind the message. In Japan roles and accountabilities are not clear but everyone works together and they are prepared to work outside their formal roles. If I am only working with Japanese people then this is not important but if I work with non-Japanese people then you need much more clarity about roles and accountability.'

There is virtue to slightly ambiguous goals. It tells the team that they are being trusted and empowered to do the right thing, rather than being measured against narrow metrics. It gives them flexibility which does not come from tightly defined goals. It is a high-trust and high-commitment model, which works in a cohesive group where everyone understands each other: team members need to be working for the common good, not just for their own good.

The drive for total clarity and simplicity can be seen as too alien from a non-western perspective. One Japanese insurance executive describes his surprise at how different cultures deal with goal clarity and ambiguity: 'When I first came here I felt that we must spend more time and effort in growing the book of business so I put the majority of my pressure in that area. Whilst I have emphasized the importance to grow the business I have never said that profit is not important. The Japanese staff perfectly understood what I was saying but it took me quite a long time until I recognized that the British people's understanding was something different. Most of the British staff felt that I meant growth comes first and profit comes next.'

*'When a Japanese leader says let's grow the business, usually that does not mean profit is not important: profit is still a must. Most of the Japanese staff would understand that both growth and profit are equally important and both must be pursued. To British staff that was a contradiction and a confusion as they felt you are asking for two different things and the priority among the two must be clear. There are many other areas I felt the difference between British people and Japanese people but probably this was the biggest difference between the two, in business practice, I had recognized during my days working in the U.K.'*173

Just as clarity is not always a virtue, nor is ambiguity. Managers may be ambiguous for good and poor reasons. The good reasons are around trusting and empowering the team. The poor reason is that the manager is weak and unsure about what to do. There are plenty of Japanese managers who fully understand the virtues of clarity. Here is Masaaki Moribayashi, Managing Director of NTT Europe: 'If top management change their minds then that is bad for trust and motivation. Clear goals are important for clear decision-making, and for getting clear roles and accountability. If the team makes a decision then top management needs to support it.' That is the classic western view of goal setting and accountability. It is also a reminder never to trust national stereotypes: there is no uniform way of doing things in any country.

In global teams, there will always be a level of ambiguity and conflict. The best managers recognise that you have to manage differently with global teams: 'clear goals are a

In global teams, there will always be a level of ambiguity and conflict.

125

co-pout because the goals for a global team are never as clear as they are for a local team. You will never have clear accountabilities and roles, so you have to accept paradox and uncertainty: you cannot simplify everything, so you need shared values which get you to the right outcome. Don't pretend it is simple.'[174]

The ability of a team to deal with ambiguity depends on its cohesiveness. If there are high levels of mutual trust, mutual commitment, shared values and a common sense of mission, then some ambiguity can be empowering and enable innovation. If the team is diverse, then ambiguity will quickly break down into confusion and conflict. Goal setting happens in a cultural context.

3. Why goal setting is harder in any complex environment

Goal setting is hard enough in a domestic context, because there are always competing priorities and the ever present risk of game playing. The popularity of the balanced scorecard[175] is testament to the challenges of goal setting. The original balanced scorecard looked at four perspectives:

▶ Financial

▶ Customer

▶ Learning and growth

▶ Internal.

Each factor has its own complexity, trade-offs and challenges, even before you start to make the trade-offs between the four factors. For instance, how much will you risk your customer franchise in pursuit of short-term financial goals? And how do you balance the need to meet next quarter's performance with the need to invest in long-term learning and growth? Are your internal business processes geared for minimum cost today, great customer service or flexibility to deal with future market and product changes? And how do you balance the demands of different products, brands and functions?

In practice, management have to make things simple. They have three tools:

The best predictor of next year's budget, strategy and goals is this year's budget, strategy and goals plus or minus a bit.

▶ Use inertia. The best predictor of next year's budget, strategy and goals is this year's budget, strategy and goals plus or minus a bit.

▶ Use the budget to force clarity. Most organisations are set up for conflict. There will always be competition between functions, geographies and products for a finite pot of budget and management support. It is through the budget process of constructive conflict that the priorities of the organisation can be fine-tuned, within the overall strategy.

▶ Focus, focus, focus. In theory, it should be possible to achieve multiple goals at the same time. In practice, most leaders prefer to focus on one thing where they can really make a difference.

What's the point of education? The challenge of goal setting in a domestic environment[176]

We were sitting with the Education Minister and his senior advisers. We had an unusual offer for him. We were highly confident of our programme: we offered to implement it at no initial cost to the government. The government would only have to pay for the results we delivered. We just needed them to define their goals, and how much they valued them in terms of payments.

Immediately, there was a meltdown on the other side of the table. The minister wanted to make sure that children aged 16 achieved good exam results. But which exams counted most? And should we look at the average results, or progress versus previous exams, or should we look at how many passed a minimum threshold? And which exams counted most: should we focus on just literacy and numeracy, or would that lead to science and languages being ignored? Then they realised they also wanted children to acquire life skills, become employable and be rounded individuals: sports, music, careers advice, financial knowledge and dealing with people are all vital. They knew that if they focused on one priority, schools would ignore the other priorities: just like most managers in most firms.

Put to the test, the government could not answer the simple question: what is the purpose of education? Before mocking the incompetence of politicians and civil servants, you might try to answer the question yourself: what goals would you set for education, and how much would you pay to achieve them? It is genuinely hard to be clear about priorities when there are so many conflicting needs. And they don't even have the complexity of dealing with other countries.

Even where the goal is clear, there is often ambiguity about how it should be achieved. There are good and bad ways of achieving goals. You might target an increase in market share, but there are good and bad ways of achieving that. Price discounting gains share fast, but does not build brand loyalty; worse, it may make your loyal customers more price sensitive in future and destroy any premium image you have. Equally, executives over the years have proven very adept at manipulating accounts to drive earnings growth in the absence of any underlying improvement in performance.

The challenge for global teams is not just to set a clear goal, but to set a goal which is not gamed by management. Management needs context, understanding and buy-in to the goal. John Ridding, CEO of the Financial Times, understood this when setting a bold global goal of securing one million subscribers globally. The magic million number could be achieved in good or bad ways. To be meaningful, he needed one million sticky and high-value customers, not one million price sensitive and flighty customers. So, in his words: 'the conversations are about how to get 1 million paid for subscribers: we are at 770,000 now. So we start by breaking that down into consumer and B2B. Then we have to work out how we build engagement with our readers and how we build habit. We can measure engagement. And we are building a new access model to encourage greater engagement.'

4. Why goal setting is harder in a global environment

Most firms can deal with complexity far better than they can deal with ambiguity.

In the global context, the challenge of setting goals rises as a result of complexity and ambiguity. To paraphrase Donald Rumsfeld,[177] complexity is about the known conflicts and uncertainty; ambiguity is about unknown uncertainty and conflict. Most firms can deal with complexity far better than they can deal with ambiguity.

Three factors drive complexity in most global firms:

▶ Different markets have different needs

▶ Geographic business units often have real power

▶ There are different perspectives between the hub and the spokes of the organisation

Firms are often good at setting the high-level global goal: it would be surprising if they were not good at this. But the real challenge comes when you drive these goals down into the organisation. In practice, it is individual teams working in different countries and functions that find themselves having to make uncomfortable trade-offs. For these teams, there is real ambiguity about how far they adapt to the global or local requirements. The goal that looks very clear at a global level suddenly looks much more ambiguous at team level.

Different markets have different needs

Different market needs drive strategic challenges around how far the firm can integrate globally versus differentiate locally. But this challenge becomes most acute when you drive down to team level. It is at team level that the conflict between global and local needs is most acutely felt. Local differences can be driven by regulation, language, price sensitivity, local tastes, market development and by different routes to market.

▶ Product and price differences: NTT has a cloud product which it developed in the Japanese market where it is the dominant player. It wanted to globalise the product, not least to serve its global Japanese customers. As soon as it did so, it ran into problems. It found that the European market was ahead of it in terms of performance requirements and expectations. Even within Europe, there were significant differences: Spain was much more price conscious than the UK. Suddenly the goal of globalising the cloud service became a real challenge: should the service be optimised for the global or Japanese market, and could pricing be varied by market without the risk of cannibalising high-margin sales? Inevitably, this creates tension between the region and the centre over priorities, specifications, pricing and product development.

▶ Customer differences: Pret, a chain of UK sandwich stores, decided to expand their unique model globally. In each market, they had to adapt. In the words of the CFO at the time: 'Paris looks the same as London but in Paris we lead with the sweet stuff: they like more sweet things in Paris. We do softer textures in Paris and offer sweeter bread. You also have to offer *jambon beurre* and the yoghurt must be slightly more sour. In Hong Kong the mid-market customer is very status conscious. They use brands as a means to promote their status and show people that they are progressive and internationalised. So the initiatives for our global brand in Shanghai included our team members having T-shirts saying "London, New York, Paris, Shanghai" – highlighting the point that Pret is proud to be in Shanghai and that Shanghai is standing shoulder to shoulder with the world's "glamour" cities, and we developed a beautifully packaged range of products to share with friends at home that allowed the customer to demonstrate his or her global credentials.'[178]

▶ Regulatory differences: a leading provider of global services to financial institutions is considered to be a 'systematically important financial institution and that brings with it much more American and European regulatory focus which has become much more intense since 2007'. Its IT infrastructure is key to delivering services which global clients want to be consistent around the world. The IT systems went through a major upgrade, driven out of the UK, US and India. But regulation drives different requirements in different places at different times: 'one of the pain points we have with German clients is the "know your customer" requirements. In Germany, we have very specific requirements and regulations which were not picked up in the American processes and systems. But if America responds to everyone's special needs then it quickly becomes a complete mess.'[179] The global team needed a smooth and consistent global roll-out of new systems; regulators made that impossible.

▶ Sourcing and branding differences: within any global team: there will be conflict within the team over key decisions around sourcing and branding. Each country is attached to its own brands, and no country wants to lose production and jobs. At a high level, the strategy may be clear. But the pain of making it happen is faced at team level. This is how the conflict played out at Electrolux in Asia: 'recently we bought a company in China. Top management decided to use the China brand which has a wider product range. But we also have a company in Thailand which builds similar sorts of kit. What do we do with our Thai business when we brand our Thai product under the Chinese brand? The initial challenge will be people's concern over the quality of China made products. So we have to balance what is right globally and what is right for the region. There are always trade-offs.'[180]

In each case above, the global goal was clear:

▶ NTT and Pret: globalise our products
▶ Global financial services: create a global IT infrastructure for global clients
▶ Electrolux: optimise our regional operations and branding.

In each case the simple global requirement became far more complicated when translated down to the level of the team. It was at the team level that the practical trade-off between going global and going local had to be made. Clear global goals do not translate easily into clear team goals.

Geographic business units often have real power

As individuals, we all like to think that we are unique and special. The same is true of every country. Every nation has its pride, and thinks that it is unique and special. This can be a source of great frustration to global organisations which operate in Europe. The Belgians will proudly insist that they are different from the Dutch who do not care for the Germans who are not greatly liked by the Norwegians; and the French think they are different from and better than everyone else, just like everyone else.

If you believe that each country is unique, you will land up with a series of national baronies around Europe and Asia. Your ability to drive global products, services, operations and consistency will be broken. This is a disaster if your clients are global and expect global service: most large professional services and IT firms have to serve global clients while dealing with national pride.

If you believe that each country is unique, you will land up with a series of national baronies around Europe and Asia.

Once the barons have power, they are hard to dislodge. This was the challenge faced by Fujitsu in Europe. Historically, they had organised by country. The new Fujitsu CEO for EMEIA[181] realised that if they were to serve global customers effectively, then they needed to organise by industry group such as financial services, or travel and transport. Only that way could they build the expertise and seamless cross-border service which clients expect.

The global goal of serving global clients and industries faced the regional reality of entrenched power barons in each country. So the CEO took them all to a two-day conference in Frankfurt to discuss change. In his words: 'We took them to Frankfurt to make the case for change not just to announce the change. On the first day, some of the country barons made the case for not changing so I offered them a choice: they did not have to change but they would have to increase their forecasts for profitability sales and cash flow. I let them think about that overnight. Next day no one had raised their forecasts so that meant we were all in for the change. That gave us nine change agents around the region.'[182]

Different perspectives between the hub and the spokes of the organisation

It is no surprise to find that what matters for a region may not even figure on the radar screen at the centre of the organisation. At the bottom of the mountain you might see children playing in the street and animals in the farmyard. At the top of the mountain you may see peaks far into the distance. The two views are completely different and both are correct. How you see reality depends on where you stand.

Ambiguity is built into these different perspectives. For instance, a Japanese insurer in London was created initially to serve the global corporate clients of the parent insurance group. Some of the business in Europe was large and viable. But it also meant that they had over 130 policies which had annual premiums of under £250. That was unprofitable business for the UK, but potentially important as part of the firm's global relationship with the client. A UK consultant advised cutting these policies, but that ran against the Japanese desire to maintain relationships. Neither the hub nor the spoke is necessarily right: ambiguity is baked into the differing views from the hub and the spoke of the firm.

Effective global leaders understand this and work hard to bridge the gap. This is the challenge which faced Paul Abrahams, who is responsible for global communications at RELX, an Anglo-Dutch media company that used to be known as Reed Elsevier. It has annual turnover of €7 billion. He has to balance the need for global and local stories with the reality that the CEO only has a limited amount of time. In Paul's words: 'Only 8 per cent of our revenues are in the UK, so we have to go out and find stories. But will our CEO understand that an interview in Atlanta, where we have many employees and we need more engineers, is needed? We don't just need the *Financial Times* and *Wall Street Journal* because if we have an article in Atlanta that will communicate with our employees and with potential engineers. So you need a clear plan about what is important and what you are going to do.'

Relationships between the hub and the spoke do not always play out so smoothly. Instead of being complementary, the views from the hub and the spoke often set up conflict. There can be a lack of basic trust which is expressed forcibly:

▶ Hub view of the spokes: we have a clear strategy, but does the spoke have the skill, capacity and will to execute the strategy properly?

▶ Spoke's view of the hub: why does the spoke not listen to our needs? How can we have any influence over vital decisions which affect us? How can we achieve our goals when we are not properly supported from the centre?

This lack of trust is explored further in the chapter on trust. A trust deficit undermines the commitment to any global goals which top management may decide upon. Clarity at the top does not translate into either clarity or commitment at individual team level.

5. How to set goals for global teams

Strategic clarity at the top of the organisation often becomes ambiguity and uncertainty within a global team which is having to make the trade-offs between global priorities and local realities. The instinctive reaction of most managers is to drive for ever greater clarity and certainty. Finding clear goals for global teams is as easy as reading smoke signals in the fog. There is a point at which the drive for certainty has to make way for another approach: learning to cope with ambiguity.

The drive for clear goals in global teams can have unintended consequences:

▶ The team ceases to be a team: it becomes a series of silos, each chasing its own very clear goals.

▶ Team members are able to hide behind narrow performance metrics, while missing the broader mission.

▶ Goal setting becomes an end in its own right, consuming management time and effort.

▶ Attempting to find precise metrics becomes an exercise in futility.

Setting goals for global teams means that you have to steer between twin perils:

▶ The search for too much clarity becomes a self-defeating bureaucratic and political nightmare.

▶ The failure to achieve enough clarity and certainty results in chaos and confusion.

To be effective, the goals for the global team must:

▶ be common and consistent across the team

▶ be based on a shared context and understanding: from 'what' to 'how' and 'why'

▶ unite the team.

Common and consistent goals

In a western team, good goals are classically SMART[183] goals. A team is not a team if everyone on it has inconsistent SMART goals.

SMART goals have become a simple way of thinking about goals since the acronym was first coined in 1981. SMART stands for goals which are: specific, measurable, assignable (or achievable, depending on who you talk to), measurable and time bound. As with all simple systems, it is open to abuse. The main abuse for global teams is that the smarter the goal becomes, the narrower it becomes. Instead of becoming a call to action and enabling cross-border co-operation, it becomes a barrier to innovation and co-operation.

The best SMART goals are not just specific; they are very simple. They unite the team behind a common purpose. The Financial Times set itself a goal of one million sticky and profitable subscribers. That is simple and clear. It gives every team a sense of purpose and direction. It means that the Financial Times has to invest heavily in digital, and in developing tools and metrics to understand levels of subscriber engagement. The high-level goal can be translated into priorities for every team.

Regardless of how specific or flexible the goals are, for a global team there is one imperative for the goal: it must be a common goal. If different team members are working towards inconsistent goals, then it is no longer a team.

Achieving goal consistency which binds the team together is essential, but difficult in a global context.

For instance, one large law firm realised that it needed to be far more global in the way it worked with clients. So it decided to make 40 per cent of each partner's pay variable, split between individual performance and global performance. Lawyers are smart and worked out what they had to do to maximise their income: ignore the 20 per cent global pot and focus exclusively on their personal performance. They could not control the outcomes achieved by 300 other partners around the world, but they could control their own performance. This is a challenge which most global professional services firms face: how, in practice, do you incentivise cross-border working?

Mandarin Capital is a private equity fund which invests in Chinese companies looking to grow in Italy and Europe, and in Italian companies looking to grow in China. This could lead to two teams optimising their own portfolio: one in Italy and one in China. Here is how Gao Zhen describes their approach: 'We have two teams: one in Italy and one in China, but we have one common goal and operate as one team. The goal is to achieve excellent returns for our investors. Each project needs joint efforts of the team across the continents. In the process, we will jointly decide what is the best way to structure each deal and work closely to create value in our portfolio. If you only focus on one side of the coin, it will lead to failure to get the best overall return.'[184] Inevitably, that causes tension when China is having a good year and Italy is having a lean year, or vice versa. One team will feel it is carrying the other team. But by having one portfolio and one carry interest[185] for everyone, it creates peer pressure both to perform and to help each other.

SMART and common goals describe what good goals look like. That is half the story at best. The other half of the story is not about what the goals look like, but how you develop them. In a global context, the process is as important as the outcome.

Shared context and understanding: from 'what' to 'how' and 'why'

Top management may have a very clear view of what is required. But not everyone is at the top of the mountain and not everyone has the same view. Further down the mountain, people are dispersed and have different views

Achieving goal consistency which binds the team together is essential, but difficult in a global context.

from each other and from top management. This can be a source of great frustration to top management: they want everyone in the organisation to buy into their brave new world, so they work harder and harder at spreading their message. And that is precisely the wrong way to communicate.

Building buy-in means that you have to switch from broadcast mode to receive mode, at least for some of the time. The best leaders, like the best sales people, have two ears and one mouth. And they use them in that proportion. They listen at least twice as much as they talk. Simply repeating the same message louder and louder does not help understanding, nor does it build buy-in. Building buy-in means that you have to switch from broadcast mode to receive mode, at least for some of the time.

There will always be a degree of ambiguity about the trade-offs any global team needs to make. The heroic leader cannot resolve all those ambiguities personally, or even with a very smart staff team. The people who can resolve those ambiguities are the global team members themselves. They have to build ownership over its goals and understanding of its context. That means that dictated goals will never be sufficient. To embed the goals in the team, you need discussion and understanding. Focus discussion on the key issues which the team will face. Understanding the challenges in advance forces discussion and understanding on what matters.

For instance, Canon Europe faces all the normal challenges of global teams: how far to adapt products to each market, and who has accountability for what. But they face the additional challenge of knowing their customer. Their immediate customers are resellers, but their end customers are consumers who buy their cameras. So that is the trade-off they focus on:

'I always ask my team: who is your customer? This is about getting clear goals and shared values. Most people think of satisfying the direct customer and that means our resellers. But that may not satisfy the end customer: we have to focus on the end customer. But if your direct customer is not happy then you never reach the end customer. So there is a real trade-off on our goals here.' [186]

This is a dialogue which never ends. And the effective dialogue is focused on the end outcome. Here is how Shane Perlman, CEO of Modern Tribe, does it for his global workforce: 'We have a series of daily mantras that we keep on using. One is how do we win? We ask our customers over and over again how they define success until everyone agrees and understands what success looks like.

Anybody on the team should be able to answer the question: how do we succeed? Everyone should also answer the question: what do I do next and why?'

Both Canon and Modern Tribe focus the discussion on the customer and what they have to do to win there. That is a productive discussion which cuts through the fog. It is the same discussion that the FT creates around its goal of one million subscribers: 'the more complex it is, the simpler your goals must be so that you can create a unifying force. That is not just about efficiency: it creates conversations about how to get there.'[187] The point about the conversation is critical. Stating the goal is not enough. For the goal to become a truly shared goal, there has to be a conversation about the goal, its context, why it matters and how to get there.

> For the goal to become a truly shared goal, there has to be a conversation about the goal, its context, why it matters and how to get there.

This is very different from the traditional command and control leader and organisation, where clarity is created through very specific goals and accountability. Global teams exist in a world which is so complex that no one can ever know all the answers. You have to set the high-level goal, and then manage the discussion about what that means and how each team member can help reach the goal. The discussion has to cover:

► what the goal is
► why it is relevant
► how it will be measured
► who is responsible for what
► how to handle likely blockers: pre-empt problems.

The last discussion could be seen as a classic difficult conversation, but is vital to preventing even more difficult conversations and situations later on. Again, this is what Jon Ridding did when the Financial Times was taken over by the Nikkei. Both sides agreed that the success of the FT depended on it having editorial independence: it could not afford to become a mouthpiece for a vested interest like some of its rivals. Editorial independence is a vital tool to helping achieve the goal of one million subscribers: the FT needs to appeal to a broad base, not a narrow base of subscribers.

Editorial independence sounds a fine principle, like democracy and liberty. Few people are against it, but what does it mean in practice? So instead of talking about principles, they talked about practice and where it might go wrong. For instance, the Nikkei and Japan have a clear view on competing sovereignty claims in the South China Sea. Would editorial independence mean that the FT could take a different view? Confronting the difficult issues before they become crises make it far easier for the team to work well. And in this case, editorial independence was confirmed: the Nikkei and FT can take different views where they see fit.

Achieving a shared understanding of the goals means that the goals have to be broken down into bite-sized chunks for the team. Help team members understand that there are good ways and bad ways of achieving their goals, as one Singapore-based leader explained:

'Even if people see the big goal they get confused about how to get there, so I have to break it down into small bite-sized chunks. You have to be very clear, especially in Asia. You need to hold their hands. You work back from the goal and set it out very clearly: sometimes you have to be a manager while leading them.'[188]

Effective goals for global teams have to be shared goals, and that means that the process of developing the goal is as important as the outcome. Both need to be right for the team to work well.

Unite the team

Setting goals is not just about plans. It is about people. Plans do not inspire people, or build commitment and belief. You need a team which not only understands the goal, but also believes in it and is committed to it. If the team is clear about the goal, then you can trust that they will build the plan to get there. If there is enough commitment to the goal from a talented team, you can trust that they will find a creative way of getting there.

For instance, Frank Fredericks decided to set himself the modest goal of reducing violence between faiths globally. He has created a network of like-minded people in his organisation, World Faith.[189] Clearly, there are many ways of reducing interfaith violence. The outcome may be clear, but there are many roads to the destination. In Fredericks' words: 'Simon Sinek points out that Martin Luther King said "I have a dream", not "I have a plan". If I find giving out hotdogs solves religious violence we will be in the hotdog business. You start from the end and then reverse engineer back to the solution.'

Teams get more excited about a dream than they do about a plan. If you trust your team to come up with the plan, there is a real risk they may come up with something new, original, creative and effective. If they believe it is their plan, not yours, they will be committed to it. People rarely argue against their own ideas, but will be more than happy to pick holes in your plan – when you are out of the room.

This matters because in a global team you have to trust that remote teams on different time zones will make good decisions. Team members clearly see the link between goals, trust, accountability, delegation and performance:

'You've got to trust that, no matter if things are being done differently in different places, it's all going in the right direction. If we all understand and agree the goals – or, better, are involved in helping set them – then we can trust people to delegate the execution.'[190]

Involving the global team in setting the goal requires investment of time: it is an investment which pays handsome dividends. Not involving the team properly in the goal-setting process is fast and easy to start with, but leads to disengagement, misunderstandings, loss of trust and a downward spiral of performance. Use the goal-setting process to unite the team.

6. What is the point of having a global team?

The challenges of managing a global team raise a simple question: why bother? The research showed that global teams work to achieve one or more of seven goals:

Desired benefit	Type of team and organisation
Serve a global client	Consulting, IT
Deliver a global product	Autos, fast food, aircraft
Reduce costs and increase efficiency	Outsourcing, supply chain, finance
Achieve economies of scale	R&D, pharma, civil aviation
Access the best talent globally	Professional services
Innovate and learn globally	All, potentially
Build network strength and scope	Amazon, Google, social media

Most of these benefits are not 'nice to have' benefits. They are 'must have' benefits. The scale of R&D and investment in building a large new aircraft and developing its engines, or creating the next generation of computer chips means that global scale is the minimum viable scale. Fujitsu's clients were more or less demanding that Fujitsu move from a geographic to an industry organisation: they wanted the highest level of industry expertise to be available to them. For the web design firms, the logic was equally simple: clients want the very best talent at the very lowest cost. If you only recruit from Silicon Valley, you may or may not get the best talent; you will certainly bake in high costs. The logic of globalisation is relentless: you have to organise globally in order to stay competitive and stay in business.

You have to organise globally in order to stay competitive and stay in business.

Two examples will make the point about how global working is inevitable in more and more industries.

Music industry: the customer imperative

The music industry should in many ways be a local industry. The music giants of Bolivia are probably a minority taste in Tokyo and vice versa. It is not obviously global. Even at the start of this millennium, account management was a national job. Music was sold in physical format, mainly CDs, which went through national retailers. In 2014, for the first time, download revenues exceeded physical sales.[191] Downloads and streaming are dominated by global players: iTunes, Google, Spotify, YouTube. For music companies like Warner Music, that changes everything:

'There was a need from our largest global retail and streaming partners. They do not want to speak to multiple, different account handlers about a major global release. What they want are central contacts who will organise the release for many countries. We have a team that looks after these accounts.' [192]

As ever, globalisation makes things harder. The global platforms such as Spotify want to work with global partners; local radio stations want local partners who can help them build relevant local playlists for their local audience. The job of the global team is to bridge this global and local divide. To make matters more interesting, each country used to have its own release date for new albums: that does not work for a global release, so every country has to agree a common release date.

IT and BPO outsourcing: the competitive imperative

At the start of this millennium, outsourcing meant handing over your IT or business processes to a specialist provider who would probably be based in the same country as your own. IBM had operations in India, but with just 9,000 people there as late as 2003. By 2015 it had over 100,000 employees there.[193] India has the skills, at a huge cost advantage versus the West. IT programmers in India might earn $5,000 to $15,000 in India, depending on experience.[194] A US software engineer might cost $50 to $150 an hour, again depending on experience.[195] That comes out at $65,000 to $200,000 a year at 75 per cent utilisation. As a client or a competitor, it is hard to ignore this huge cost differential.[196]

Inevitably, once one major outsourcer starts to offer American levels of quality at Indian prices, it becomes impossible for competition not to follow. The result has been a rush to India. By 2015, all the main outsourcers had built large operations in India, from more or less a standing start in 2000, including:[197]

Number of India-based employees, end 2015, estimated:

Cognizant 140,000

Accenture 80,000

Cap Gemini 40,000

This is in addition to Indian IT and BPO[198] providers such as Tata Consulting Services (350,000 employees),[199] Infosys (195,000 employees)[200] and Wipro (170,000 employees).[201] Going global is not a free lunch. These outsourcers face huge challenges in making sure the needs of the remote client are understood and met; that goals are properly understood and that all the challenges of making global teams work are met.

More and more firms and industries are finding that going global is not an option: it is a matter of survival. This means that more and more firms face the challenge of making global teams work.

Conclusions

Goal setting is about substance and style. How you set the goals is as important as the goals themselves.

How you set the goals is as important as the goals themselves.

Substance

The obvious, but frequently missed, starting point is to be clear about what you are trying to achieve by being global. This vision is critical context for your teams. When you translate the vision into specific goals, you will naturally try to make them SMART goals to achieve the greatest clarity and focus. But inevitably, there will always be ambiguity about priorities, especially for a global team which has to balance global and local needs. This is where clarity of the overall vision matters: when the team has to make a trade-off between competing stakeholders and demands, then a clear vision helps the team decide what to do.

There is a trade-off around detail. Classical management would set detailed goals and manage tightly against them. In a global context it is often better to set broader goals for the team because micro-managing against detailed targets is neither possible nor desirable. Micro-managing is not possible because conditions vary so much around the world and you cannot know what is happening everywhere all the time. Micro-managing is not desirable because it shows lack of trust in the team; that leads to demotivation and lower performance which can trigger even greater micro-management and a death spiral of performance starts.

Style

Too often planning becomes a black-box exercise led by staff and management at head office. Instead of being a black-box exercise, goal setting needs to be open. It has to involve teams around the world, for three reasons:

▶ An open process builds buy-in and commitment to the goals.

▶ Being open forces discussion, which then allows the team to understand the context and why the goals matter.

▶ Once the team understands the context, they are better able to make the right decisions at moments of uncertainty and ambiguity; that in turn builds trust and confidence between the team and head office.

Goals which appear clear at the top of the firm are rarely clear by the time you reach the global team. You have to work hard to make sure the global team understands not just the goal: the team also needs to understand the context for the goal and why the goals are important.

7

Systems and processes
The building blocks of success

Management systems provide the plumbing of the global firm. Plumbing is unglamorous, and you only discover its true value when it goes wrong. These are hygiene factors, not motivational factors. No one is motivated by management systems which work well, but when they don't work you are likely to feel demotivated: 'just because it's the small stuff, it can be what upsets people the most.'[202] So it is important that management systems work, but you cannot rely on them alone for the success of the global team.

Global team members recognise this distinction. Management systems are rarely their top concern: leadership, trust and communications were more important. But when systems and processes are mentioned, they are a source of real frustration to the team.

Here is how often global team members rated different management systems as one of their top five issues:

▶ Roles and accountability   33%

▶ Processes and procedures   25%

▶ Decision making   19%

▶ Budgets   8%

▶ Rewards and recognition   6%

▶ Any of the above   62%[203]

In addition to these, one more management system came up unprompted: learning and innovation.

This chapter explores the following:

▶ Why systems and processes are harder in a global team

▶ Accountability

▶ Decision making

▶ Learning and innovation.

Technology is notable by its absence. This has been covered, where relevant, under communications. Budgets and rewards and recognition will be mentioned in passing in this chapter, but are not seen as pressing issues by most global teams.

Why systems and processes are harder in a global team

Any team needs clear roles, accountabilities, systems and processes. Even on a domestic team, there can be challenges in achieving clarity across the team about who does what, and about how different priorities and perspectives can be resolved. The challenges for a global team are far greater than for a domestic team. There are three reasons for this:

▶ Global teams find themselves dealing with inconsistent processes and procedures.

▶ Domestic teams find it easier to adjust to any process problems.

▶ There are high barriers to fixing process problems on a global team.

Global teams find themselves dealing with inconsistent processes and procedures

Most firms struggle to have consistent processes around the world. Differences may be driven by different customer or regulatory requirements. More often, they are driven by history. Each location creates its own processes. Even if they start out the same as elsewhere, over time they diverge as each country conducts its own process improvement and re-engineering exercises and adapts to local needs.

Within a domestic team, everyone will be working with the same processes and procedures. In theory, the same should be true on global teams. In practice, global teams find they struggle with the challenge of consistency:

▶ 'There is no point in two locations each improving their own processes in their own ways because you will still be inefficient.'[204]

▶ 'You cannot assume that if it works here then that is how it works over there. So consistency of organisation is a hurdle.'[205]

▶ 'Consistency is really important because we are on the admin side. If both teams go about the same goal in different ways you'll end up with a nightmare.'[206]

▶ 'It is all about creating consistency in the void: figuring out the patterns that set people up and getting the daily habits right.'[207]

The need for clarity is felt most keenly by front-line team members who suffer the consequences of lack of clarity: 'Across our organisation we need to know who does what. If a server falls over we can patch it, but headquarters will refuse the patch that we want to put in: so who is responsible for the resulting outage?'[208] Clarity is required not just on one-off decisions, but also on routine administration. High volumes and high complexity drive the need for clarity of roles, processes and account- ability: 'Unclear roles and accountability really screw you up on adminis- tration. You have to know who is supposed to do what, especially on the administration side because there are high volumes and it operates much like a factory.'[209]

Team members at the spokes of the firm are 48 per cent more likely to mention processes and procedures as a challenge than people at the hub.[210] Junior team members were 60 per cent more likely than bosses to focus on processes and procedures.[211] This is unsurprising, but challenging. It is unsurprising because it is people in the front line who are most affected by any problems: they are the people who have to resolve the problem. At the top of the organisation, these challenges are often regarded as noise: irritating but not vital. But when process prob- lems are not addressed, front-line team members quickly become demo- tivated and feel unsupported by top management. As we shall see, fixing process problems can be hard for any team, and especially for a global team.

Domestic teams find it easier to adjust to any process problems

If a process goes awry on a domestic team, it is fairly easy to fix: you can pick up the phone or you can walk across the floor. The problem can be identified and fixed in real time, before it spirals out of control.

On a global team, the problem may not even be apparent until it is too late. For instance, if a trade is logged incorrectly in New York at 1pm local time, London may not even find out about it until 9am the next working day: too late. And when London discovers the problem, they have to wait until New York comes back online four or five hours later. And fixing the problem is not a matter of walking around the floor and finding the three or four key people who can fix the problem. If the processes between New York and London are not consistent, it may be hard to pin down who needs to be involved, and then it is even harder to actually get them together on a conference call or video call. Even after the formal call, it is harder to do the informal follow-up to make sure that the solution is sticking, and to give support and help where needed. At least New York and London speak the same language (more or less): once you factor in differences of language and culture, the challenges escalate even further.

Every step of addressing a process problem is far easier on a domestic team than on a global team, which makes it even more important to have clear and consistent processes. Unfortunately, there are significant barriers to achieving such consistency.

There are high barriers to fixing process problems on a global team

All firms are prisoners of their past. Firms, teams and individuals are naturally reluctant to change a successful formula: if it has worked in the past, why risk changing it? Don't mess with success. Even struggling firms find it

All firms are prisoners of their past.

hard to change: the risks and effort of process change (which can seem dull and boring) outweigh any perceived benefits, which are often hard to quantify.

This inertia can be seen in all sorts of small ways, even in the language of the firm. For instance:

▶ P&G is famed for its brand management. But within P&G, brand management has always been referred to as the Advertising Department. It might make sense to change the name, but no one sees it as a battle worth fighting.

▶ British Telecom was set free from government control over 30 years ago, but staff still use public sector language from the past: they refer to vacation as 'leave'.[212]

Changing processes and procedures is far harder than changing the way language is used. The problem is one of inertia, which comes in two forms: emotional and rational.

Emotional inertia is about people and teams getting stuck in a familiar routine. It may not be the best routine, but if it more or less works then people will stick with it. Any change to the process is risky. Adapting to a process brought in from another part of the global network can feel like a sell-out. The result is that people do not want to change: 'It is incredible how two groups of individuals trying to do the same thing stick to their own way fanatically.'[213] Inevitably, the team will find plenty of rational reasons for not changing, but these are a smokescreen. People avoid change because change is risky: it means adapting to new and unfamiliar ways, with uncertain consequences in terms of time, effort and outcomes.

The second reason for inertia is at least partly rational. While it may be in the interests of the firm to optimise its processes, it is not in the interests of any individual or team to do so. Any one team or individual lacks the authority, capacity, skills, budget and time to effect the complete process change, so it is rational to keep on going with a sub-optimal process. This means that process change has to be driven from the top. But as we have noted (above) senior management see process change as a much lower priority than frontline workers, because they are less affected by the consequences of poor processes. This challenge was clearly expressed by a country manager in SE Asia:

'Processes are given and they are taken for granted especially in large companies. People think that processes are set and cast in stone and it is not worth their while trying to change it and there is nothing you can do about it. But there is always a better way of doing things.' [214]

In a domestic team, you can see where there are process problems. In a global team, the process problems are harder to see. One of the jobs of the team leader is to make sure you see these problems clearly and respond appropriately.

Accountability

Clear roles and processes enable clear accountability and high autonomy

If you do not know who is responsible for what, you cannot hold anyone to account. This means that accountability and clear processes are two sides of the same coin. Clear roles and processes enable clear accountability and high autonomy: they were all seen as part of the same idea:

▶ 'If you are not clear about roles then accountability cannot follow.'[215]

▶ 'Accountability goes with autonomy.'[216]

Accountability is not just a systems issue: it is a deep cultural issue as well. Different cultures have different attitudes to accountability, and that causes confusion on a global team. There are four aspects to the accountability challenge:

▶ Accountability and personal autonomy

▶ Accountability: culture and mindset

▶ Accountability: individual or collective?

▶ How to drive accountability in a global team.

We will explore each of these themes in turn.

Accountability and autonomy

It is reasonably obvious that if you want to be autonomous, then you have to be accountable for your decisions and your actions. As an autonomous person, you cannot blame your decisions and your actions on someone else. This should reflect a simple equation where autonomy = accountability. On global teams, nothing is simple.

In practice, there are three challenges to the accountability and autonomy equation on global teams:

Many leaders find it hard to delegate

Autonomy does not always follow accountability. Many global teams fudge accountability and autonomy. The team leader is happy to grant accountability, but then puts in a series of checks and balances which erodes autonomy. There are checks around decision making and there are process checks in terms of reporting, monitoring and measuring. These checks limit the autonomy of the team member, and also limit the amount of accountability the team member feels. This leads to team member frustration: they have the accountability, but lack the autonomy and authority which their accountability requires.

Many cultures prefer to delegate upwards

Team members want more autonomy, but often prove very adept at delegating problems upwards. In the words of one frustrated team leader: 'People say they want more autonomy and then you give it to them but then they want more leadership. So this is a cultural change which has to take place.'[217]

▶ 'India can be hierarchical and that can be a challenge as decisions get passed upwards.'[218]

▶ 'In Indian firms the owner makes all the decisions and you can only make suggestions.'[219]

▶ 'In Thailand they just won't make decisions. They might make a recommendation.'[220]

▶ 'Everything gets delegated upwards in Thailand.'[221]

Too much autonomy leads to the creation of power barons

Ultimately, too much autonomy leads to the creation of power barons who work in their own castles. On a global team you need people who want to share and to learn and to help each other: if this does not happen, then there is not much point in having a global team. If you want to serve global clients, build global expertise and learn across borders, then geographic power barons have to be challenged (see text box below).

Chris[222] was appointed to run the European operations of an IT firm. She faced considerable resistance because:

▶ she was a woman

▶ she did not come from Europe

▶ she wanted to organise around industry groups, not geography.

▶

She could possibly have been forgiven for being a woman and being foreign. But the power barons were not going to let her destroy their geographic power bases. So they all came up with sophisticated arguments to show how Italy, Germany, Poland and the UK were completely different.

Chris knew that clients wanted cross-border support and that they wanted deep industry expertise, not just local generalists. So she took stock. She realised that some power barons could be useful in her new world, and others would simply try to block progress. So she re-organised along industry lines. The power barons who had been given European-wide responsibility for an industry suddenly discovered eloquent arguments as to why industry expertise trumped local knowledge. The other power barons found themselves looking for jobs elsewhere.

If you want to make progress, you have to challenge the power barons.

The challenge of accountability and autonomy is not just a rational issue. It is also about culture and politics. As a team leader you have to balance what you believe is the ideal solution with what is the practical solution in your context. What works in practice is better than what works in theory.

Accountability: culture and mindset[223]

Accountability means different things in a domestic and a global setting: there is a big step up in accountability for global team members. The standard of accountability required of a global team member is higher than that of a domestic team member.

There are three different levels of accountability at which you can operate:

▶ Victim mindset
▶ Corporate mindset
▶ Accountable/global mindset.

The differences between these mindsets are set out in the table below:

	Accountable (global) mindset	Corporate (domestic) mindset	Victim mindset
Locus of control	I control my destiny, and use influence beyond my formal role	My control is defined by my formal role and accountability	My destiny is shaped by decisions and people beyond my control
Self-efficacy	I seek out new opportunities to learn, grow and perform	I perform well within my role definition	I avoid unfamiliar, ambiguous and difficult situations

Most firms like to promote the accountable mindset. The reality is that corporate and victim mindsets are very common. Maintaining the accountability mindset is a real challenge. We will look at each of the mindsets in turn.

The victim mindset

The victim mindset is toxic to success. Complaining about poor communications, about being excluded from decisions, about not having enough support is natural. Everyone complains from time to time. But complaining does nothing to help the team. Complaining sets up exactly the wrong culture. It creates an 'us' and 'them' culture which is divisive; it legitimises complaining as an alternative to taking control; it fosters a sense of grievance. Complaining, not acting, is classic victim mindset: the victim feels shaped by events they cannot control.

The victim mindset is not confined to junior staff. It is surprisingly easy for even senior and successful people to fall into the victim mindset. Here is one global team leader talking about some highly paid masters of the universe:

'The overseas often feels excluded. They will say that they cannot get access to someone at head office and they can't meet so-and-so. But then I say: why don't you just fly over and meet them? I would happily pay for their flight. If they fly over they can get more connected. Instead of complaining and feel linked like a victim they should take responsibility and make the connection themselves.'[224]

As a global team leader, you need to let people vent their frustrations and hear their complaints, otherwise

You need to let people vent their frustrations and hear their complaints.

you will never hear what is going on. The challenge is to then help the 'victims' discover that there is an alternative. You have to help them take control of their destiny; and if they cannot control their destiny, they can at least learn how to influence it.

On global teams the absence of control is normal, which makes it easy to fall into the victim mindset. But there is an alternative to control: influence. Team members have to learn to influence people and decisions who are outside their control. If they can do this, they move from the victim mindset to the accountable mindset. The accountable mindset does not complain: it acts.

The corporate mindset

The corporate mindset traditionally matches responsibility with authority. In large and complex organisations this creates stability and control. This is how machine bureaucracies work. It also creates a bureaucratic mindset: a tick-box culture in which each person complies with the system, but does not challenge the system and will not take initiative outside their narrowly defined role.

The corporate or bureaucratic mindset does not work on a global team. Global teams exist in a more ambiguous environment than many domestic teams. If you are to control your destiny, you have to influence decisions, people and events which happen far away and out of sight. If you stick within your narrow role definition, you are in danger of adopting the victim mindset where you complain about being a victim of circumstances beyond your control.

For a global team member, the corporate mindset is not enough: they need a truly accountable mindset which believes it can influence decisions, events and people which are outside their formal responsibility.

The accountable mindset

Perhaps the best book you never need to read is called *Control Your Destiny or Someone Else Will*.[225] The reason you do not need to read the book is that the message is in the title, and it is a good reflection of the accountable mindset.

The accountable mindset is powerful on global teams. It does not accept that power is constrained by formal job titles, budgets or role descriptions. The accountable mindset takes control where it can, and where it cannot take control it uses influence. The accountable mindset does not use the complexity and ambiguity of global teams to hide or to complain: instead, the accountable mindset will use ambiguity as an opportunity to build influence and push forwards.

The accountable mindset will use ambiguity as an opportunity to build influence and push forwards.

The accountable mindset is confident to take on new challenges, to seek new opportunities and to learn and grow: these are the qualities you need when taking on the challenges of working in and with different cultures around the world.

The domestic corporate mindset is a comfort zone which is not available to global team members. Global team members either have to step up to the true accountability mindset, or they default back to the victim mindset. The corporate mindset is not a sustainable option for global team members. The complexity and ambiguity of a global team requires using influence to control events that are beyond your formal responsibility. Failing to step up and influence leads to acting like a victim who complains about being controlled by events and people.

Accountability systems matter, but they have to be supported by the right mindset as well.

Accountability: individual or collective?

Strong individual accountability is a basic building block of western management. Many people can share responsibility, but ultimately one person has to be accountable. However, we have learned in the past 20 years that western management is not the only way of working.

There is an alternative to personal accountability: collective accountability. Collective accountability is not just a different system, it is a different culture: 'In Japan roles and accountabilities are not clear but everyone works together and they are prepared to work outside their formal roles. If I am only working with Japanese people then this is not important but if I work with non-Japanese people then you need much more clarity about roles and accountability. If orders from top management are not clear then American people do nothing, but the Japanese will think what it is that management really want and how they can help.'[226]

153

There are three reasons why some level of collective accountability can be desirable on a global team:

▶ Global teams are emergent: there is always some degree of change and ambiguity for the global team to deal with. This means that team members must be ready to cover for each other, fill in the gaps and improve the process. This is as important for westernised global teams as for any other: 'An ability to deal with ambiguity is really important. It drives me potty when people want total role clarity, because then they just spend the rest of the time defending their turf.'[227]

▶ Global teams need teamwork. Accountability can be an excuse to hide in a silo, which is the opposite of team work. At the extreme, if you have complete clarity over processes and accountabilities, then you have no need for a global team: you can simply throw work over the wall from one silo to the next. By having a team, you recognise that the whole is greater than the sum of the parts: there are areas where you need collaboration across the team. That leads to collective accountability. Anyone who has seen Japanese teams working late into the night to support just one team member will realise that collective accountability is not a soft option. It creates a huge amount of peer pressure to perform: no one wants to be the person who lets the rest of the team down.

Accountability can be an excuse to hide in a silo, which is the opposite of team work.

▶ Narrow accountability encourages short-term thinking and is an obstacle to innovation. For instance, Europol plays a vital role in dealing with cross-border crime. It needs to keep ahead in terms of the technology and techniques of criminals and it needs to work on long-term programmes against drugs, people trafficking and terror. But the accountability regime does not enable this: 'senior officers have very short performance cycles of perhaps just six months so it is not in their interest to look five years ahead. They get moved often, so they focus on operations today and they get very resistant to change because change will not help them today.'[228] Short-term and individual accountability encourages individuals to focus on polishing their résumé, not on tackling the long-term collective challenges they face.

Making collective accountability work is a cultural challenge. In the wrong culture it leads to the wrong behaviour:

▶ Everything is up for challenge by everyone, so debate never stops.

▶ Everyone jumps on any success.

▶ Everyone runs from problems.

▶ Performance management is hard because it is not clear who did what, especially on a global team where performance cannot be observed directly.

Given these cultural challenges, collective responsibility works best in homogeneous cultures where the rules are understood and observed. Global teams are normally a cultural melting pot, with high degrees of complexity and ambiguity. Under these circumstances, most global teams have a natural desire to seek greater clarity around roles, responsibilities and personal accountabilities.

The challenge for the team leader is to balance personal and collective accountability. The key is to work out where the team needs to work as a team, and where team members can operate independently. Key decisions are the concern of the whole team; routine work is for individuals. Between these two extremes there is a wide grey area.

How to drive accountability in a global team

The tools for driving accountability are broadly the same in global and domestic teams. But in one area, some global firms are starting a quiet revolution in the use of technology to deliver both accountability and autonomy.

The traditional tools for driving accountability are the budget, a RACI analysis[229] and a team charter. We will look at each of these, and then at the radical use of technology.

Budgets and accountability

Budgets drive accountability. A budget is essentially a contract between two layers of management. The higher level wants the best outcome for the least resource. The lower level wants the minimum outcome for the maximum resource. It is a game which is played countless times in countless firms, and most of the budget negotiation games are well known and do not need much rehearsal here.

Budgets drive accountability.

However, it is much harder for global teams to negotiate budgets well. The team is not hard-wired into the key stakeholders; it may not understand the budget process and more or less certainly will not be involved in the vital early planning discussions which set the budget framework. The budget-setting process, like most processes, is far harder in a global team than in a domestic team. A good budget should not just reflect a good outcome for all parties, it should also reflect a fair process. The need for fair process as well as a fair outcome was widely perceived:

▶ 'This is really hard if you are working remotely because it is very difficult to renegotiate the budget.' Web design, Argentina[230]

▶ 'The flow of the budget is unclear: is it through the SPU or the region, and if we need more resource is it clear where you are meant to look?' NGO India[231]

▶ 'The key is to get everyone from the ground up involved in the budget so that it is their budget not just a top-down imposition and then they understand the context and purpose and they see alternative perspectives.' Financial services, North America[232]

Used well, the budget process can help you force a discussion on both sides about priorities and resources. For the global team, this depends critically on having a team leader who is well connected with the informal and formal decision-making networks and processes. Equally, top management have to ensure that the budget is owned by the team: an imposed budget will not be owned and there will be a low sense of accountability.

Transforming losses into investment: the art of budget negotiation in a global team[233]

The one-way ticket to Japan looked less attractive when it turned out that the local business had no sales, no sales prospects and no active business. But it did have a lot of bills which needed to be paid.

The Japan business was part of the American subsidiary of a French firm, and was led by an expat from London. It was clear that if the financial team in New York or Paris saw the Tokyo numbers, they would close the business. That would make it a short and less than successful posting for the expat. Instead of the victim mindset, he adopted the global accountability mindset and bought a series of round the world tickets. In both directions. He then spent the next few months finding excuses to visit New York and Paris, while trying to find clients in Tokyo.

The visits to New York and Paris were to spin a story: the firm could create an integrated business in Japan for $4 million over four years to serve global clients. Or it could exit Japan and lose global clients worth far more than $4million. Or it could invest $5 million in buying another firm in Japan, which is risky and might not integrate. Top management decided to invest $4 million in building an integrated Japan business.

The $4 million investment was an excuse to make a loss of $4 million over three years in the consulting business. Losses are bad, investment is good. But in consulting, they are the same.

As a global team, you have to stay connected to the budget process and influence decisions in your favour. It is far harder, but it is essential if you are to control your destiny.

Team charters and RACI matrix

Objectively, team charters and a RACI matrix offer a good way of defining who does what: clarity helps on a global team.

A RACI matrix defines who is responsible, who is accountable, who needs to be consulted and who needs to be informed with regard to different tasks. There are variations of RACI, such as RASCI, which also identifies whose support is required on each task. We can leave aside the variations of this matrix: the purpose is to drive role clarity into the team.

The team charter takes a broader look at the goals of the team, its mission, values and the key processes and protocols it will follow. A team charter can take any shape you want it to take. Like the RACI matrix, it is there to help your team achieve clarity of purpose, process and direction.

These are valuable outputs which should require modest effort. And yet most global teams hate them. They see them as a bureaucratic waste of time, loved by consultants but not by managers. These tools are hated because:

▶ they take too long to negotiate, leading to pointless debates and wasted time

157

- they move the focus from work to talking about work
- they never fully capture the ambiguity and complexity which the team faces
- events mean that everything changes, which leads to further time spent reviewing the charter and the RACI matrix.

Where team charters have been useful, the value has been in the process, not in the outcome.

Where team charters and a RACI matrix have been useful, the value has been in the process, not in the outcome. The team has recognised from the start that it will not achieve a perfect definition of roles, processes or even priorities. But it has used a short process, often at an offsite event, to work through the major challenges facing the team, and to agree how they will work together. Where the tools are used to build mutual understanding and respect, they work. Where they are used to build a detailed contract between team members, it becomes counter-productive.

Use of technology

In previous chapters we have seen how small and innovative global firms such as Groove, Modern Tribe and The House are using technology to drive accountability and autonomy.

The effect of technology is to bring total transparency to the work of the global team.

The effect of technology is to bring total transparency to the work of the global team. Transparency is easy in a domestic team: you can see what everyone is doing in real time. On a global team there is no visibility of what everyone is doing. Technology enables the global team to re-create the visibility of being on a domestic team.

Four types of technology enable this collective visibility:

- Project management software such as Trello, where progress is open and visible to everyone on the team
- Chat forums such as Slack: this is open and visible to everyone, as opposed to email which is a private communications platform. It allows the office chat to happen online
- Document editing such as google.docs. This is open to everyone on the team; changes can be seen in real time. In contrast, Word is a private

editing tool, and sharing it often leads to different people working on slightly different versions

▶ Video conferencing allows people to see each other and pick up the visual cues which are not apparent when using email or the phone.

High visibility, by definition, makes it hard to hide. Everyone knows how everyone else is working. This drives much higher levels of accountability, and can lead to a highly coercive or highly supportive culture: technology can be used well or poorly.

This use of technology has strong echoes of TQM.[234] A typical example from a car factory[235] shows that huge amounts of performance data is made available in real time to the teams on the assembly line. The teams then self-manage both the work, their performance and the improvement process. The result is a revolution in trust and performance. The emerging use of technology in global teams is creating the transparency, performance data, accountability and autonomy which are the hallmarks of successful TQM on the factory floor. If office productivity can be transformed the same way, we may be on the brink of another productivity revolution.

Decision-making systems

Decision making for global teams is a challenge for three reasons:

▶ Informal decision-making networks load the dice against the global team

▶ Formal decision-making processes also load the dice against the global team

▶ Decision making varies by culture, which makes decision making within the team difficult.

This section explores these challenges, and what can be done to address them.

Informal decision-making networks load the dice against the global team

In theory, good decision-making systems should be rational and formal. In theory, there should not be war, disease and poverty. In practice, decision making is both emotional and political, and this hurts global teams because it is hard to manage emotions and politics at a distance.

Politics of decision making

The problems of decision making start because individuals, of all cultures, are not good at making decisions. As one team leader put it: 'Some people find it very hard to make decisions, even if it is: "shall we go out for a pizza this evening?"'[236] There is a good reason for people disliking making decisions. Making a decision is risky, and the risk is asymmetric. If you make the right decision, then you get no credit for it: either it is seen with hindsight as an obvious decision, or everyone else claims the credit. If you make the wrong decision, you find you are in a very lonely place. But there is no harm in being catastrophically wrong, as long as everyone else was also backing the same course of action. The result is that decision making is not a purely rational act: it is a political act in which you have to build consensus and commitment.

The politics of decision making tilts the playing field against global teams. Research shows that there is real home nation, and home state, bias when it comes to tough decisions:

'Dismissals of divisional employees are less common in divisions located closer to corporate headquarters; and firms appear to adopt a "pecking-order" and divest out-of-state entities before instate.' [237]

Emotions and decision making

Business schools attempt to teach rational decision making, and force students to study things like Bayesian analysis. Most managers go through their entire careers without ever using or understanding Bayesian analysis.[238]

Human decision making is not all rational, and executives are humans. There is a large body of evidence, notably from Nobel Prize winning economist (and psychologist) Daniel Kahneman,[239] that we all use short cuts to make decisions. These rules of thumb, or heuristics, are useful because they save time. They are also dangerous, because they can lead us astray. We are easily biased by the first evidence we find, by what other people think, by what we want the answer to be, by how vivid the evidence is. And we are led astray by risk aversion: we do not want to make a decision which will make us look dumb.

In practice, decisions are often made informally and they are intuitive, emotional and political. Data is used in decisions the same way that drunks use a lamp post: for support, not illumination. This matters for global teams. If decision making was purely rational and followed formal processes, then global teams would be at no disadvantage compared to domestic teams. But where decision making is based on personal perceptions, personal agendas and per-

Data is used in decisions the same way that drunks use a lamp post: for support, not illumination.

sonal biases, the global team is at a huge disadvantage. You can only discover the bias and agendas of each stakeholder through continual dialogue, preferably face to face and in private where you are more likely to hear the truth. This is relatively easy if you are in the same office as the other stakeholders; it is close to impossible if you are in a different time zone in a different culture with a different language.

Politics and emotions are best managed in person and in private. They depend on having good bonds of trust with each stakeholder. That means that a global team has to be linked into all the power networks. Normally, that is the role of the team leader who has to be able to bridge the gap between the hub and the spokes of the firm.

Formal decision-making processes also load the dice against the global team

Formal decision making also works against global teams. Most formal decision-making systems are geared up to saying 'no'. Corporate approval systems are, in effect, disapproval systems. Formal decision-making systems require sign off from multiple stakeholders such as Finance, HR, Legal, Sales, Marketing and more. Each person with sign-off rights has the right of veto. They can stop the decision, but they cannot approve it; they can only approve their own small part of the decision. Managing this decision-making process is time-consuming and frustrating for domestic teams: it is far harder for global teams who do not have the ability to walk round to each stakeholder and argue their case in person. It is even harder if the decisions and the paperwork are all in a second language.

The more formal and bureaucratic decision making is, the harder it is for global teams. Any process which is hard for a domestic team will be harder for a global team to manage. The two enemies of simple decision making are silos and hierarchy. The experience of dealing with silos and hierarchy remotely is not pleasant:

▶ 'You have to get the right approval with the right information at the right time. But different groups need different processes and different protocols. For instance engineering versus financial versus legal versus marketing: America versus Japan versus Europe. They all have different ways of thinking, expressing and working.'[240]

▶ 'Here, we have product managers who understand the end-to-end process. But at HQ it is a much more silo organisation, so at manager level they cannot decide. Each manager has a boss who is not in the meeting. So they then have to ask their boss for permission and nothing happens.'[241]

▶ 'I talk to HQ, and they simply say "I want to talk to my boss so please wait two days while I make a report for my boss".'[242]

▶ 'There are too many layers, too many silos and no one talks to anyone else, so it is impossible to make a decision.'[243]

The solution for most global teams is the same as for most domestic teams: work the informal systems: 'we just go round the formal process and use the back door'.[244] Working the back door is an uneasy balance of respecting the formal processes while working the informal channels. Managing the balance and working the informal channels remotely is hard:

'In making decisions there are always company rules and procedures. People naturally follow these written and unwritten rules. Unwritten rules means lobbying, we are not robots we are people. People may not understand what you really want, so we have to work at it. We need to show passion, to show why each decision is important.

I go to Japan about 14 times a year: face-to-face meetings are essential. Of course we have our business meetings but then we have drinks and we get to know each other and trust each other as well. So much decision making is difficult by phone: you can't have a drink, you can't have an honest conversation, you can't have a one to one meeting, you can't have a relaxing time, you can't find out what people are really thinking.' [245]

Working the back door depends on having a team leader who is an insider, not an outsider. The team needs someone who knows all the stakeholders, has their trust and knows all their agendas, and can speak their language culturally and literally.

Head office also needs to play a role in managing decisions around global teams. Just as the global team leader needs to be an insider who understands HQ, so headquarters needs to be populated by managers who understand the global context. This can be very hard for firms which are prestigious in their home country and have a home country bias: they will have low global awareness. As one executive complained: 'these people don't know other countries, simply don't know. They don't understand different cultures and different customer needs.'[246] Global teams need to deal with a globally aware head office: that opens up a wide agenda around talent management and culture.

Working the informal networks is consistent with also working the formal process and making the rational case. The global team leader needs to be an advocate marshalling the facts and numbers to make the case: the rational case gives the key decision makers the excuse to approve the decision, and makes it more embarrassing for them to oppose the decision. If following the formal process requires drawing up NPV, ROI or IRR[247] calculations, or doing a SWOT and sensitivity analysis complete with a risk assessment, then that is what the team has to do. The team needs to start with the desired answer and work back from that: start at the bottom right-hand corner of the spreadsheet with the 'correct' answer and then work out plausible assumptions which will enable that answer to be shown. The global team has to work harder and shout louder to be heard: being balanced and nuanced rarely helps.

The global team has to work harder and shout louder to be heard: being balanced and nuanced rarely helps.

Decision making varies by culture

All decisions exist in a cultural context, which affects the way the decision is made. As long as everyone comes from the same culture, this is relatively unimportant because everyone is playing to the same rules. On global teams, there are different cultures and different ways of making decisions. This is a recipe for misunderstanding and conflict.

Cultural differences are not correlated to distance. If you travel between continents, you expect the culture to be different and you expect to adjust. But big differences can happen over a small distance, and can catch out the most culturally capable executives. If you drive just four hours from German-speaking Zurich to German-speaking Frankfurt, you find a completely different way of doing things and making decisions:

'When I came back to Germany I just found it so different. In Zürich 25% of the population is not Swiss and most of the Swiss population have strong international experience. The way they operate in Switzerland is much more subtle, so you need to listen, and decisions are much more consensus-based. But Germany is much more hierarchical. So in Switzerland you have to involve people much more, but once they are on board you can move ahead with astonishing speed. In Germany, they look to delegate issues upwards to the leadership because they want to clear stuff off their desks. In the international organisation I see a lot of management committees, but the real conversations and the real decisions do not happen in the committee.' [248]

With big differences between Zurich and Frankfurt, it is no surprise that global differences are also great. Major fault lines exist between individualistic and collective cultures, and between hierarchical and democratic cultures. But each country creates its own decision-making culture, which has to be understood and respected.

Country	Decision-making style	Advantages	Disadvantages
France	Descartes, intellectual tradition: conflict and debate	Intellectually robust solutions	Exclusive to top management; alienation, lack of buy-in
Japan	Consensus built on private one-to-one discussions	High buy-in, rapid implementation	Excludes outsiders; can be risk averse and slow
USA	Leader led, based on input from team and stakeholders	Fast, pragmatic, flexible	Continuing challenge to decisions

These differences in approach affect how team members see each other. The more consensus-based cultures will be seen as weak; the more individualistic countries will be seen as poor team players. The classic western view was described by one more traditional leader this way: 'you can try to pretend it is a democracy, but ultimately it is always a dictatorship. We can debate issues, but ultimately someone has to make decisions. And that's me.' [249]

The classic western view is in contrast to the Japanese view:

'Western managers think that it is their job to make decisions. In the West the organisation is a pyramid, but in Japan it is a village where everyone's idea counts and harmony is very important. So there are different views of what makes a good leader. Some Japanese leaders do make decisions, but others try to create consensus. Western people often think that Japanese leaders are being weak when they try to create consensus and they do not deliver clear decisions. So I often have to explain to Japanese managers why they are going to a global meeting and what is expected of them, and that is very different from what is expected when they attend a Japanese meeting.' [250]

These differences come to the surface in decision-making meetings. In Japan, meetings make public the consensus which has been reached in private: challenge at this point would be very unwelcome. In western firms, initial meetings are there to explore options: so they will be disappointed when someone from China or Japan does not challenge and offer views. That looks weak and implies that they have nothing to contribute. But in respect-based cultures, differences should be aired in private, not in public.

Western executives have a bias that tells them decisions are leader led. The obvious conclusion is that the best way to get a decision made is to approach the leader. In the West, this works very well. If the CEO likes an idea, then all the staff will suddenly discover that they like the idea as well: approval becomes a formality. In a hierarchical culture like Japan and China, it should be even more obvious that going to the leader directly is the way to short-cut the decision-making process. This can go wrong for two reasons:

▶ A hierarchical culture can also be consensual: the leader will want to know that the views of people lower in the organisation have been heard.

▶ In a hierarchical culture, leaders like to speak to leaders. Each level of the hierarchy faces off against its counterpart. Gaining access to a senior leader is not easy for someone who is perceived to be less important.

This means that western executives can charge in and then get very frustrated by the decision-making process. Patience is required:

'Decision-making in large Chinese companies and state-owned enterprises can be very long and involve many different departments and people who you may not think are important, but you have to meet them and get information from them all: this is often overlooked by foreigners.' [251]

There is not a single 'correct' approach to decision making globally. The only correct process is the one which works in each cultural context. A good decision-making process is one which gets a good decision for the global team: that means the team has to adapt to the culture.

Innovation and learning

A critical role for global teams is to foster innovation and learning across the global firm. Innovation and learning represent two different agendas:

▶ Learning: how global teams spread best practice across the world

▶ Innovation: how global teams develop new products and services.

The two agendas differ in the degree of change they represent. Learning is about incremental improvement to existing processes and products. Innovation represents more of a step change. This difference matters because effective learning is different from effective innovation. For this reason, we will look at the two agendas separately.

Learning

Any global team and global organisation contains a vast amount of knowledge and experience. Knowledge is relatively easy to codify and share: most organisations have a knowledge base and other forms of sharing knowledge. Experience, or tacit knowledge,[252] is harder to codify and harder to share. Knowledge is 'know what', which Google or Wikipedia can provide. Experience is 'know-how' and is more valuable.

In practice, the best knowledge-sharing system is not technology: it is people.

In practice, the best knowledge-sharing system is not technology: it is people. Even where there is a strong knowledge or experience base which is captured online, the first instinct of most managers is to see who posted the knowledge and then call them up to find out what the real story was:

'For new ideas we have a system called E gate. But the problem is how many people actually use it? Why should people unselfishly share their resources? And even if you find something on E gate, you still need to find the people who have the real expertise and talk to them and get them involved.' [253]

In practice, the knowledge that is most valued is the tacit know-how knowledge of experience. The easiest way to move that around the world is through people. There are two ways of doing that. First, you can move individuals around the world: they can then transfer their experience from one region to the next. This is simple and effective, as shown in the example in the text box below, which shows how a new regional manager for Pepsico in the Middle East was able to transfer learning from East Asia.

Transferring knowledge and success around the world

'I inherited a business with nearly 90 per cent share of the soft drink market. But it was all based on a totally artificial basis which was the Arab boycott. This had kept our very formidable competitor Coke out of the market for some 20 years. As I arrived, Coke had finally broken this barrier and their invasion fleet was launched. Unfortunately Pepsi senior management had milked the market for profit, seeing no threat and no long-term potential from investing in the region.

'I saw that there was no infrastructure to defend us: no fridges, no vending machines and no poster sites. I had come from the Far East, where in our strongest market Thailand, the bottler had done it very well. They had shown that increased availability of cold product actually grows per capita consumption. I had learnt that you can not only defend share but also grow the markets with good infrastructure.

'So my innovation was to spend on infrastructure to build per capita consumption. We funded this by a massive increase in marketing. We funded our share of this by increasing the price of concentrate and reinvesting the gains. On top of that, we persuaded the bottlers to match our spending. We showed them a vision of what would happen with and without the investment. Before, they had always resisted any rise in the price of concentrate. But when they saw the vision and the need, they supported it.

'The happy ending is that Pepsi saw off the Coke invasion and is still, 30 years later, the outright market leader with a vastly bigger business based on real business success not on artificial boycotts.'[254]

The other way of moving knowledge through people is to bring people together. The function of firm-wide gatherings is often ostensibly driven by business planning and some training. The softer needs of socialisation and transferring knowledge are at least as important. Knowledge transfer does not happen naturally: there has to be a structure to make it happen. Knowledge fairs and competitions are two simple ways to encourage knowledge transfer. As with all group meetings, there is a predictable bias in the way knowledge is advertised: Americans are the most forthcoming with contributions to knowledge bases and fairs; then the Europeans and finally the East Asians where a mixture of language and cultural barriers leads to low participation. Finding the knowledge cannot be reactive: there has to be proactive effort to find knowledge wherever it is.[255]

Even when the knowledge has been found, there is a challenge in transferring it. Each country thinks it is unique; there is risk aversion to new ideas and a lack of commitment to ideas which people do not own. Lack of ownership is also the 'not invented here' syndrome. Successful global teams need a culture based on a growth mindset: be open to learning and new ideas. SECOM, the security company, sends 12 of its best UK staff to learn about service in Japan each year: 'I tell them that the training starts when you check-in at JAL to see how good the service is. They see that at Narita and Haneda airports the guards look far more professional than UK security guards. I tell them to look at how professional the train guard on the Narita express is.'[256] Learning is not just about formal training: it is about observation.

SECOM case: transferring know-how

SECOM is a Japanese security company with over $7.8 billion revenues worldwide.[257] When it started in the UK, it decided to compete as a service-led model of commercial and domestic security. It faced all the classic challenges of resistance to innovation and change. Minoru Takezawa, the UK Managing Director, takes up the story:

'There was big resistance to start with. Typically security is sold as equipment not as a service in the UK. If an alarm starts ringing, it is just left to ring. But in Japan we sell security as a service: the kit is rented, not bought. Hardware is just

▶

a small part of our service system. So I started the idea of QSP: changing the company from a hardware installer to Quality Service Provider.

'People used to use a magic phrase in the UK: "but in this country", which is used to make a Japanese expat quiet. They say that the market is different, the culture is different, and customer expectation is different.

'So I needed to prove that we can win with service-focused strategy. In 2003 I started the QSP campaign. We are the largest security company in Japan and our business is based on a monthly charge: you pay, we protect you. We only sell on quality services. In the UK, over 90 per cent of the alarms which police respond to are false alarms. But that does not happen in Japan, Korea or Taiwan because we are the first response: we get there first to confirm if it is a genuine crime, so the police do not waste their time on false calls and the customer is protected.

'UK regulations are different. So if I try to bring a Japanese model in I will be banging my head against a brick wall. But I realised that if you could provide security as a good service, keep your promises, then you could be a big winner. The most important thing in building the strategy. how to provide good service, was the involvement of the employees. We went round the country, brainstormed with staff asking: if you were a customer what and when would you feel was good quality service? We then came up with simple ideas such as answer all calls within three rings; bring a vacuum cleaner to sweep up the dust after installation. So we reinvented all the best ideas from small to big. We started with some small and simple wins. We made our QSP Bible which contained all the best ideas.

'I always got staff to put themselves in the shoes of the customer. We put up posters to communicate the message. We had a long, hard campaign to change the mindset, until each person believes in their heart rather than just doing it because that is what the boss says. We focus on the small things such as calling the customer if you are running late. So I started to celebrate and publicise good cases. When I started I only got complaints from customers. But slowly I started to get letters saying what went well. So I would find out who did it and I would then praise them in public. Recognition of good work is vital to build a strong team to support good-quality service.

'So I introduced QSP awards and I would always go to the local depot to make the award, make a picture taken and would put it in the newsletter. I also started sending 12 employees to Japan every year to witness all the quality services in action. I called it the Japan Study Tour. Seeing is believing. It has greatly helped my team to fully understand our Quality Service ethos.

If a customer likes you they get new business for you without any commission, so then the staff saw that QSP works. My job was to change mindset and give pride to people. "Our job is to protect customers. We make it harder for the bad guys to win. We forced the bad guys to go to towns where we are not present. Let's take a pride in our job."'

Minoru Takezawa knew the innovation he wanted to introduce: service-based security systems. Instead of mandating it as the new CEO, he got the staff to reinvent the idea themselves, so they thought it was their own idea. People may argue against an idea from the boss, but they rarely argue against their own ideas.

Transfer of knowledge and know-how requires a comprehensive approach. There is no single magic bullet that enables a team to become a learning team. The comprehensive approach has to include both formal systems for identifying and codifying experience, and informal systems which bring people together so that they can learn from each other.

For instance, CRU is a global research firm which focuses on extractive industries. Sharing knowledge and experience is essential for them, and they use a suite of methods to manage this:

'We use four main tools to spread knowledge and experience:

▶ First, there is an expert directory which points people to experts in products, countries and languages.

▶ Second, twice a month we have global lunch-and-learn sessions which bring in internal or external speakers and let us share our knowledge.

▶ Third, we have the eHub, our cloud-based collaboration, communication and community of practice tool. It is a platform which encourages learning across business units.

▶ Fourth, we have embedded knowledge champions for each market.'[258]

Innovation

There are many theories of innovation in firms, and many of them are excellent.[259] The purpose here is to understand the role of global teams in innovation.

Traditionally, innovation came from the centre and then global teams deployed the innovation around the world. In many global firms this is still broadly the case. Auto manufacturers do most of their new car development in their home country. Hugely successful brands and formats maintain a consistent approach globally. McDonald's and Starbucks vary their offering somewhat by geography, but the fundamental format is one that was created in America and rolled out globally. Part of the attraction of these global brands is that they are seen to represent the best of the home nation: Coca-Cola and the American dream; Mercedes and German engineering; Lexus and Japanese quality.

Traditionally, innovation came from the centre and then global teams deployed the innovation around the world.

In all of the examples above, the approach to managing global teams is to create a clear divide between the role of the centre and the role of the local operation. This is most explicit in the franchise operations of the auto manufacturers, Coca-Cola and McDonald's. The franchisor provides the trademark, brand, copyright, training, quality control, supply chain and perhaps marketing and advertising; the franchisee provides the capital, staffing and daily operations locally. The franchisee may occasionally come up with good ideas, but they are not the driving force of innovation around the world.

The home-nation approach is resource intensive, and can lead to breakthroughs. Bell Labs created revolutionary products, from transistors to lasers.[260] Du Pont global research developed Kevlar and Lycra. Xerox at its Palo Alto Research Center (PARC) developed endless breakthroughs including the Ethernet and the GUI[261] interface; they took up neither because they were blinded by their focus on copiers.

This home-nation approach works where the product or service is relatively consistent across geography and stable over time. The home-nation approach struggles where more local variation is required, or the speed of innovation and change is high. Inevitably, this leads to conflict between the home nation and the global teams. Each geography always thinks that it is unique and wants special treatment; the home nation typically drives for consistency. The boundaries between what has to be consistent and what has to be local keep on shifting, so the conflict is never fully resolved.

The alternative approach is much more open. In the words of Google's Head of Games and Apps:[262] 'the ecosystem is smarter than any of us'. This is a fundamental mindset shift, and one which changes the role of the manager and the global team.

Home-nation closed innovation model	Global and open innovation model
We know best	The ecosystem knows more
We control our IP	We create IP with partners
We employ the smartest people	We engage with the smartest people anywhere, anytime, anyhow
Value comes from controlling IP	Value comes from accessing IP to support our business model
We research and develop new ideas	We co-create new ideas with customers, suppliers and partners
We invest heavily in R&D	We share investment risk widely

Apple and Google represent contrasting approaches, because they have different strategies. Google's mission is to organise the world's information. That contrasts with the mission Steve Jobs defined for Apple: 'To make a contribution to the world by making tools for the mind that advance humankind.'[263] Apple is more focused on their products and design. This means Apple is driven to a proprietary model driven from the hub. Google is much more open in its approach to innovation which harnesses the talent of third parties wherever possible.

Most firms will combine elements of closed and open innovation. P&G's Connect and Develop programme has more than 1,000 active agreements with innovation partners including universities/institutes, sole inventors, emerging companies, SMEs, MNCs and competitors. These have to be managed through dedicated staff in over ten countries. P&G estimates that over half of its new product initiatives now involve significant external collaboration.[264]

Moving to the global innovation model depends on creating engagement platforms where the knowledge and experience of global teams can be harnessed. Each platform needs to create a dialogue of discovery. For global teams these platforms are both virtual and physical, and are similar to the platforms for learning. Expert directories, knowledge bases, global conferences, external partnerships are all relevant platforms. To move from learning to innovation requires a step change in the way the global teams work and collaborate. Teams at P&G and Google have an active mandate to go and forge external partnerships and to bring the best ideas from the rest of the world into the firm, in a focused manner.

Conclusions

As a global team leader, you should ask three questions about learning and innovation:

▶   How can I foster learning and innovation within the team?

▶   How can the team contribute to the learning and innovation of the firm?

▶   How can I learn and innovate?

Learning and innovation is as much about mindset as it is about systems. You can no more force people to learn and innovate than you can force them to be happy and passionate. But you can create the conditions for learning and innovation. The starting point is you: you are the role model from which the team will take its cues. If you are seen to focus on personal growth and learning, and you encourage others, then the team will follow. A very simple habit, outlined in the chapter on communications, is to debrief consistently with the team using a simple two part formula:

You can no more force people to learn and innovate than you can force them to be happy and passionate.

▶   WWW: What Went Well? Start with this. This is how the team can consciously build its success formula. It allows you to reinforce good behaviours by recognising what works.

▶   EBI: Even Better If ... The evil twin of WWW is what went wrong, and it quickly leads to in-fighting and discord. EBI avoids this, and focuses on action, learning and improvement.

The more consistently you use this formula by asking these two questions, the more learning and innovation becomes a habit. Beyond this, you can layer on top systems for learning: the team meetings and the technology and knowledge bases. These only work if you have created a culture of learning, and if you show a commitment to learning and growing yourself.

The final piece of the jigsaw is to have a team which is open to learning and is flexible and adaptable. Creating the right team is the subject of the next chapter.

8

People and skills
Global talent, global mindset

Great people achieve great things. They will turn crises into opportunities, turn mountains into molehills and turn ideas into action. In contrast, the 'B' team is a recipe for sleepless nights and stress for the team leader. In global teams, the need for the best people is even greater, because the stakes are higher and success is harder to achieve.

Global team leaders are keenly aware of this challenge: 'In the Middle East I knew I could go on holiday. Out in Russia, when it was just emerging from communism, I never went on holiday because I was not convinced that my team would cope.'[265]

For the team leader, the challenge is to know what makes a good global team player, how to recruit them and how to build a balanced team. Global team players need a different skill set and mindset relative to domestic team players: domestic success does not convert automatically into global success.

For the firm, the challenge is to recruit and develop a pipeline of talent that can work globally. This forces the firm to make a clear decision about how it wants to work across the world: does it want a relatively cohesive organisation culturally, or does it want to build a truly diverse global talent pool? The rhetoric in the media is all about diversity; the reality on the ground is that many organisations prefer cohesiveness.

The rhetoric in the media is all about diversity; the reality on the ground is that many organisations prefer cohesiveness.

This chapter will explore two sets of people challenges. The first poses a fundamental choice for the firm and the way it manages talent: how will the firm manage the trade-off between diversity and cohesiveness? The next three talent questions explore why global team members need a higher and different skill set as well as a different mindset.

The five issues for this chapter are:

1. Choosing between cohesiveness and diversity
2. Global team members need higher skill sets
3. Global team members need new skill sets
4. Global team members need a distinct mindset: autonomy, accountability, ambiguity
5. Building a team with the right mix.

There are many challenges regarding how to manage the global team, and these are covered in other chapters. How to build trust and communications within the team has been covered in chapters on trust and communications; how to manage performance will be covered in the chapter on systems; how to build a common set of values and culture will be dealt with in the chapter on values. This chapter focuses on the talent challenge.

Where needed, this chapter draws out the differences between two types of global team player:

▶ Team members who work on a global team from within their home country
▶ Team members who work on a global team from outside their home country.

Where the difference is not explicitly stated, the findings apply to both types of global team member.

1. Choosing between cohesiveness and diversity

The media is relentless in trumpeting the virtues of diversity; few voices are raised in opposition to diversity. In terms of society, fairness, equality and diversity are clearly good in their own right.

And yet many global teams and global firms have a different principle from diversity: cohesiveness. Even firms which celebrate diversity of race, gender, faith and sexuality will trumpet the fact that they are a 'one firm firm'[266] or have 'Blue Box values'[267] around the world. In other words, diversity is skin deep: you can be of any race, colour or gender, but you have to conform to a certain set of values and ways of thinking. Those values are normally deeply rooted in the values of the home nation. It can be remarkably effective: Goldman Sachs, McKinsey and American Express have forged cohesive cultures which have served them very well. The values unite a truly global workforce. As we shall see, there is another way of building cohesiveness: ensure that most senior management come from the home country. This is effective in the medium term, but is hard to sustain in the long term.

The choice between cohesiveness and diversity is a critical part of the firm's talent strategy: do you hire the best regardless of where they come from, or do you prefer to build a cohesive elite based out of the home country? Successful global firms can follow either strategy. The table below summarises the case for and against each strategy.

	Cohesive teams	Diverse teams
Advantages	• High trust • Ease of decision making • Ease of communications • Collective accountability	• Top talent • Good skills spread • Idea generation • Challenge to status quo
Disadvantages	• Risk averse • Weak innovation • Weak personal accountability	• Misunderstandings • Co-ordination and communication • Building trust

This is a fundamental choice which determines what sort of talent the firm will recruit, develop and promote; it is a choice about the culture and nature of the firm; it affects how decisions are made and how learning is enabled. To understand the choice we will explore four themes:

▶ The case for diversity

▶ The case for cohesiveness

▶ Building cohesiveness: exporting the home nation around the world

▶ Building cohesiveness through a one-world approach.

The case for diversity

McKinsey made a heroic attempt to see whether diversity makes a difference to performance. Their conclusion was that firms in the top quartile for ethnic diversity were 35 per cent more likely to outperform, and those in the top quartile for gender diversity were 15 per cent more likely to outperform.[268]

The critical advantage of having a diverse global team is around idea generation and challenge. Anyone who works on a global team will be familiar with finding that colleagues think and act differently: that is both a challenge and an opportunity.

Diverse groups are far better at creating good new ideas than cohesive groups Professor Burt of Chicago Booth[269] has studied how good ideas are generated and acted on. The consistent, and unsurprising, finding is that diverse groups are far better at creating good new ideas than cohesive groups.[270] In one study, he asked supply chain managers at Raytheon to write down ideas for improving operations, and then had those ideas rated by independent managers. The best ideas came from managers with contacts outside their immediate work group: the different perspective generated better ideas. In his words: 'People who live in the intersection of social worlds are at higher risk of having good ideas.'[271]

The critical insight from Burt's work is that the size of your network is not what matters when it comes to generating ideas: it is the diversity of your network which makes all the difference. For global firms this is an important distinction. At global conferences it is normal to see everyone sticking with the functional and geographic networks which they already know. Travelling halfway round the world to meet people in the office next to you misses the point of the conference. The conference should diversify, not simply reinforce, your network.

Diverse teams also help in the war to recruit and retain top talent: a firm which is genuinely open all the way to the top to the best talent from anywhere in the world is much more attractive than a firm which operates a glass ceiling for foreigners. The glass ceiling is self-reinforcing: top talent avoids firms where they see they cannot reach the top, which makes it impossible for the firm to find talent which it can promote to the top.

One Japanese manager has seen both diverse and cohesive cultures. He sees the cohesive Japanese culture as not being truly global. The firm may be prestigious in Japan where it attracts top graduates, but struggles outside Japan where it is not so prestigious and is seen to have a glass ceiling: 'Japanese companies think that they are global but they are not. This means that they are not attractive for top-notch foreign people. When I advertise a position I get 100 people all with PhDs from Oxford, Harvard and other leading universities. A PhD is like a driving licence: it is not enough even to get short-listed. My Japanese friends are very surprised because they have never seen people like that at all. Japanese firms may be famous in Japan but not over here.'[272]

Several executives challenged whether you can be truly global if you are not diverse: 'You don't need a global team if you don't have diversity. I cannot have someone who sounds American in Japan. Diversity is as simple as how people talk. For instance, the Americans will talk in superlatives but the Japanese will talk in euphemisms.'[273] If you are not diverse, then you are simply the home nation exporting your products, values, services and staff around the world. But there are plenty of cases where largely uniform products and services succeed globally: Apple, Microsoft, McDonald's, BMW and Boeing, to name a few. In practice, there are many varieties of what it means to be global.

The case for diversity is strong. The main benefits are:

- ▶ Generating new ideas
- ▶ Challenging the status quo
- ▶ Attracting the top talent globally
- ▶ Outperforming less diverse firms.

But the research also shows that managing a truly diverse global team is exceptionally hard in terms of decision making, trust, communications and fair process. Diversity is not a free lunch. For some firms, the bill is too high and cohesiveness is preferable.

The case for cohesiveness

Given the case for diversity, it is surprising that any global firm would not want to embrace diversity. But there is a powerful alternative: cohesiveness.

Here is CEO David Novak[274] on driving performance across 1.4 million employees spread across 117 countries: 'when we first started our company, the single highest priority I had was to create a global culture where we can galvanize around the behaviours that we know will drive results in our industry'. This cohesiveness has worked, to the extent that Yum! Brands' earnings per share grew fourfold in ten years to 2015.

Firms which have a fairly standard product around the world are going to value consistency and cohesiveness. Microsoft and McDonald's do not want to have to reinvent their entire business model every time they enter a new market. They may make adjustments to the core product, but these will be relatively minor. When clients work with McKinsey or Deloitte, they want to know that they will get the same service quality around the world. Consistency counts.

To deliver consistency around the world, you need not just a consistent product and service: you need also a consistent set of values which creates a cohesive workforce. The question is how firms achieve cohesiveness. Global firms take one of two approaches:

▶ Home nation cohesion
▶ Whole world cohesion.

We will look at each approach briefly.

Building cohesion: exporting the home nation around the world

This has been the traditional approach to building a global empire, be it military, political or commercial. The Roman Empire was built by Romans, the British Empire by the British: cohesiveness was achieved by developing and recruiting an elite that ruled: arguably, the purpose of British public schools in the nineteenth century was to develop an elite with a common set of experiences and values.

This is also the way most firms initially go global. One of the first great global firms was the East India Company: it was effectively the commercial arm of the British Empire and was run exclusively by British. It was also, as the Chinese will attest, the world's biggest drug runner. It arranged for the export of vast amounts of opium from India to China at a time when opium was legal in the UK, but not in China.[275]

The home nation approach continued through the twentieth century. Harold Geneen was the legendary CEO of ITT, a huge conglomerate with operations which spanned the globe. Geneen took a simple approach to the world: he would not adapt to the world, so the world would have to adapt to him. That meant he kept to East Coast time all the time. Even when he visited his overseas businesses, he would stay on East Coast time, which led to meetings starting at 2am. His colleagues got jet lag without getting on the jet.

There are still plenty of firms which operate on the home nation approach. There are two signs of a home nation global firm:

▶ How many members of the executive committee are from the home nation?

▶ What proportion of key overseas roles are led by expatriates?

This approach may be increasingly old-fashioned, but it is powerful because it:

▶ drives consistency across the globe

▶ enables easy communication between head office and overseas units

▶ creates a network of trust where ideas can be exchanged and decisions made quickly and informally.

The problem is that it creates a caste system. If you are not from the home nation, then you know you are a second-class citizen, however talented you may be. This leads to huge frustration: you know your promotion prospects are limited, and you are excluded from key decisions which you cannot influence. You are not in control of your destiny.

It is hard to break down the home nation model. Outside the home nation, top talent is deterred from joining because they can see they will be second-class citizens. This means there is no diverse talent pool to promote to the top positions. At the top, the network is hard to break into. If the home nation is Japan, then all the senior executives will speak Japanese: that immediately creates a very high barrier to entry for non-Japanese speakers. In contrast, firms with an English-speaking home base find it much easier to identify and promote diverse talent to the top, because English is so widely spoken. Language makes diversity easier for English-speaking firms. At the last count, 39 per cent of the CEOs of the top 100 public companies in the UK were foreign:[276] that is unimaginable in most non-English speaking countries around the world.

The weaknesses of the home nation approach are significant:

▶ Inability to recruit top talent

▶ Low awareness or responsiveness to local needs and opportunities

▶ Cost and risk of expatriates: up to 40 per cent of expats do not complete their tour of duty because they fail to adapt to local conditions[277]

▶ Tension between the high-caste home nation staff and the rest.

The problems of the home-nation approach are such that many firms are now reaching out for an alternative: the one-world approach.

Building cohesiveness through a one-world approach

The whole-world approach is based on two principles:

▶ Recruit the best, wherever they may come from

▶ Develop a single, unifying set of daily values.

These two principles balance each other out. Recruiting the best talent globally leads to diversity; the unifying daily values leads to cohesion. Done well, this allows the firm to achieve both diversity and cohesion.

The whole-world approach reverses the approach to expatriates. The home-nation approach sends an elite cadre out to manage the firm globally. The whole-world approach reverses the flow. Microsoft, for instance, has a 'reverse expat'[278] programme where high potential managers are moved from China (for instance) to Redmond and elsewhere to absorb the Microsoft way of doing things. Small firms as well as large can do this. CRU, a global research firm based in London, brings its new China hires to work in London for a few months, for exactly the same reason: to learn the CRU way of doing things. Both CRU and Microsoft foster a culture of creative thinking and challenge: these are not consistent with the culture of Chinese education which respects hierarchy rather than challenges it, and is better at gathering information than generating insight. The benefit of this approach is that it allows operations in China to be more or less completely localised and led by local talent, while creating a global elite that is cohesive enough to work together well across borders.

Finding the right talent can be especially hard for ambitious firms from lower wage Asian nations. In the first instance, they send a trusted senior executive to open the way in America or Asia. They then find that the cost of hiring locally is prohibitively expensive and will compromise: they find lower cost staff who can more closely fit with the pay policies of the home nation. By picking B or even C grade team players, they doom the venture to failure and/or even greater dependence on expatriates from the home nation. Accepting diversity means that you have to accept diversity in terms of pay and conditions, if you are to find the right talent.[279]

Creating a cohesive culture across a diverse workforce takes more than recruiting and developing the right talent. Other key elements include:

▶ Clear and consistent values which are acted on globally

▶ Frequent meetings, both virtual and physical

▶ HR systems which identify and manage the careers of global high potential managers

▶ Appropriate coaching and internal mentoring.

Creating a cohesive culture will be covered in the chapter on values.

2. Global team members need higher skill sets

Being on a global team raises the stakes for team members. They need high skills, and they need new skills.

The skills bar rises for global teams for four reasons:

▶ Global teams are recruited from a global talent pool.

▶ The trust bar is higher on global teams.

▶ Expectations are higher on a global team, both internally and externally.

▶ Everything is harder on a global team.

Global teams are recruited from a global talent pool

The global war for talent cuts both ways. Firms find it harder than ever to recruit and retain top talent. But equally, talent around the world is now competing more directly with each other. This is obvious in the gig economy where you can outsource work, using sites such as guru.com or elance. com. It may cost $40 an hour to develop your website or translate a brochure in developed countries. It may cost just $4 an hour in emerging countries. And you will be able to see portfolios of work for each freelancer to check their quality.

The gig economy is mirrored within global organisations. Globalisation 'exposes staff in high cost countries such as the US to lower cost, high quality, and hungry staff who will compete for their jobs from the base of a low-cost location'.[280] The outsourcing option is the same within a firm as it is outside: do you want work done at $40 an hour or $4 an hour? Workers in high cost countries have advantages of proximity to the customer, but the cost differential puts real pressure on them to show that they are worth the premium.

The trust bar is higher on global teams

The chapter on trust showed that distance raises the need for trust, and especially for credibility. Within an office, you can see if someone is struggling, and you can shift work around the team to compensate. Working at distance you have to trust that each team member will deliver. You cannot see how they are performing in real time, and it is harder to shift work around. Global team members have to perform without a safety net.

Remote working requires high trust, which in turn requires high skills. Teams around the world saw that remote working requires high trust, which in turn requires high skills: you can only trust people to do the right thing if they have the right skills:

▶ SE Asia: 'Trust is the main problem; if you get the right people in the right job then you don't have to hold their hands.'[281]

▶ North America: 'If you have someone remote without the right skills then it just won't work.'[282]

▶ Serbia: 'Remote working has a lot of downsides. I could understand that our boss needed to micro-manage because we were new and we did not have the trust from him.'[283]

▶ Japan: 'You have to trust them when you don't see them and can only communicate by telex or fax.'[284]

Expectations are higher on a global team, both internally and externally

This is particularly true for global team members who have to work outside their home country. If you become an expatriate, you have to show you are worth it. Externally, you need enough credibility to represent the firm. Internally, you have to show local team members why you are worth all the extra cost of moving around the world: do you really have a type and level of expertise that is not available locally?

It is not just your team members who will be judging whether you bring anything of value to the team. Your boss will only select people who have something special in terms of skills: 'they have to have higher level expertise to enhance the level of skill of our people'.[285]

That is a tough expectations bar to jump.

The performance bar has risen relentlessly. In the past, it was possible to have global executives whose main skill was an ability to bridge the gap between head office and the local team. It is still important to be able to do this. But if a global team member works outside their home country, they need to be more than the generalist who represents head office: 'The era of the gifted amateur is over. You need professionals, we have to be much more focused and we need to develop deep skills.'[286]

Everything is harder on a global team

Anyone who has worked overseas is familiar with the panic of trying to deal with daily life. Even buying a subway ticket for the first time can be confusing. At work, it is even harder. New arrivals don't know how things work; they are not familiar with the local culture and they are cut off from all the networks of influence and power that let them succeed in their home country. They do not start on a level playing field: odds are stacked against them, and they are expected to outperform. To do all that, they need exceptional skills.

Bhavit Mehta[287] describes the challenges of organising a book fair in Guadalajara in Mexico. Any book fair has challenges to test the organiser – suppliers let you down, prima donna authors wreak havoc[288] – but he describes how these challenges escalate when working in an unfamiliar country, culture and language where you do not have the networks of support which get taken for granted domestically:

'Everything is harder globally. Just getting a poster printed at short notice is very hard. Who can do the design, and who can do the printing? This was not a budget issue, but a capacity issue. Everyone must have a can-do attitude because inevitably not everything will go to plan: the local caterers let you down, taxi drivers won't arrive, luggage will get lost and authors go missing. This is inevitable. It's about

being able to deal with that and not panic. You need a calm and positive and can-do attitude and not everyone has it.'

3. Global team members need new skill sets

Having a strong technical skill set is not enough. Working on a global team puts a premium on team working skills. A selfish player is toxic on a global team, as one Chinese team leader found: 'We have hired very good professionals but they cannot work in this global environment if they are dedicated to their own interests. They may be good professionals but they must also be good team players.'[289] On a global team, these skills include being adaptable, listening and influencing. These are soft skills which not everyone has.

In addition to team working skills, global team players need to keep their technical skills refreshed and up to date. This was a constant refrain from across industries and geography:

▶ 'It is more important to have people who can learn fast than have years of experience. People who were advanced three years ago are substandard now. You have to keep on learning.'[290]

▶ 'We need industry experience, but we will choose the brain that can learn over someone who is more experienced but does not learn.'[291]

▶ 'Global experience is not key. Some executives with vast global experience have not learnt anything.'[292]

The need to keep skills fresh is driven by two factors. First, skill sets are changing all the time. Even within a domestic team, up-to-date skills are essential to staying relevant. On a global team, expectations are higher: you have to show that you bring something special to the team which other local team players do not have. Stale skills are not going to keep you in the global race.

4. Global team members need a distinct mindset: autonomy, accountability, ambiguity

Global team members need a distinctive mindset, whether they work on the team from within or outside their home country.

Professionally, working on a global team offers much greater autonomy, accountability and ambiguity than you would have on a domestic team.

These three differences mean that global team members need a different mindset from domestic team members.

Autonomy and accountability

Autonomy and accountability walk hand in hand. On a global team, you do not have other team members watching over you all day. You have freedom and responsibility: you have to deliver, and how you deliver is up to you. In the words of one experienced global team leader, that means 'not everyone is suitable to work in a distributed workforce. You need self-management, discipline, you have to balance loneliness, and at the end of the day there is accountability: they have to set expectations with themselves accurately.'[293]

Clearly, domestic team members also need autonomy and accountability: the difference is in the degree of autonomy, accountability and ambiguity which global team members experience. On a domestic team, there is a process of constant mutual adjustment between team members. There is a constant dialogue and direct observation of what is happening, or not happening. This happens informally and naturally on a domestic team. Where it happens on a global team, the dialogue is less frequent and more structured.

Ambiguity

Ambiguity also rises dramatically on a global team. On a domestic team, the cultural norms are well known and well established. Team members know how much challenge is appropriate and how to challenge; they know how decisions are made and how to influence decisions; they know how their colleagues like to operate and how to work with them. None of this is obvious on a global team. No one knows what the rules of engagement are. They have to be discovered. To some people this is ambiguity, which causes stress; to others it is freedom, which is liberating.

Mindset

Autonomy, accountability and ambiguity drive the mindsets which are especially important on global teams:

▶ Flexibility and adaptability: learn to adapt to new cultures and new ways of working

- Curiosity: be open to new cultures, respect the culture and learn from it; read the local news, try the local food

- Learning: keep professional skills current; see differences as a chance to learn and grow, not as a failure to conform

- Humility: recognise that 'my way or no way' does not work on global teams; what works in one country may not work elsewhere

- Positive regard: especially when things go wrong, be supportive not critical.

Curiosity, humility and learning go together. You can only learn if you are humble enough to recognise the value in how other people work, and you have the energy and curiosity to discover the local culture. Working globally requires a global outlook, which takes effort:

'To be credible you have to have global perspective: that means Europe, America and Asia. So I read the Financial Times, Wall Street Journal *and* South China Morning Post *every day. You have to know what turns people on and off, what you can and cannot say and do, when to buy a gift and when not, when to invite people to dinner: it boils down to 100 specific behaviours that you must adopt. If you do not have global perspective you are not globally credible. Above all, that means you need humility.'* [294]

These mindsets cannot be learned. They are part of how you are. It is as simple as being open to trying new foods, listening to new music and tapping into foreign media. This global mindset is a good way of selecting team members, and in practice many people self-select on global teams. People who prefer the comforts of home and familiar ways of working are not suitable for global team working, and normally avoid volunteering for global teams.

I have made the mistake of hiring people who were talented but had the wrong values and I always regretted it.

If you cannot train for mindset, then you have to recruit for mindset. Hedge funds recruit some of the most talented people on earth, occasionally referred to as 'rocket scientists'. But even they recognise that intellectual talent is not enough, as one hedge fund boss noted: 'I have made the mistake of hiring people who were talented but had the wrong values and I always regretted it.' [295]

In the course of the research, it became clear that many of the most global executives are effectively global citizens. Being global is part of their identity, as one firm found: 'everyone on our team has a very international background: they are all global citizens'.[296] This often came from their education or their family background. Goro Yamashita, channel manager of Mitsui OSK Lines, exemplifies this. His family has been in the global shipping business for over 100 years with the eponymous Yamashita[297] shipping line, and he himself was partly educated in the UK and brought up in France. With that background, it would not be surprising to find that his DNA now contains a unique globalisation gene.

Even where being a global citizen is not in the family DNA, global executives soon find that they cannot imagine going back to a domestic setting. They find it hard to give up the freedom that comes with autonomy, accountability and ambiguity. For many, going global is a one-way career step: there is no going back to a domestic role.

5. Building a team with the right mix

A good team is a balanced team. A football team made up of the 11 best goalkeepers in the world would not be a good team. The need for balance may be stating the obvious, for domestic as well as global teams. But, as ever, it is much harder to achieve on a global team because:

A football team made up of the 11 best goalkeepers in the world would not be a good team.

▶ you do not know the people on the team
▶ you may have limited ability to select who joins the team
▶ cultural noise makes it harder to understand differences between people.

The lazy way out is to recruit people who are like yourself. This takes the argument for cohesiveness to an extreme. This approach may be simple in the short term, but it is also ineffective: 'If everyone is similar then it is very easy to manage. But in practice you need a combination of different skills and different personalities because you want different approaches and different perspectives.'[298]

The sort of balance that you need to work on includes he following:

▶ The right mix of skills. Most teams understand this need. You may need a wide mix of technical, administrative and market facing skills. The goals of the team will determine the skills required.

▶ The right mix of personality types. This is where the trade-off between conformity and variety is most acute. The highest-performing teams are often the hardest to manage, because they choose variety over conformity. This means there should be some tension in the team: 'Teams only work as well as the most difficult person on the team. You need some difficult people because you need to have grist in the mill, but you don't want too many.'[299] Equally, you need to balance thinkers and doers; leaders and followers; risk takers and risk minimisers; people-focused and task-focused team members: the number of potential trade-offs is limited only by your own creativity in identifying potential personality types.

▶ The right mix of experience. The natural instinct of many team leaders is to hire experience, especially on a global team. If you have to trust someone to act and decide for you remotely, you have to trust that they have enough skills and experience. But in practice, you need a balance. Less experienced team members bring energy, hunger and challenge to the team. More experienced team members cost more and it is harder to keep them all happy: 'If the team is too experienced then you cannot meet their expectations in terms of responsibility and career growth.'[300]

The need for balance may be self-evident. Achieving balance is less obvious. At the outset, many global teams are essentially mandated. The team leader has limited opportunity to select people from around the world and has to trust that HR and the local countries have identified suitable team members. But this is where the problems start: HR and the local countries will naturally place onto the global team people who are available. The inevitable suspicion is that anyone who is available is not good enough: either they are inexperienced or they have had mediocre experience and need a second chance. As a team leader, you want the best people. By definition, the best people will be in high demand elsewhere so they will not be available.

In practice, it takes time to evolve to the right team. The team you start with will not be the team you finish with. You will be engaged in a constant juggling act of trying to keep the best people and replacing others.

Conclusion

Building the right team is one of the basic requirements of any successful leader in a domestic or global context. In a global context, the 'right team' means a team with the following characteristics:

▶ High-level skills: you have to trust that the team can perform without you micro-managing them remotely.

▶ Global mindset: you need people who

  ▶ are comfortable with accountability and autonomy

  ▶ can manage the ambiguity and uncertainty of working across borders

  ▶ have cultural intelligence: they do not assume that their way is the best way

  ▶ are open, flexible and adaptable to new ideas and new ways of working

  ▶ learn constantly.

▶ The right mix in terms of skills, personality and experience.

Team building is hard enough in a domestic context, where you probably know the potential team members and you know the decision makers who can allocate people to teams. In a global context you don't know the potential team members and you don't know the decision makers, but you do know that the skills and mindset requirements for your global team are higher than for a domestic team. It is another perfect storm for global teams.

In reality, team building takes time. Balance does not come from day one, and the needs of the team and the expectations of team members keep on changing. Building the right team is a never-ending task. It is probably the most important investment of time the team leader can make.

Building the right team is the most important investment of time the team leader can make.

Finally, as the team leader you have to be the role model for the team. You have to show that you have high-level skills; you have to role model the global mindset; you have to be the bridge that unites the team and the firm. Leading a global team is an exceptional challenge which requires exceptional people.

9

Culture
Building cultural intelligence

This chapter addresses the invisible challenge of cultural differences. For a global team, this is a three-part challenge:

▶ Understand the cultural differences within your team

▶ Bridge the differences within your team

▶ Build a common set of values across all teams in the firm.

The focus of this chapter is on understanding the cultural differences within your team. We will then briefly explore how you can deal with those differences.

The nature of the cultural challenge

Travel opens the mind to new cultures. The obvious differences assault our major senses. They can be seen, heard, felt, tasted and smelled: clothes and buildings look different; people talk in a different language or accent; the food smells and tastes different.

In business, the biggest differences escape our senses. Business culture is about habits of mind which are shared across a group or society. These habits of mind are invisible to both visitors and residents. For the residents, their habits of mind are based on assumptions which no one questions or thinks about, until they come into contact with visitors who think and act differently.

These cultural differences matter much more than liking or disliking the local cuisine: they make the difference between failure and success. Some simple examples will make the point:

▶ Is escalating a problem good or bad? The Germans were used to hierarchy and escalating issues; their new American owners expected to delegate challenges down.

▶ Should we share documents or not? European managers were frustrated by colleagues from an authoritarian state who would not go onto google.docs or any other open platforms: they had learned that too much sharing is dangerous.

▶ Should we drink or not? The Midwestern firm had a clear no alcohol policy; in Kazakhstan their partners expected to build personal trust over many drinks before starting the business discussion.

▶ Who should talk to who? The Italian sales manager needed to speak with the Chinese CEO. It was never going to happen: the mismatch in hierarchy was too great.

For most of the twentieth century, American culture was the default culture of business. Any conversation with a global executive quickly throws up examples of surprises and conflict. Traditionally, the more powerful culture is the one which has been followed. For most of the twentieth century, that meant that American culture was the default culture of business. In the twenty-first century, things have become more complicated as we enter a multi-polar world of business. The rise of new and emerging economies has created more equal players globally; the rise of integrated global supply chains has created a world of deep interdependence, not dependence. Adjustment is no longer a one-way street: it has to be mutual.

You can only adjust to a different culture if you understand what the differences in culture are. This is a huge challenge which has taxed practitioners and academics alike for a long time. In 1965 Geert Hofstede founded the personnel research department of IBM. Between 1967 and 1973, he led a vast survey of 117,000 IBM employees across fifty countries and three regions to understand and quantify the cultural differences between cultures.[301] Initially, he identified four major dimensions on which cultures vary; he then grew this to six. Erin Meyer of INSEAD has identified eight critical areas where culture affects business.[302] Most practising managers can probably identify dozens of cultural differences. There is a real danger of getting lost in a cultural swamp.

For our purposes we will look only at national level differences. There are also major variations in culture between regions, firms and individuals. A tech person from Silicon Valley, a bond trader from New York, a professor in

Chicago and an engineer in Houston are all likely to have very different outlooks even if they do all come from the same country.

This means that any cultural analysis runs the risk of stereotyping. Stereotypes are a useful shorthand which alert us to common differences, but they can be as dangerous as stereotyping people based on colour, race, gender or sexuality. Ultimately, we have to understand and respect the individual.

The good news is that at the level of a single team we do not have to worry about stereotyping: we can focus on discovering the different assumptions and mindset of each team member, treating them as individuals. You could discover these differences by trial and error over weeks and months of interaction: that is a painful way to learn through misunderstanding. The faster way is to put the critical cultural stereotypes to work. You can use them to identify the different assumptions and working habits of each team member.

Who has the mysterious culture?

It was getting late and the beer was flowing. In Japan, this is when the truth can be spoken without fear and you will be forgiven in the morning. The senior Japanese executive leaned over and whispered in my ear: 'Jo-san, there is something I need to ask you.' I leaned towards him. It sounded like we were about to get down to the real business.

The executive then asked: 'How do you shake hands in America?'

'??!!???' I replied. Shaking hands? It's obvious, isn't it? Now try explaining the rules. When do you shake hands and with whom? How do you know they are ready to shake? How do you show you are ready to shake? How long should you shake hands for, and how firm should your grip be? Suddenly, the mysteries of bowing in Japan seemed trivial. For bowing, there are clear rules and methods. But for shaking hands? And let's not even start on Europeans and kissing . . .

We may find other cultures mysterious, but never forget that we are the culture which is mysterious to others.

Never forget that we are the culture which is mysterious to others.

Understand the cultural differences within the team

The research for *Global Teams* identified 20 cultural differences which can impact the work of the team. These cultural differences can be divided into five broad categories:

▶ Attitudes to authority and hierarchy

▶ How team members communicate with each other

▶ How team members relate to each other

▶ Mindset and beliefs

▶ Cultural context.

The first step for the team is to understand these differences. Work through the differences below: the easiest way is via a survey. Where there is consensus around an approach, there is no need for discussion. For instance, if everyone thinks trust is best built professionally and that personal trust will follow, there is no need to discuss trust. If the team is split, you need to work the issue further.

The table below summarises the cultural differences. Below the table is a short summary of what lies behind each one. Most teams and team members do not exist at the extremes of these trade-offs. But there will be sufficient differences to cause misunderstanding which impedes the work of the team.

Simplified cultural differences

Individual	Collective
Follow the process	Focus on the goal
Hierarchical	Egalitarian
Principles and reason	Pragmatism and practicality
Open and rational	Private and personal
Expressive, open	Restrained, closed
Direct and simple	Layered and nuanced

Individual	Collective
Professional	Personal
Direct	Indirect, avoided
Visible	Invisible
Tolerate ambiguity	Eliminate ambiguity
Optimistic	Pragmatic
Task focus	People focus
Open	Closed
Linear	Flexible
Long term	Short term
Process	Outcomes
Impersonal	Relationships

We will briefly explore each of these differences in turn.

1. Decision making: individual versus collective

In every organisation there is a balance between individual and collective decision making. Even in the most hierarchical organisation, the leader will normally seek the views of colleagues and team members before making a decision; even the most egalitarian organisations have some form of hierarchy in which some decisions get passed upwards. So this question is one of balance:

▶ How far do big decisions get delegated up or down in the organisation?
▶ How much do management consult before taking a decision? And is this advice listened to and acted on? Or is it a façade of 'touching' and 'involving' staff to build 'buy-in' to a decision which has already been made and the only question is how it is executed.

The text box on extreme delegation shows how far delegation of authority can go.

Extreme delegation

The Brazilian company Semco has taken egalitarian decision making to an extreme. It started when the founder and CEO, Ricardo Semler, got fed up hearing complaints about the canteen. So he let the staff run it as a way of getting rid of the complaints. It worked, and from there delegation snowballed. Now staff set their own hours and pay; managers are evaluated by their teams; teams make all the day-to-day decisions. In Semler's words: 'the only way to manage is by firing all the managers'.[303]

Even the traditionally hierarchical P&G can be democratic. Their Chicago plant was facing a crisis:[304] it was old, with out-of-date working practices, and was struggling to attract business. So the management left the plant and let the staff make the bid for the next major manufacturing contract. The staff were more radical than management had dared, to be with the result that the plant won the contract and stayed in business. Management then had the tricky task of negotiating their way back into the plant . . .

How far do management trust the collective wisdom of your teams?

Each global team needs to understand where they are on this trade-off. If team members expect consensual decision making, then they will become highly frustrated if the team leader starts making all the decisions unilaterally. Equally, a more hierarchical culture will expect to delegate problems upwards and will be unnerved if they do not get clear direction: they will start to think that they have a weak boss and will lose confidence.

2. Accountability: individual versus collective

Accountability is closely tied to decision-making rights. If you can make a decision, you are accountable for its consequences. A good test of accountability is to see what happens when things work well and not so well.

▶ When there is a success, does the team share the credit, or does one person get the glory?

▶ When one member of the team is struggling, does the team feel it has to help out, or does the team feel let down? In Japan, it is not uncommon to see the whole team staying late to help out if that is required.

The chapter on systems showed that teams can work well with either strong individual accountability or with collective accountability, but not both: all team members need to be playing to the same rules.

3. Compliance: follow the process versus focus on the goal

Compliance cultures vary dramatically across firms and industries, as well as across geographies. At one extreme there is the classic bureaucratic culture which will enforce rules and regulations, even if they clearly are pointless. This is process compliance: follow the process and do not worry too much about the outcome.

At the other extreme are the goal-focused organisations, where achieving the goal is everything and no one is too concerned about the process. At the extreme this leads to ethical problems in some sales teams and some types of business. But any system with strong goals and high rewards or sanctions for achieving those goals will lead to game playing. Even the UK school system has suffered from head teachers playing the exam system to achieve government mandated goals.

Playing the game

If you have a high stakes accountability system, do not be surprised if people start to game it. We might expect some gaming to happen in business, but even in mission-driven organisations, extreme goal focus can lead to game playing. The UK has a strong system of accountability for schools, and head teachers know that failing will probably lead to their losing their job.

The core metric for high schools is exam results. Exam results can't be gamed, can they? Yes, they can. Here's how:

▶ Encourage low performers into home schooling: move them out of your scores.

▶ Quickly remove any troublesome pupils: move the problem onto someone else.

▶ Enter pupils into easier subjects worth more points in the system.

▶ Focus on pupils on the key threshold: ignore the high performers who will pass anyway and the low performers who will fail anyway.

> ▶ Put most effort into pupils in their exam year, not before, which works if you have been drafted in for a short-term contract.
>
> None of this improves education, but it improves results. Most businesses play similar games.

Process-driven compliance ignores the big picture; goal focus leads to game playing and even to ethical problems.

Both extremes are dangerous. Process-driven compliance ignores the big picture; goal focus leads to game playing and even to ethical problems. Most cultures are somewhere in between.

Global teams need to understand differences here. A team with a goal-focused culture will expect individual team members to have some autonomy and flexibility to do what it takes to achieve the goal. A process-driven team will want to avoid surprises which come from individual team members doing something unexpected and different. This trade-off should lead to a discussion about how much independence and initiative each team member is expected to show.

4. Style: hierarchical versus egalitarian

Hierarchy is not just about bosses bossing. Some very hierarchical cultures can also be very consensual: Japan has a strong culture of hierarchy in relationships and a strong commitment to consensus in decision making and collective accountability.

Hierarchy is most easily judged through communications:

▶ How do team members address team leaders? In Anglo countries first names will be used; in China the team leader will be addressed with the honorific '*zong*', or 'boss'. In between these two, France will use the more formal '*vous*' rather than '*tu*'.

▶ How open is dialogue across the hierarchy? In more hierarchical cultures it is difficult even to arrange meetings where there is a real mismatch in hierarchy, and the junior person will not expect to speak unless they are asked to speak. In Anglo countries, speaking rights go to whoever believes they have the expertise to speak: if junior people do not speak up, then that raises questions over why they attended the meeting and whether they have anything worth saying.

Understanding this difference is essential for a global team. Each team member needs to have the same expectations about when and how they are expected to contribute in meetings.

5. Persuasion: principles and practice

At its simplest, reasoning has two types: inductive and deductive. Different cultures take different approaches (see the text box below).

▶ Inductive thinking starts with concrete, practical observations and then attempts to draw conclusions from that.

▶ Deductive thinking works in the opposite direction. It starts with first principles and the theory. It then works out the practical implications from those principles.

This causes chaos when inductive and deductive thinkers meet and try to persuade each other. The inductive thinker will be driven to distraction by the theorising and impracticality of the deductive thinker. The deductive thinker will dislike the lack of intellectual rigour of the inductive thinker.

On global teams it helps to have a mix of the two types of thinking. Between them, the two approaches can reach an intellectually robust and practical decision. Team members need to understand and value these different approaches, so they can build on their mutual strengths.

England and France: one thousand years of misunderstanding[305]

England and France have been the best of friends and enemies for the last thousand years or so. Only a large ditch separates them: the English Channel or *la Manche*, depending on where you live. This large ditch conceals a huge gulf in how the French and English think.

France is proud of its intellectual heritage and that is reflected in the way executives go about making decisions and persuading people. They tend to start

▶

with first principles and work down to the detail from there. French tradition is based on Cartesian logic.[306] Robust challenge is expected.

The English also have a proud intellectual heritage, but they hide it. Calling a manager an intellectual implies that they are impractical, theoretical, out of touch and probably arrogant. Instead of starting with the theory, the English are more likely to start with a list of bullet point facts and work towards a conclusion from there.

The English way looks intellectually lazy and unreliable to the French. The French way looks theoretical and impractical to the English. So the two sides rarely understand each other. But they are making progress: they have given up invading each other for the last 200 years or so.

6. Dealing with problems and differences: open or private

No culture enjoys airing problems.

Global teams need an agreed way of dealing with problems as they arise. No culture enjoys airing problems, but there are very different ways of doing so.

In high respect cultures across much of Asia and the Middle East, there is an emphasis on not causing offence. This makes it difficult to raise a problem or a difference. Raising the issue will be seen as destructive of team harmony and will damage personal relationships. If issues are raised, they will be raised in private, obliquely and as a last resort. Where there is also a strong sense of hierarchy, it means that the boss rarely hears bad news. 'Don't give your boss bad medicine' is a good rule of thumb in most cultures, and even more so where there is hierarchy, respect, desire to save face and avoidance of conflict.

In more open cultures, problems and differences must be raised and discussed. Transparency avoids surprises and that helps build trust and improve the relationship. As long as the discussion is kept rational and does not become personal, then this open dialogue is seen to be very healthy for the team.

This is an area of real culture clash. The respect-based team will be aghast when a team member raises problems and issues in public. The team from an open culture will quickly lose faith and trust in a team member who does not raise issues promptly: they will be regarded as evasive, dishonest and unreliable.

With some cultural differences (such as inductive versus deductive thinking), diversity strengthens the team. That is not the case when dealing with problems and differences: diversity weakens the team. The team needs an agreed way of dealing with differences and problems. That in turn will require active support for the team members who have to change their approach: it is very unnatural for respect-based cultures to be so open. Equally, team members from more open cultures will be highly frustrated by not being able to raise issues openly.

The team can choose to deal with problems and differences either way: the important thing is that the whole team needs to use the same approach.

7. Body language: understanding diversity

Body language is a very visible expression of cultural differences. For the purposes of the global team, you can add personal appearances and personal space into the discussion about body language. There is no right and wrong answer, but there is plenty of opportunity for misunderstanding. Three examples make the point:

▶ Indians may shake their head when agreeing; other team members may interpret the shake of the head as disagreement.

▶ Japanese may laugh with embarrassment when a mishap occurs; others may think they are laughing at the mishap, causing resentment all round.

▶ British people traditionally display very little body language. This makes them hard to read and can feel unfriendly, when that is not the intention.

Collectivist societies tend to mask negative feelings. Different cultures amplify or de-amplify key emotions such as anger, fear, sadness and contempt. A controlled study of Japanese, North American and Russian body language found:[307]

▶ Russians and North Americans display anger and contempt more than Japanese.

▶ North Americans expressed happiness more than Russians or Japanese.

▶ Japanese amplified fear and surprise more than Russians.

These reactions are culturally conditioned. Experiments showed that in private Japanese would register emotional expressions similarly to North Americans; in the presence of others, negative expressions in particular would be de-amplified.

Displays of anger and contempt are highly discourteous in one culture, but are a sign of strength in another.

These differences matter. Displays of anger and contempt are highly discourteous in one culture, but are a sign of strength in another.

Personal space also varies by culture. One study[308] looked at the average conversational distance between students from three countries:

- ▶ Japan   1.01 metres
- ▶ USA   0.89 metres
- ▶ Venezuela   0.81 metres

These differences may not sound much, but they are dramatic. If the Venezuelan meets the Japanese, it will look like the Japanese is being chased backwards round the room. The Japanese will keep on retreating to maintain distance; the Venezuelan will keep approaching to maintain contact. Friendliness on one side feels like intrusiveness on the other.

Finally, every tribe and every culture has its own dress code. It is easy but dangerous to rush to judgement based on dress. Consider this situation: on a beach in Dubai two women pass each other: one is in a burka, the other is in a bikini and sunglasses. What might they think of each other?

- ▶ Bikini woman looking at burka woman: 'Poor woman, virtually everything covered except her eyes. What a sexist, male-dominated society.'
- ▶ Burka woman looking at bikini and sunglasses woman: 'Poor woman, virtually nothing covered except her eyes. What a sexist, male-dominated society.'

In the office we can equally easily rush to judgement. If someone wears a suit, it does not make them respectable and trustworthy: politicians wear suits. If you see someone in dirty jeans, they are not layabouts: they may have been working all night to sort out a tech problem.

Dress codes vary by nation, by level within the firm and even by function. And all the dress codes vary over time as well: few people dress as their parents used to. The global team can afford to celebrate diversity in dress, saving an agreed dress code for key events.

The global team should not try to prescribe appropriate body language, personal space or dress codes. These things are deeply rooted in each culture. Instead, the team has to foster cultural intelligence which enables each team member to understand and respect each other's cultural styles.

8. Communication style: high context versus low context cultures

High context and low context cultures misunderstand each other easily.

The difference between the two styles of communication come down to the relative weight given to maintaining the relationship versus moving to action:

▶ High context cultures (Asia, Middle East): maintaining the relationship is a key part of the communication. This makes communication, especially around problem solving and differences, very oblique.

▶ Low context cultures (Anglo world): the focus is on the actions not on the relationship. This enables communication to be direct and transactional.

In low context cultures messages can be taken at face value: 'I say what I mean and I mean what I say.' In high context cultures, much is left unsaid. As the Japanese say: '*kuuki o yomu*': you have to read the air. Novelist Amy Tan put it this way: 'I try to explain to my English-speaking friends that Chinese language is more strategic in manner, whereas English tends to be more direct; an American business executive may say, "Let's make a deal", and the Chinese manager may reply, "Is your son interested in learning about your widget business?"'[309]

Managers from low context cultures like Germany or North America find it difficult to read what is meant by the nuanced and indirect nature of communication by people from high context cultures. But even if you are from a low context culture, you will have plenty of experience in dealing with a high context culture. Every day, you deal with a high context culture at home: within the family much is said beyond the words which are said. The feeling and intention behind the words can be felt on both sides.

Clearly, there is huge scope for misunderstanding here. High context managers can be offended by the directness of low context communications, and that can harm the relationship. Low context team members can get very frustrated by what they see as the avoidance tactics and inaction of the high context team members.

In practice, managers do not change the way they speak. But they can change the way they listen, so that they can pick up and respect the different style of their colleagues.

9. Trust: personal versus professional

All cultures eventually reach the same end point on trust where the trust equation (see the chapter on trust) is satisfied:

$$ t = \frac{i \times c}{s \times r} $$

As a reminder: trust (t) is built by a combination of intimacy (i) and credibility (c), but is negatively impacted by self-orientation or selfishness (s) and the perceived risk of the situation (r).

The big difference is in how trust is built. The difference broadly follows the split between high context and low context cultures.

▶ High context cultures across much of Asia, the Middle East and Latin countries put emphasis on building the personal relationship first. They want to find common interests and common values, and develop a personal understanding and rapport first. They work on the intimacy part of the equation first.

▶ Low context cultures, such as the Anglo world and North Europeans, want to get down to business straight away. In this culture, trust comes from credibility: show that you can do what you say. Any personal trust and relationship will come after the professional relationship has been established.

Although the sequence of building trust differs, the end result is the same. Trust comes from a combination of personal trust (intimacy) and professional trust (credibility). The sequencing causes missteps on both sides. The classic Anglo view was expressed by one frustrated manager who found the only way of dealing with the relationship challenge was to delegate the relationship building to someone who understood how to do it:

'Our Turkish distributer was like a child and always wanted to talk for hours on end. So I hired an old Lebanese who would do the talking for me. The Turk would tell the Lebanese "tell your boss this or that". The Turk just wanted to be listened to by someone who had the ear of the boss, so that's why I hired the Lebanese.'[310]

In practice, nearly every global team finds it useful to meet in person as soon as possible. Trust levels and the ease of communication rise dramatically once people have met in person. Even in low context cultures, meeting and knowing your team makes a big difference.

> **Trust levels and the ease of communication rise dramatically once people have met in person.**

10. Feedback: direct or indirect

Most cultures are comfortable giving positive feedback. Praise and flattery are universally appreciated. But equally, most cultures dislike giving negative feedback. The kickback against formal appraisals is strong. In 2015, Accenture ditched its annual appraisal process for its 330,000 staff. GE was famous, or infamous, for its 'rank and yank' appraisal system which would weed out the bottom 10 per cent of performers. They have also decided to ditch annual appraisals. Dropping appraisals does not mean less feedback; it requires managers to give more frequent feedback. Janice Semper, leader of GE Culture, explains the shift: 'It is really a shift from what we have historically done at GE. The focus is much more on the people, developing them, and much less on rating and ranking people.'[311]

The difference between direct and indirect cultures is both in what they say and in how they say it.

Managers in direct cultures, including Netherlands, Russia, Nigeria and France, say it as they see it:

▶ Be explicit about perceived failings

▶ Don't cushion the blow by discussing strengths

▶ Focus on the task, not the person

▶ Use power words: absolutely, always, worst, never, must. . .

Managers in indirect cultures, including Japan, Thailand and Indonesia, say it differently:

▶ Avoid any negative feedback

▶ Focus on strengths, and leave the listener to realise that the omissions are the weaknesses. For instance: 'You are very good at communicating with your boss' may mean 'You are terrible at communicating with your team'

▶ Focus on maintaining the relationship

▶ Use soft words and qualifiers: sort of, may be, like, could, possibly.

There are many cultures in between. Many of these are the 'I love you, but . . .' cultures where the bad news is sugar-coated with lots of positive statements which come first. Both sides know the rule that 'everything before the "but" is bull****'. But it is still a ritual which shows respect while being explicit about the negative feedback.

Both cultures work internally. The robust Dutch culture means that feedback can be two-way: the team member can give negative feedback to the boss. Giving negative feedback to the boss is unimaginable in countries like Thailand and Indonesia, where team members learn to read between the lines to hear the real message.

When cultures clash, problems emerge fast:

▶ Direct to indirect culture: giving robust and direct feedback will be a relationship breaker. The team member from the indirect culture will feel humiliated and distressed. This will signal to the team leader from the direct culture that the team member is weak and ineffective. Disaster follows.

▶ Indirect to direct. The team leader will be so positive and indirect that the team member will believe that they are doing a great job. They will not read between the lines or hear any of the danger signals which are being flagged obliquely by the team leader.

Feedback demands huge cultural intelligence from the global team leader, who has to radically adapt they way they communicate the message depending on who they are talking to. Within the team, norms have to be established about how team members give feedback to each other. Awareness of different styles helps, and simply discussing this challenge in the group makes a start in reducing the intensity of misunderstandings when they occur.

11. Status: visible or invisible

Visible status cultures are very easy to spot. In the Philippines, the major brewery had a lift for the sole use of the chairman; and the lift had a dedicated lift attendant to push the button for the chairman twice a day as he went to his personal office on his personal floor. This was a chairman who enjoyed and expected a high degree of respect and deference from staff. In high status cultures, the carpet is deeper, the flowers are fresher and the furniture is more expensive as you go up through the organisation. In these cultures leaders are used to being respected, and have forgotten what it is like to be challenged.

Respect status[312]

The boardroom looked like it had been designed for a James Bond villain: it was an exercise in power projection, with flags and microphones at each seat. Even getting into the boardroom required negotiating a phalanx of executive assistants, flunkies and sharp-suited security guards with bulging muscles and bulging pockets.

I had been asked to wait for the CEO. He came in, with bulging eyes and bulging veins. He was furious: 'I'm going to fire Kristoff! He is useless!' I gently suggested that a sales director who spoke seven languages might be useful in some upcoming global negotiations. 'I'd rather have someone who is smart in one language than dumb in seven!' he snapped back, giving the classic defensive riposte of monoglot leaders.

Further enquiry showed that the sales director's error was that he kept walking through doors in front of the CEO. This showed total disrespect for the CEO who felt humiliated and upstaged in front of visitors.

Later that day, Kristoff left the building for the last time, escorted by four of the security guards. If leaders crave status, let them have it: they have the power and you don't. You have to learn the culture as well as the language.

For better or worse, the rules of the game are clear in high status cultures: the leader expects to lead, and the followers have to follow and show respect. In practice, this makes it difficult to have open dialogue, or any dialogue across more than one level of the hierarchy.

The real challenge comes with cultures where status is hidden. Many tech CEOs in particular favour a desk in an open-plan office. This is the ultimate democratic statement: aside from the odd billion dollars in the CEO's bank account, 'we are all in it together'. A brief web trawl will throw up pictures of Mark Zuckerberg (Facebook), Max Levchin (PayPal co-founder and founder of Affirm) and Dennis Crowley (Foursquare) with cubicles in the middle of an open-plan office.[313] Their dress code is as democratic as their workspace: everyone wears the same uniform of individualistic dress-down styles.

The democratic culture is more open and there is less need to show overt deference. In place of deference and loyalty, you have to show that you can add real value fast through insight or delivery. As one more democratic CEO said, 'anyone can see me at any time. . . once. If they make a difference, they can see me again.'[314] The threat was clear: you can waste his time once, but you will not get a second chance.

The two status cultures lead to very different sorts of interactions. One puts a premium on loyalty and deference, the other on insight and action. It is for the leader of the global team to set the style well.

12. Ambiguity: tolerated or eliminated

Across most cultures there is a big divide in attitudes to ambiguity between large businesses and entrepreneurs.

Large businesses dislike ambiguity, even though they accept and manage risk well. Large businesses dislike ambiguity, even though they accept and manage risk well. Film studios take risks on films; oil firms take risks on exploring for new oil fields and all banks are in the business of taking calculated credit and trading risk. But ambiguity and uncertainty are unwelcome: a plan which tells the CEO 'we are not sure, but we could try this or that. . . ' will not get much further than the waste bin. Entrepreneurs are the opposite: they embrace ambiguity as an opportunity to try new things, innovate and change the rules of the game.

Most global teams are also reasonable at managing risk: that is what risk logs and mitigating actions are designed to deal with. But ambiguity divides global teams.

Most global teams find ambiguity hard to handle. The more direct cultures (the Anglo world) crave clarity: they want clear goals, clear roles, clear accountability and clear processes. The more indirect cultures (Asia) are more comfortable with ambiguity. Ambiguity gives the team autonomy to decide on the best way forward, who should do what and how things should be done. In these cultures, uncertainty is not resolved through formal structures and processes. It is resolved through mutual adjustment and social norms.

Ambiguity creates a dividing line between those who put clarity and formal processes first and those who put autonomy and social cohesion first. Both approaches can work separately but not together. You have to choose one approach or the other, explain it, and make it happen.

13. Outlook: optimistic or pragmatic

Levels of optimism vary wildly by nation. Ask yourself this question: 'Is the world getting better or worse?' The most optimistic nations were (percentage thinking the world is getting better):[315]

▶ China 57 per cent
▶ Indonesia 51 per cent

The least optimistic nations were:

▶ France 14 per cent
▶ Finland 28 per cent

Most nations scored slightly above 30 per cent, so the French and Chinese are true outliers. Clearly, the question you ask and the sample you choose will yield different results. Whatever the methodology, global teams clearly see that different cultures bring very different perspectives. The only sort of challenges that Chinese executives have faced in their lifetime have been the challenges of growth: finding and retaining the best staff, managing cash flows, building capacity. The lifetime experience of many western managers has been more balanced, or even the opposite: how to maximise efficiency, reduce costs and headcount, and change ways of working to achieve the holy grail of business competition: betterfastercheaper.

These conflicting views are useful, but hard to handle. The optimistic cultures will push for the best and most positive outcome: they simply will not conceive that failure is an option. The more pragmatic cultures will be more risk aware. The two sides should help each other: the optimists will stretch the team, and the pragmatists will avoid crazy risks. But the two sides will not understand each other. The optimists will feel disdain for the pragmatists who will sound like losers; the optimists will look like fantasists to the pragmatists.

A simple way to explore these differences is to let every team member take an optimism survey.[316] Professor Martin Seligman, the founder of the positive psychology movement, has several good online resources available for use through the University of Pennsylvania.

The research on optimism is fairly conclusive: optimists live longer and better than pessimists; they recover from setbacks better and they are more successful. A classic study at MetLife[317] showed that life insurance sales people who failed the initial skills test but were highly optimistic outsold recruits who passed the skills test but were less optimistic. This research has been confirmed in many subsequent trials, in life insurance and in other industries.

If your team is full of pragmatists it will work, but it is unlikely to overachieve. Optimists can take the team to another level, and can show the pragmatists a different way of thinking and living.

14. Focus: tasks versus people

Task versus people focus is both a cultural bias and an individual preference. In task-focused cultures, such as Northern Europe and the Anglo world, you can still find plenty of people-focused leaders. And in cultures which focus much more on relationships, you can still find plenty of task-focused leaders. Within a global team you need a balance of these skills. The differences are summarised below.

	Task	People
Focus	Achieve results	Maintain relationships
Nature of work	Routine	Ambiguous
Outcomes	Efficiency	Innovation and learning

	Task	People
Control	Measures	Motivation
Incentives	Formal rewards, measures	Recognition
Team skills	Low	High

This difference has echoes of Douglas McGregor's classic theory X versus theory Y types of management.[318] Theory X is traditional command and control of low skilled workers who cannot be trusted; theory Y focuses on motivating higher skilled staff. The difference is between achieving compliance (X) or commitment (Y). Clearly, the world is moving from one dominated by X type task-focused leaders to one requiring Y type leaders who are more people focused.

Nevertheless, research shows[319] that task or people focus is contingent: it depends on circumstances. A people-first style is more appropriate where:[320]

▶ individuals are highly capable and have a high need for autonomy

▶ the task itself is self-satisfying

▶ the leader wants to achieve more cohesion across the group

▶ learning and innovation are valued outcomes.

These are fairly common conditions in global teams, which indicates the sort of leadership style which will work best for the team. The global team leader needs to be highly effective at bringing people together and building bonds of trust across the team. The leader also needs enough task focus to assure the right outcomes from the team.

Within the team, a mix of skills is productive when managed well. This is where the team and the team leader need to have cultural intelligence. At a simple level, introductions can lead to misunderstanding. When North Americans ask 'How are you doing?' they don't expect much of an answer. Anyone from the Middle East would expect this to be the start of a personal discussion, especially if it is a first meeting.

Cultural styles are just that: they are styles which the global team has to learn to work with. There is no best approach. Within the team, task-focused people can keep the project moving along, and the people-focused team members can help ensure the team works well together. Value the differences.

213

15. Openness: open versus closed

Global teams find it far easier to work in open cultures. Some cultures are very open to outside influence, others are far more closed. Global teams find it far easier to work in open cultures.

At one extreme stands London. In the 2011 census just 44.9 per cent of the population was white British (including many from Scotland, Wales, Northern Ireland and the rest of England).[321] At least 300 languages are spoken in London and over 50 nationalities have more than 10,000 residents in London.[322] It is a culture which is very open and adapts to many different influences: it is far easier to find a foreign restaurant than an English restaurant in London.

At the other end of the spectrum from London are cities such as Beijing and Tokyo which are culturally homogeneous. A short trip to Roppongi in Tokyo on a Friday night will show that there is a thriving foreign business community there, as in Beijing: outside these small foreign ghettos both cities are overwhelmingly homogeneous.

It is normally easier for global teams to work with open cultures than closed cultures. The closed cultures create barriers to outsiders, unintentionally or otherwise. Closed cultures assume that they are the best culture. Japanese often say '*Nihon chigau desu*' which literally means 'Japan is different', and that is true. It also implicitly means 'Japan is better'. Such closed cultures approach globalisation by replicating their practices around the world and staffing foreign subsidiaries with expatriates who can be trusted. Foreigners find it very hard to gain any traction with head office, even if they can speak the language.

Similarly, China referred to itself as *zhōngguó*[323] which can be taken as the 'Central State' or the 'Centre of Civilisation' where the Great Wall keeps out all the barbarians. Historically, the West also had a fixed mindset in which it believed it was superior. The political empires of Europe in the nineteenth century and the business empires of America in the twentieth century were both based on the assumption that the home nation knew best. These empires did not make many concessions to the locals.

The closed culture works where you clearly have a superior way of doing things. The closed culture works where you clearly have a superior way of doing things. This was the case for the nineteenth-century European empires (technology), twentieth-century American businesses (brands, operating models) and the Japanese in the late twentieth century (autos etc). The closed culture still works where the firm has a very clear business model which you can roll out globally with low adaptation to each country. Starbucks has such a model and it succeeds with a relatively homogeneous leadership team: of its fifty-seven senior executives just seven were educated outside the United States. Those seven came mainly from the Anglo world of Canada, UK and Ireland.[324]

The closed culture does not work where there is more even competition globally and a greater need to adapt to local conditions. Coming from a closed culture does not prevent a firm from forging an open culture for itself. Nissan has opened up. Four out of five board members are non-Japanese, including Carlos Ghosn, who is President and Chairman.[325] Twenty out of fifty of its most senior executives are also non-Japanese.

Nissan and Starbucks show that culture is not destiny. A firm can come from an open society and have a closed but successful firm culture (Starbucks) and you can come from a closed society and have an open and equally successful firm culture (Nissan). The difference between the two is that Starbucks is internationalising a success ful model; Nissan is trying to build a truly global firm which does not depend so heavily on the skills and experience of the home nation.

If a firm wants to be truly global, it has to open up: that will be reflected in who gets promoted, who runs the firm, who makes decisions and how far it learns and adapts with each market it enters. If a firm simply wants to internationalise, then it can remain homogeneous.

16. Growth: fixed versus adaptive

Individual team members need to be both open and adaptive. This is often called the growth mindset.[326] It is one of the seven mindsets which the most successful leaders display.[327] The growth mindset is open to learning, is interested in new ideas and new ways of working, and is prepared to take risks to learn and grow. These are very useful attributes for team members to have.

In contrast, the fixed mindset is toxic to a global team. It is averse to new challenges and new ways of working; it will avoid risk by sticking with a proven successful

The fixed mindset is toxic to a global team.

formula from the past and will not learn. There are some technical roles where this can work for a while: it is not always good to have book keepers who start to get creative with the books. But most global teams need members who adapt to each other, respect each other and learn from each other. The growth mindset and the global mindset are closely aligned.

Fixed and open mindsets display different personal and professional preferences, and are easy to spot.

	Fixed	Adaptive
Food	Stick with what's familiar	Try new foods
Music and films	Golden era when person was 18–30 years old	Likes new and different styles
Risk appetite	Avoid failure	Embrace chance to learn
Other cultures	They need to adapt to my way	How can we both adapt?
Dealing with problems	Problems mean failure and someone is at fault	Problems are a chance to learn and grow
Dealing with criticism	Deny; fight back; spread the blame	Take responsibility and learn

Different cultures are more or less open to learning, adapting and growing. Even closed and homogeneous societies are quite capable of learning very fast from foreign influences. Japan industrialised at breakneck speed after the Meiji restoration in 1868, driven by the realisation that they were far behind the West technologically. Japan learned so fast that by 1905 they defeated Russia comprehensively in a conflict over territory in Manchuria and Korea. Japan repeated the learning trick more peacefully after the Second World War when they took the quality lessons of Edward Deming to heart and achieved huge success in autos, consumer electronics and office equipment. More recently, China has proven very fast at absorbing ideas from the West following the reforms started under Deng Xiaoping.

In contrast, some open societies are much more resistant to adapting. France is keen to protect its cultural, linguistic and intellectual heritage in the face of rampaging English language and Anglo values. The French Toubon law not only specifies the use of French in all official documents, but also sets a French quota for radio and television broadcasting;[328] the Académie

Française[329] is the official custodian of the French language. It is hard to imagine Congress mandating what words are permissible or not in English, or telling television stations where their programming should come from.

Each firm and each team crafts its own culture. For the global team, recruiting people with the right mindset is essential to the success of the team.

17. Time discipline: linear or flexible

Your colleague has asked to meet you at 3pm. What time is it acceptable for you to turn up:

▶ 2.57
▶ 3.00
▶ 3.05
▶ 3.15
▶ 3.30
▶ Any time, provided you send a text message explaining circumstances
▶ Whenever you can get there.

Different cultures will give very clear and very different answers. These different approaches can lead to unnecessary clashes and conflict on global teams.

In Japan, 3.00 means 3.00 regardless of who you are meeting. Even social events are managed with time precision. Imagine you are invited to dinner from 7pm until 10pm. At 7pm precisely all the guests will appear; at 10pm all the guests will depart. In time-sensitive countries, turning up late is a very bad sign. It shows disrespect for the other person's time; it implies that you are inefficient and disorganised; it is a way of saying that you do not value or care for the person you are meeting.

The Japanese, Germans and Swiss are at one extreme on time sensitivity. It is perhaps no coincidence that they also have reputations for being very precise in terms of quality and engineering. At the other extreme is South Asia and the Middle East. In between come the Anglo countries where some slippage is allowed, but within narrow limits and depending on circumstances.

Time-sensitive cultures see time as linear; it is a finite commodity with real value. Professional service firms bill by the hour (or less) and are time sensitive. In these cultures, people organise themselves around time, which must not be wasted.

More flexible cultures do not see time as being the primary organising principle of the day. Relationships and events determine priorities. If you are engaged in something important, it makes no sense to

Flexible cultures do not see time as being the primary organising principle of the day.

stop it before completion because some arbitrary point on the clock has been reached. In Southern Europe or the Middle East it is far more important to finish the conversation than to cut it short to go to another meeting. Events as well as relationships shape how time is used in flexible cultures. In Japan and Switzerland, the bus leaves according to a timetable, regardless of whether it is full or empty. In South Asia, Latin America and many parts of Africa, the bus leaves when it is full: that makes economic sense and means it helps the most people travel.

These cultures clash over small distances: the Swiss are highly punctual and linear, the Italians are far more flexible. North America and Mexico have very different views of time keeping.

Time discipline

	Linear, rigid	Flexible, adaptive
Examples	Japan, Germany, North America	Italy, Mexico, Middle East
Deadlines	Precise	Guidelines
Respect	The clock	The relationship
Priority	Be punctual	Finish the task or conversation
Sequencing	One thing at a time	Multi-task

Time in most cultures is sensitive to hierarchy. India has a fairly flexible view of time. Meetings will start when the most senior person appears and is ready to start. Harassed officials can keep supplicants waiting for hours for a meeting. But even in India, if you are invited to a meeting with the Prime Minister at 3pm, it is best to turn up at 3pm. The more important the person is, the more important it is to keep time: this is universally true. Don't try to keep the President of the United States waiting while you send that very urgent text message. And even time flexible cultures understand that when the plane leaves at 7.25, it leaves – unless you are a government minister in a kleptocracy who has the power to order the airline to wait. Flexible cultures can be time sensitive when they need to be; they will be flexible with your time when it suits them.

Time cultures also vary by discipline and generation. Engineers in manufacturing and creative types in advertising have different views on most things, including time. The engineers value organisation, discipline and managing tasks in a logical sequence. Creative types are more flexible and adaptive; they will respond to challenges as they arise. In their own context, both approaches to time work. Put them together and you have a recipe for misunderstanding.

Generations also have different attitudes to time, driven by technology. Before the age of mobile phones, there was no way of telling a date you would be late, so you had to turn up on time. Now that technology allows us to say we will be late, we do so. The technology may enable us to be late, but it does not give us permission to be late. Curiously, one technology works to keep people prompt: scheduled Skype calls tend to start when scheduled, even with time flexible cultures.

The time challenge for global teams is obvious where you have time sensitive and time flexible people on the same team. The time sensitive team members will turn up on time to team meetings, and then feel very offended when the time flexible team members keep them waiting, repeatedly. The time flexible team members will not understand what the issue is and will be aggrieved by the hostility being shown to them.

If the time of a global team is valuable, it makes sense to agree expectations which minimise wasted and waiting time. But the important thing is that the whole team has to agree to the same set of rules and then enforce them.

Time tempo

Robert Levine has studied the tempo of time across cultures.[330] He has found that the pace of life, literally, varies dramatically. People walk faster in the more prosperous (and cooler) climates. The fastest walking paces are found in Northern Europe and North America: England, Germany, Netherlands and the US. The slowest walking paces are found in poorer and warmer countries, including

▶

Mexico, Kenya, Brazil and Indonesia. Observation also shows that people walk faster in the prosperous centre of the main city, and slower outside in the countryside.[331] In the city, there are fewer social interactions and more task focus.

Although he has shown correlation between walking pace and prosperity, he has not shown which way causality flows (if at all). If we start walking faster, will we get that pay rise? Will the firm become more profitable? Will the global team achieve more?

18. Time horizon: long term or short term

Time focus varies by culture and hierarchy. Typically, entry-level staff will focus on the second hand: they have to worry about delivering today's results and this week's results. Middle managers will worry about today, but also about this quarter and this year. They focus on the second hand and the minute hand of the clock. Senior managers will worry about today and this year, but will also be laying plans to make a difference over the next few years: they are tracking the second, minute and hour hands of the clock.

Different cultures also have different time horizons,[332] and these cultures differ by nation and by industry:

	Short term	Long term
Nation	Anglo world: US, UK	Japan, China
Industry	Financial services, retail	Oil, aerospace, pharma

These different time horizons affect how individuals, teams and firms operate:

	Short term	Long term
Results focus	Quarterly earnings	Competitive, strategic position
Change	Measurable outcomes	Building blocks for future
Decision making	Fast	Measured
Staff assessments	Past performance	Development for future

We will explore each of these differences in turn.

Results focus: quarterly earnings versus competitive and strategic positioning

The United States is famous, or infamous, for the non-stop treadmill of quarterly earnings reports which are scrutinised 24/7 by the talking heads on various financial TV channels. Similarly, in the UK there has been a debate for the past 40 years at least about the problems of 'short termism', which is generally viewed negatively. Short-term focus is seen as being alien to building long-term successful businesses. It puts pressure on managers to meet the numbers, and in many cases to manipulate the numbers where they can. The evils of short termism can be overblown. Some of the UK's strongest industries are oil, pharma, aerospace and telecoms (Vodafone) all of which require huge investments which only pay off over the very long term. Long term and short term are not always at odds with each other.

In contrast, Japan takes the long view. The concepts of strategic intent and core competence both take a very long-term view of how a firm can succeed. It is no coincidence that the original work on these ideas focused on Japanese companies which were disrupting western industries. The Japanese had very long-term and revolutionary strategies: the classic examples included Canon against Xerox, Komatsu against Caterpillar and Honda in engines.[333]

The long-term and short-term view changes how firms manage themselves. It also changes how teams and projects work, as we shall see in the next section.

Change: measurable outcomes versus building blocks for the future

Change projects are often dramatic and visible in the Anglo world. Restructurings, re-engineering, mergers and acquisitions all lead to dramatic changes in a short amount of time. This is consistent with the quarterly earnings perspective: get results fast. It also fits with most performance management systems. Everyone, in particular the CEO, wants to show that they are making a difference.

Japan has a different approach: 'open the backdoor and close the front door'. Instead of having a dramatic restructuring once every four years where 20 per cent of the workforce are made redundant, the Japanese take their time. Productivity improvements of 5 per cent a year let them reduce headcount by 20 per cent over four years by not hiring (close the front door) and natural wastage (open the back door). This is less dramatic and is more collective as an effort, which means there are fewer heroes to take the glory.

In practical terms, this can have a dramatic effect. Panasonic was a leading consumer electronics company. It still has strong consumer brands such as Lumix cameras. But Panasonic decided to take its consumer DNA and convert it into a B2B business.[334] Instead of serving retail customers directly, it serves them indirectly by creating real technical competencies in core electronics which it can sell to other firms. Moving from B2C to B2B is a huge shift. The result is that over 75 per cent of its business is now B2B: change achieved over the long term with less dramatic projects all pulling in the same direction.

'We always overestimate the change that will occur in the next two years and underestimate the change that will occur in the next ten.'
Short-term cultures want immediate gratification and immediate results. Long-term cultures will manage change more slowly, but equally dramatically. In the words of Bill Gates, founder of Microsoft: 'We always overestimate the change that will occur in the next two years and underestimate the change that will occur in the next ten. Don't let yourself be lulled into inaction.'[335] The long-term view drives dramatic change if done well.

Decision making

Short-term cultures value fast decision making. Because time is money, delaying a decision costs money and it looks like weak and indecisive management. A good decision is one which moves to action: if the decision needs to be revisited later in the light of unfolding events, that is no problem: make another fast decision and keep moving forward.

Long-term cultures are ready to take more time over arriving at a decision. They want to explore every avenue: the goal is to find the best solution, not just a pragmatic solution for today. They also want to ensure that the whole team is committed to the idea. This normally means that the decision making is far slower, but the implementation is far faster.

Neither approach is correct, although mixing them up on the same team causes confusion. Short-term cultures will be frustrated by the tortuous and long-winded approach of the long termists. The long termists will be appalled by the apparent sloppiness of the short termists and their disregard of fair process: failing to build buy-in and commitment from the team as a whole.

The team can decide which approach it prefers to take: what matters is that they understand the difference and make a clear choice.

Staff assessments

We have already noted that annual appraisals are falling into disrepute, with leading employers such as GE, Accenture and Deloitte ditching them altogether. But feedback is still expected, even if the long-term and short-term cultures drive in opposite directions.

The short-term culture expects to see measurable results, with each team member accountable for specific outcomes. This is seen to be a high-performance culture: clear outcomes, clear accountabilities and clear deadlines. It is fundamental to how western firms work.

Long-term cultures see things differently. If the firm and the team are to make deep change, like Panasonic moving from a B2C to a B2B firm, that requires a sustained collective effort over the long term. Building the required competencies takes time for the firm, the team and the individual. In this world, performance and outcomes over the last quarter are not the only metrics that matter. As important is how the firm, the team and the individual are developing: are they building the right skills, processes, capabilities and structures to thrive in the future? The long-term culture is more forward focused than the short-term culture which is rooted in the present and looks backwards as much as forwards.

Within the team, it is vital that everyone understands what good looks like:

▶ Will I be measured on personal achievements over the last three months?

▶ Will I be measured on my contribution to the team and my personal development?

These two forms of assessment drive fundamentally different behaviour. The first focuses on delivering short-term outcomes and is highly individualistic. The second is about teamwork, learning and growth.

Ideally, a global team will achieve all of these outcomes: strong individual outcomes, short-term performance, great teamwork, and learning and growth. In practice, the team has to choose how it will hold itself to account.

19. Meetings: process versus outcomes

'Meetings are a wonderful opportunity to sabotage the agendas of other ministries', declared the gleeful *chef de cabinet* of a major French government department.[336] This was the moment that I realised meetings are like sweets: they come in all shapes and sizes. Meetings can serve an endless variety of functions. On global teams, there is a strong sense that there are just too many meetings which lower productivity and are often poorly run:

▶   'It's an accepted practice that meetings are good, but I look at my day and it's rammed full of meetings.'[337]

▶   'I spend my whole day in meetings anyway just to understand what is happening and to update my team on what is happening.'[338]

▶   'Let them work without interrupting them with burdens like meetings.'[339]

▶   'There needs to be more communications but fewer meetings.'[340]

▶   'I have been to meetings where there are not clear goals. That is bad when the meeting is face to face, but worse when you are meeting remotely.'[341]

▶   'So many meetings have no leadership and have people just chipping in.'[342]

A large part of the problem is that team members often do not know what the meetings are for, and this is where there can be a huge cultural gap.

Effective meetings in the Anglo and Germanic worlds are assumed to have clear outcomes which may be decisions, or they may be about assigning accountability, planning projects and checking on progress: 'You need regular meetings at regular times of the day and you need to assign clear ownership.'[343]

This outcome focus contrasts with the process focus of other cultures. In Japan, decisions are made outside the meeting, not inside it. Meetings either confirm in public the consensus that has been achieved in private, or they are there to gather information which can support a later decision:

▶ 'Of course we have our business meetings but then we have drinks and we get to know each other and trust each other as well.'[344]

▶ 'The real decision makers don't attend the meetings.'[345]

These different assumptions cause problems on global teams. Where team members expect clear outcomes and decisions from the meeting, they will not just be frustrated by the lack of clear decisions in the meeting: they will be frustrated that they do not understand the decision-making process and they will suspect that they are being excluded deliberately. The meetings will feel like a waste of their time and their motivation will decline.

In contrast, team members from more process-driven cultures will be alarmed by meetings which make decisions in public. They will feel that they have not had the chance to express their true opinions in private; they will feel that they have been forced into a decision without due process and they will lack confidence in both the process and the outcome.

Both approaches work, but not together. As with many cultural challenges, transparency matters. The team needs to be aware that there are different assumptions about meetings, and then the team needs to decide what they want meetings for, and how decisions will be made.

20. Law: impersonal or personal

The law operates in very different ways around the world, which can come as a shock to business people when they fall foul of the local way of doing things. For instance, the rule of law is seen in quite different ways in Europe and China:

You do not have the rule of law, you have the rule of relationships.

'Then there is the issue of the rule of law. Europeans have a sense of rules, but the Chinese don't think like that. They think it is all about relationships. So in China the courts are irrelevant. The Chinese will not even mention the word court. You do not have the rule of law, you have the rule of relationships.'[346]

Each culture will be judgemental about the deficiencies of other cultures' legal systems. Cultural intelligence is about learning and understanding, not judging. There is much for global teams to learn from the Chinese approach to the law, which more closely reflects how decisions are made and how justice is administered within firms.

In theory, governments and firms make decisions impartially, independently, objectively and impersonally: in other words, they decide in the same way a judge decides in Europe or America. But practice is not like that. Decisions in firms are not made rationally: they are made for emotional and political reasons, based on relationships and trust. Even governments and the civil service do this. Most European governments are still medieval in the way they operate. Each government will have a large civil service with rules and procedures around decision making and procurement. But if you, as a courtier, can get the support of a key minister, you suddenly find that all the civil servants, rules and procedures start to work for you instead of trying to stop you.

Rational decision making?[347]

It was late on a Friday and a call came in from 10 Downing Street.[348] A civil servant explained that the Prime Minister was going to give a speech on Monday announcing a major expansion of Teach for Britain. We gently explained to the civil servant that we were called Teach First, not Teach for Britain. Less gently we explained that he could not announce our expansion because we were an independent charity and we did not have the funds to expand.

The civil servant became quite uncivil. No one ever says no to the Prime Minister, unless they want to say goodbye to their career. If the PM wants to make a speech, he makes the speech. The discussion became quite tense: the unstoppable force of the PM against the immovable object of Teach First.

By the end of the weekend, the PM had his speech and Teach First found it had government funding for several years of growth: all the procurement rules, ministerial papers and submissions and all the careful checks and balances disappeared in a puff of smoke. The Prime Minister still called us Teach for Britain: you can't win every battle.

When you have the ear of the boss, the machine will do whatever it can to help you.

Most firms are like government: they are medieval in decision making. They carry the veneer of sophisticated processes and protocols around decision making. But these processes support the decision which top management want to make anyway. The CEO is the monarch and the senior executive team are the monarch's ministers. As a courtier, you have to find your way around court to get the support of the ministers and monarch. For a global team this is a huge challenge. The team will be remote from the monarch's court, has limited access to courtiers and does not know what all the gossip at court (head office) is. The team needs an influential courtier (senior executive) who wants to represent the team: there has to be a personal gain for the courtier in helping the team. Goodwill helps in good times, but something stronger than goodwill is needed in tough times.

> **Most firms are like government: they are medieval in decision making.**

As with decision making, so with promotions and justice. Medieval justice was personal, like the mafia: stay on the right side of the boss and all is well; cross the boss and bad things happen to you. Even in the best run firms it is exceptionally hard to make comparisons between staff from different departments: the lobbying power of the departmental boss goes a long way to helping or hindering the prospects of team members. On a global team it is hard to see how the team is performing, let alone how individual members are contributing. As with decision making, this makes it essential for the global team to have a powerful sponsor who has an active interest in supporting the team and each member in the team.

The lesson of the law is simple: don't trust your future to the vagaries of the law. Firms may appear to be objective like western law; in practice decisions are made politically and emotionally from the top, like the law in many other cultures. That means each global team needs a powerful sponsor at head office who wants to influence decisions, promotions and budgets in their favour.

Conclusions

Culture can be a huge source of misunderstanding and conflict within a global team. There are three ways you can manage culture across your global team:

▶ Build cultural intelligence, not just cultural knowledge
▶ Understand and manage the cultural differences
▶ Build a common culture across the team.

Build cultural intelligence, not just cultural knowledge

Anthropologists can spend an entire career attempting to understand how just one culture works. That is about building cultural knowledge. You do not have the time or capacity to build deep cultural knowledge and understanding of all the different cultures you will work with. Cultural intelligence is different from cultural knowledge. Cultural intelligence is about building a mindset which:

▶ seeks to understand, not to judge
▶ is open to new ideas and new ways of working
▶ adapts to different circumstances fast
▶ respects and has positive regard for differences.

A simple way of building cultural intelligence and cultural knowledge fast is to create a buddy system. Every time you start work with a new culture, find a buddy who can guide you through the culture and explain the local rules of the game: for instance, if you know that in some countries a red traffic light is taken just a guidance, not as law, that might just save your life. The buddy does not have to be local: sometimes a foreigner is better able to see the differences than a local. Your buddy can build your cultural knowledge. You need to match their knowledge with your intelligence: you need to cultivate the mindset which allows you to make the most of the differences, rather than fighting the differences in culture.

Understand and manage the cultural differences

Cultural differences are real and cannot be brushed away. It is no surprise that preventing cultural misunderstanding is better than repairing it: prevention is always better than cure. When most teams set out, they normally have a start-up meeting where they agree the basics of what, who, when, how, where and why. This start-up meeting is even more important for a global team, because the ambiguity and uncertainty are even greater when tasks and roles are being shared remotely across borders; also, there is much less chance for informal adjustment in the weeks that follow because team members cannot see each other day to day. But global teams are often the worst at having start-up meetings: the time, cost and logistics mean that this vital first step is often missed. Don't miss it.

Within the start-up meeting, hold an explicit section on culture and ways of working. Here are two simple things to help you:

▶ Work through the list of 20 cultural differences in this chapter. With each difference, your team can choose to recognise, understand and accept the different ways of working: no one needs to change. Or the team can agree on a preferred way of working: this is necessary when the two ways of working clash with each other.

▶ Work on a cultural appreciation exercise for each nationality. Most people naturally focus on negative stereotypes, which is divisive. Ask the team to focus on positive appreciation: what strengths each culture brings to the team; you might then ask what each culture can do even better or differently to help the rest of the team work well.

Build a common culture across the team

For a team to be effective, it has to be cohesive: shared goals, shared values, shared ways of working help the team succeed. While differences matter, it matters even more to find what binds the team together: 'Sometimes we get bogged down in the differences, not what is the same between people.'[349] As a team leader, you have to build a common culture which transcends country: you cannot impose your own culture on everyone else. But you can find common values and beliefs which can help bind the team. These values may be as simple as committing to excellence and not shouting at people.

The need for a common culture was put well by Carolyn Koenig, Head of HR at Laird: 'When we come to work we are part of a different culture from when we are at home. We are who we are, but when we are in Laird then we know what is appropriate: our culture trumps local culture. If you allow the local norm to trump the company values, you will both lose and always be at odds with each other. When you do that, you just become 50 different companies in 50 different countries.'

Building a common culture is a journey of discovery. At the start of the journey, everyone on the team can sign up to high-minded ideals such as 'integrity', but that word can mean different things to different people.

Building a common culture is a journey of discovery.

Does integrity mean that you speak up when there is a problem or the boss is making a mistake – or do you keep quiet and help the boss save face? Different cultures will have different solutions: within your team you need to make sure everyone has the same solution regardless of background: 'You must have a team that does not see the world by country.'[350]

Use each minor culture clash as a chance for your team to learn and to agree a common way of working. Do not tell your team the solution: let them discover the solution which works for them.

10

Structure

Co-ordination and conflict

The structural challenge for global teams is around co-ordination and conflict. Any structure optimises co-ordination in one way but creates conflict in others. For global teams, the classic clash is between head office and the local team: between the hub and the rim. This clash is felt in five ways:

▶ Respecting each other: cultural intelligence

▶ Trusting staff

▶ Understanding customers

▶ Setting goals

▶ Making decisions.

This first part of the chapter will explore each of these conflict zones and suggest how the conflict can be reduced: it will never be eliminated.

The second part of the chapter will look at the structural choices open to the global firm, and how to make those choices. The choice of structure optimises co-ordination in some dimensions of the firm, but hard-wires conflict into other dimensions: the only choice is where and how that conflict is expressed.

Conflict between the hub and the rim

There always has been, and always will be, tension between the head office and the field. The head office is usually seen to be staffed by idle, overpaid paper pushers who have no idea what is really happening on the ground. Meanwhile, it is common for the hub to doubt the quality of staff at the rim and to suspect that the rim actively sabotages the initiatives which the hub has carefully crafted.

This is a fundamental challenge of structure: there will always be distance between the hub and the rim. This challenge plays out in terms of cultural differences, trust, goal setting, understanding and responding to customer needs, and making decisions.

For the global team, the structural challenge is greatest. The global team is often required to bridge the gap between the hub and the rim. The team does not feel that it is part of the hub, from which it may be far removed. Nor does it feel part of the rim, because it is trying to follow a global agenda.

Each of these structural challenges is explored below:

Respecting each other: cultural intelligence

Structural challenges disappear fast where there is respect and trust on both sides of the structural divide. Where that respect does not exist, the divide quickly becomes a chasm. Each culture and each head office that it is the

Structural challenges disappear fast where there is respect and trust on both sides of the structural divide.

centre of the world, and thinks that it is therefore superior to the rest of the world. It is a malaise which is common to most head offices: some head offices are aware of the problem, other head offices and cultures are not. The more prestigious and successful the firm is in its home market, the greater its prejudices are about the rest of the world. Domestic success can be a global curse. This challenge cuts across cultures and firms:

▶ 'Europe still thinks it is the centre of the civilised world. The Americans think that they still have global hegemony, while the Chinese think that they will buy the world: they believe they can buy the Colosseum in Rome and the sad truth is that they probably can.'[351]

▶ 'Some Japanese companies, especially if they are successful in their home market, push what they do in Japan everywhere with no autonomy for a different approach. I call that Success Poison. Some expatriates are just messenger boys from head office. Those expats, who are being pushed to sell the exact same product or service as in the home market and become very frustrated that HQ does not understand the market, often feel OKY: 'omaega kite yare' (you come here and do it!).'[352]

▶ 'There had been an arrogant head office approach: if it works here it must work there. But the key was to change this view. We had to understand

232

the nuances about product, design and teamwork were all different in every market.'[353]

▶ 'I work for an American organisation: they are full of ignorant people who just want to take control and tell me that they know how to work in Japan.'[354]

▶ 'Our Japanese style is very organised, but many of our employees are very domestic. They do not understand abroad: they think they are the best.'[355]

▶ 'Our Tokyo office is over 99 per cent Japanese. Everyone has a good education. We are a difficult company to join because we are very prestigious. But few people have languages or foreign experience. They think the world comes to them and they do not have to go to the world.'[356]

The structural rift between hub and rim can be bridged by respect and trust. But that requires people who have cultural intelligence and global perspectives. This does not come when head office is staffed with the best and brightest people from the home country, who have all made their careers in the home country. This is, in the words of Tadashi Yanai, President of Japanese retailer Fast Retailing, 'superficial globalisation'.

You have to change the traditional head office mindset which is 'head office knows best' and 'our country and culture is best':

'Many Japanese people believe that their country is special and best. You can go to a bookshop and find a lot of books praising Japan. They disgust me, I want to give the Japanese headquarters the global mindset of being a "foreign company based in Japan."'[357]

Changing the culture will not come from workshops and conferences, although they can help at the margin. If the firm wants to become truly global, it needs truly global leadership. That means it has to have talent policies which identify, recruit and develop the best talent around the world and ensures high potential managers from the home country gain significant experience globally and that there is no glass ceiling to foreign talent.

When head office and global teams are global in outlook, the structural divide can be bridged far more easily.

Trusting staff

The respect problem is compounded by a trust problem. The relationship between the hub and rim of the firm will only work if there is mutual trust, as Richard Harpham of Harris & Hoole explains: 'You have to trust head office will deliver for you. If you are in head office you need to trust that each market will deliver for you as well.' The problem is that such trust is often in scarce supply: neither side fully trusts the other:

'Everyone in the hub thinks that people on the rim have gone native; everyone on the rim thinks that the hub does not understand them.' [358]

The problem of trust is not symmetrical. Each side distrusts each other for different reasons. The rim does not believe that they are understood by the hub, or that the hub will look after their needs and interests. The hub does not have confidence that the rim can deliver: the suspicion is that staff on the rim are lower quality than staff in the hub:

'We either attract someone who wants to be a big fish in a small pond or someone who wants a lifestyle change. But the really A* people want to be a big fish in a big pond and it is hard to attract them.' [359]

If we return to the trust equation, we can see that lack of trust between hub and rim is inevitable in most global firms:

$$t = \frac{i \times c}{s \times r}$$

Trust is driven by a combination of values intimacy (i) and credibility (c). Within the hub it is easy to build intimacy, which is about shared values, shared agendas and shared experiences. Because people see each other often in the hub, there is plenty of opportunity to go through a process of mutual adjustment and learning about each other. It is also easy to see who is doing what, and who can be relied on: that builds credibility (c). This visibility does not exist between the hub and the rim and so the trust building never gets off the ground.

You cannot mandate trust through policies and procedures. You cannot mandate trust through policies and procedures. This structural challenge can be bridged through people. The firm needs a cadre of global executives: they need to rotate between global team work and work at the hub. These connectors are the vital bridge between hub and rim.

In the early stages of globalisation, this global elite all came from the same home country. That made sense: if you want to replicate your domestic business globally, then you need trusted staff from your home country to do that. This is the 'superficial globalisation' referred to by Tadashi Yanai (above). To achieve deep globalisation, your trusted global elite need to come from anywhere in the world: fishing in a global talent pool offers more choice than fishing in a domestic talent pool.

> **To achieve deep globalisation, your trusted global elite need to come from anywhere in the world.**

Understanding customers

Spy writer John Le Carré wrote in *Tinker Tailor Soldier Spy*:[360] 'a desk is a dangerous place from which to view the world'. Some executives clearly understand this. Doug Oberhelman, CEO and Chairman of Caterpillar, has Le Carré's words on a sign at the entrance to his executive suite.[361]

From behind a desk you can read all the reports, but that does not mean you understand the market or that you can hear the voice of the customer clearly. John Ridding, CEO of the Financial Times, encapsulated the problem:

'You have to have a clear line of sight from the product to the customer and back again and you need a clear line of sight from management to the customer and back again. But the matrix breaks up that connection: however you cut it up, there is going to be a gap.'

When there is a gap between management and market, there will also be a gap between management and the global team. Management at head office may see the big picture from the top of the mountain, but they will not understand the messy reality of daily life at the bottom of the valley far away. It is for the global team to bridge this structural divide between the top of the mountain and the bottom of the valley. At the top, the focus is on achieving global integration; at the bottom the focus is on responding to local needs. Global teams often have the unenviable task of achieving both global integration and local responsiveness. At the firm-wide level, Ghoshal and Bartlett show that there is a trade-off between integration and responsiveness: it is the global team that is often required to make that trade-off on a daily basis.

> **Global teams often have the unenviable task of achieving both global integration and local responsiveness.**

From behind a desk, global integration and local responsiveness appears to be an interesting strategic, intellectual and organisational question. For the global team that is in front of the customer, not behind the desk, it is an operational quagmire. The clash starts when head office wants to roll out a standard product at a standard price. Non-standard products create complexity and raise costs, while non-standard pricing creates the opportunity for price arbitrage by customers buying across borders, or at least create pressure to meet the lower price. Meanwhile, the local organisation will be facing customer pressure to meet their product needs, and will face competitive pressure on pricing. The global and local views are at odds with each other.

Global teams often feel a deep sense of anger and frustration that their local needs are not understood and not met, with the result that they are asked to market the wrong product at the wrong price. This anger is voiced strongly:[362]

▶ 'Those people who don't know other countries simply don't know. They do not understand the different cultures and different customer needs. The first thing to do is to understand the differences. They should not pretend that they are global. We used to have a team in Japan that tried to build all the products and services, but it did not work because they did not understand the requirements of other markets.'

▶ 'Head office thought that they had to tell the US all the answers and did not see that local markets could be doing things better than us and they did not understand the nuances of each local market. So there was an ever widening chasm between head office and the local markets.'

▶ 'The problem is that Japan has 3,000 customers and we have just 60, so every time Japan wins on requirements. We are always on the back foot chasing the market.'

▶ 'There was a US perspective to everything and non-US people felt devalued and excluded. There was a presentation on TV trends, but the US is a very unique TV market. They have no public service broadcasting and they have lots of cable.'

▶ 'Would you develop wine in Japan and export it to France? Japan should export sake. They want us to sell their product, but it does not meet our needs.'

Differing and incomplete customer perspectives are inevitable. No solution will be perfect. But you can reduce the pain:

▶ Make a clear choice about which perspective comes first: do you want to build deep industry expertise or local expertise, or export the successful domestic business? Depending on your choice, you will organise your teams around industry groups or geography, or you will become an export/franchise arm of the global headquarters. Being clear about the choice will not make everyone happy, but it will help everyone make clear and enable informed choices to be made.

▶ Move talent around. If you want intelligent conversations about the customer, you need people who have worked with customers across the world: relying on dry reports is never enough.

▶ Listen to the voice of the customer. Invite customers to your annual offsite meeting; listen to what is being said on social media; require executives to go and meet clients, even if they are not in traditional client-facing roles.

Listen to the voice of the customer.

Setting goals

Ambiguity is greatest for the global team. The global team has to bridge the views of the hub and the rim, which are fundamentally different. At the most senior level, goals are reasonably clear: achieve the profit, sales or market share goals. At the most local level, goals are also reasonably clear: each sales person knows what their target is. In between, there is the ambiguity which all middle managers face: conflicting pressures and goals from different parts of the matrix. The global team has all these pressures, plus the ambiguity that comes from distance, misunderstandings and multiple stakeholders.

Structure increases ambiguity and misunderstanding for two reasons. First, distance and complexity makes communication of the goal and its context far harder. Second, the global team inevitably is serving multiple stakeholders both internally and externally.

Communication and context is harder because of distance:

▶ 'The goals are not clear. The reality of what people want versus what they say is different. I have no idea about what our global objective is.'363

▶ 'Goals come from board level, through a department down to us. The goal may be clear, but if you do not know why or the context then often it makes no sense.'[364]

▶ 'If everyone is far away, then the scope for misunderstanding and going off track is great, but even when people are sitting next to you confusion can occur.'[365]

Serving multiple stakeholders, internally and externally, reduces clarity:

▶ 'This is about getting clear goals and shared values. Most people think of satisfying the direct customer – that means our resellers. But that may not satisfy the end customer: we have to focus on the end customer. But if your direct customer is not happy then you never reach the end customer. So there is a real trade-off on our goals here.'[366]

▶ 'Clear goals are a copout because the goals for a global team are never as clear as they are for a local team. You will never have clear accountabilities and roles, so you have to accept paradox and uncertainty: you cannot simplify everything, so you need shared values which get you to the right outcome; don't pretend it is simple.'[367]

The chapter on goals noted that clear goals will always be a challenge on a global team. While it makes sense to strive for clarity, not ambiguity, the team needs to mitigate the inevitable uncertainty by:

▶ understanding not just the goals, but the context, so that the right trade-offs can be made

▶ creating a shared understanding of the goals and context, even if that is just a shared understanding of the ambiguity and trade-offs

▶ building a sense of shared values so that the team can trust each other to make the right decisions about the trade-offs.

Making decisions

If you live in head office, you know how decisions get made and you have a reasonable chance of influencing the decision: you see the decision makers and influencers; you know their agenda and you know the gossip. The global team member is at a huge disadvantage and has to work far harder, as one seasoned global executive explained:

'You have to keep close to head office. I made sure I met all the people who reported to the big boss to get their advice and their support on what I was doing. I wanted them to help me presell my idea. I made sure I went to New York at least twice a year and whenever there was a big decision. There are all these characters in head office who gossip and make trouble so you have to manage them. These head office courtiers are potentially dangerous so you have to align the team and get them to visit you.' [368]

The structural distance means that every chance has to be taken to build networks between the global team and head office: 'When we have people visit from head office, I take them out because it is important, not just as being a host, but it is important professionally.'[369]

The challenges of making decisions in global teams are covered fully in the chapter on systems. The relevant point here is that any structure inevitably leaves a gap between the hub and the rim: decisions are easier to influence if you are in the hub than if you are on the rim of the firm.

Any structure also creates a bias in decision making:

Any structure also creates a bias in decision making.

▶ A geographic structure will create national barons who protect their turf fiercely.

▶ Functional structures create silos, which slows down decision making.

▶ Industry- or customer-based structure creates industry expertise but loses local knowledge and adaptability.

▶ Matrix structures can achieve balance, at the cost of complexity and political intrigue.

Seasoned executives see the corporate carousel turn round regularly: from industry to functional to geographic and back to industry focus again as the inevitable matrix gets tilted one way and another. The re-organisations are not in pursuit of the perfect structure, because there is no perfect structure. Instead, re-organisations are a search for balance, and they are a way of forcing change by moving entrenched power barons. Structure is about control, and re-organisations are a battle for control: they are a good way for a new leader to take control.

From the top, decisions to change the structure of the firm make political sense and can be rationalised financially or competitively. The effect that the restructuring has on the global team is no more than an afterthought. But for the global team, each restructuring can be a life or death affair. Networks of trust and influence which the global team has carefully nurtured from a distance suddenly become irrelevant. This matters because significant decisions about priorities and focus are often made in the wake of a restructuring: the global team finds that its influence is at its lowest ebb just at the moment when it is most needed.

The rise of the truly global firm

The nature of globalisation has been changing. In the past, globalisation was about a strong hub projecting its power around the world. This hub and spoke model leaves the home nation dominant: operations may span the globe but the

The nature of globalisation has been changing.

firm retains all the characteristics of its home. The firm may have a global footprint, but in terms of structure, control and management it remains a home country player.

There were at least four versions of this hub and spoke model:

▶ Traders, such as the East India Company and Dutch East India Company, had global reach but were very much creatures of their home nation and of empire.

▶ Exporters, exemplified by Japan in its boom era. Initially, Japan did not have significant overseas operations: instead it relied on the quality and scale economies it could achieve by concentrating production at home. When it started to build global operations, these were dominated by expatriates: this helped with communications and trust, but ensured that firms remained very much Japanese, not global.

▶ Portfolio managers, such as ITT and Hanson in the 1970s and 1980s, which bought up vast portfolios of businesses around the world. The goal was never to integrate them, but to apply financial and management disciplines which would lead to superior returns. These disciplines were consistent around the world and reflected home nation practice. Each country and each business was a separate entity. Private equity firms are spiritual heirs to the conglomerates of the past.

▶ Internationalisation. These businesses, exemplified by P&G in the twentieth century, looked global and they had a global brand management system. The focus was on replicating and internationalising the American success model, not on integrating operations and brands globally.

International or global: replicate or integrate?

Internationalisation and globalisation are often seen as the same thing: they are not. International firms seek to replicate their home country model around the world; global firms seek to integrate and co-ordinate their businesses around the world. This is a subtle but important difference in how the firm works, so it is worth drawing out the difference by using the example of P&G.

P&G made its first foray overseas when it purchased Thomas Hedley in Newcastle, England, in 1930.[370] It was a sort of coming home for P&G, which was founded by William Procter from England and James Gamble from Ireland. Thomas Hedley carried on with its own business and own brands and did not even change its name to P&G until 1962. It was close to being a portfolio investment, but it provided important learning for P&G.

Walter Lingle became P&G's Manager for Internal Operations in 1945.[371] He looked at the Thomas Hedley operations and realised that different countries had different needs and different heritages: selling the same thing in the same way around the world would not work. Instead, he took the view that 'the best way to succeed in other countries is to build in each one an exact replica of the United States Procter & Gamble organisation'.[372]

By replicating the Cincinnati headquarters around the world, Lingle created a lot of mini P&Gs which copied the US management formula all the way down to the one-page memo which brands would use to summarise the progress of their business. This replication model required low global integration. Each country could develop its own brands: the UK continued to develop unique products from its past such as Fairy Liquid, Fairy Toilet Soap and Flash. The equivalent of Flash in other markets was known as Mr Propre in France; Meister Proper in Germany; Maestro Limpio in Mexico and Don Limpio in Spain. In other words, there was not much global co-ordination or integration.

The international model is about replicating a business model into largely standalone country units.

In contrast, the global model is about integrating management, operations and brands across countries. And this is the journey which P&G has taken over the past 30 years. Brands, operations and manufacturing are increasingly integrated across Europe from Geneva, which has 3,000 employees from 68 different nationalities and is responsible for more than 120 countries.[373]

The need for global integration and co-ordination has been rising. This need has been driven by six trends:

▶ Global customers
▶ Global scale
▶ Global needs and tastes
▶ Global markets
▶ Global communications
▶ Global supply chains.

These trends reinforce each other. Here is why each one is important.

Global customers

Global businesses want global support. In the past, professional service firms such as lawyers, accountants and consultants organised by geography. Increasingly, they organise by industry groups which cross borders so they can build deep industry expertise and serve global customers globally. Duncan Tait, Head of EMEIA[374] and Americas for Fujitsu, explains how the remorseless logic of the customer forces a global approach:

'We have moved from being a collection of autonomous entities to becoming more global because our customers are global. Now we are building global consistent processes and delivery. And our customers are saying: 'why didn't you do this earlier? This is what we always wanted.'

Global scale

The minimum efficient scale for some industries is global. Where the cost of R&D and other initial investments is very high, the only way to break even is to market globally. Gartner estimates that the cost of building a leading edge semi-conductor fabrication plant will be $15–$20 billion by 2020,[375] up sixfold in 20 years. These costs can only be recouped by selling at global scale. Similarly, the cost of developing the new Airbus A350 is estimated at $15 billion:[376] global sales are required to break even.

> **The minimum efficient scale for some industries is global.**

Global needs and tastes

Market segments used to be drawn within countries, largely on the basis of socio-economic background. But segmentation is changing: marketers realise that similar segments exist around the world and are not based on socio-economic background. Mothers want happy babies, which means dry babies: Pampers is a global solution to a global need. Fashion has always been used to express status: LVMH and other luxury goods makers provide a statement for those who want to be part of the global elite. Brand identity can be powerful and global. Apple sharply divides those who want to be part of the brand and those who do not, and it is a global divide.

Global markets

In 1960, US nominal GDP was larger than the next ten economies combined.[377] By 2020, the US economy will still be large, but it will be half the size of the next ten economies combined. In the past, if a firm succeeded in the US, it was well on its way to global success: it would have enviable scale economies and would already have taken most of the available global market. Now, no single market is globally dominant. Global success requires global operations and a global mindset. Needs and tastes transcend borders, which means firms have to follow them.

Global communications

Clearly, social media is global. There are over 3 billion internet users and 2.5 billion users of social media,[378] and over 1.5 billion people use Facebook.[379] The traditional media is also going global. The *Daily Mail* is a mid-market UK tabloid paper. After six years of testing, in 2009 it launched its current online edition with a mix of hard news and celebrity revelations.

Within three years, it had become the most popular online newspaper in the world, according to comScore[380] and it now has over 200 million users each month.[381]

Global communications has three effects:

▶ It makes it easier to communicate a consistent global message through global media

▶ It makes inconsistent messaging harder

▶ It facilitates co-ordination and integration of supply chains.

The national media is being subverted by web-based media, which transcends borders. The advent of global media makes it harder to have distinct messaging for each country. For instance, when Sean Connery became the face for Suntory Whisky in Japan, he was not too keen on this being seen in Scotland. He is a fervent Scot, and supporting Japanese whisky is not the most patriotic thing he could do. That was in 1992,[382] before the advent of social media, so his dalliance with the Japanese was not widely known. With social media, such discretion is not possible, and Connery's performances for Suntory are now widely available on social media such as YouTube.

Global supply chains

Forty-six per cent of all US imports, and 70 per cent of US imports from Japan, occur between related parties.[383] This happens when a global firm creates a global supply chain and offshores some of its production. A large part of the rise in global trade is driven by trade within global firms, not trade between firms. This is especially true of trade between advanced economies.[384] Global supply chains take advantage of lower costs and different skill sets globally. This is a source of competitive advantage which no competitor can ignore: this means that whole industries have to go global to stay competitive.

Structural choices for the global firm

The forces of globalisation are compelling firms to integrate more closely across borders in terms of systems, processes, culture and structure. But the world is not yet homogeneous. There are still plenty of centrifugal forces which mean that firms have to differentiate across borders. Even the most global firms find that they have to adapt, at least in part, to local conditions.

For instance, McDonald's has over 36,000 outlets worldwide.[385] It appears to be the paradigm of global consistency: you know what to expect when you enter one of its outlets. In terms of service, quality, management and concept, it may be consistent. But even McDonald's has to be responsive to local tastes and varies its menu accordingly:[386]

- Philippines: McSpaghetti
- India: Maharaja Mac, which is made of lamb or chicken, and Veggie McNuggets
- Canada: McLobster
- Japan: Teriyaki Burger and Camembert teritama
- France: hot banana drink.

Similarly, Coca-Cola is not all about selling a uniform product in a uniform way around the world. In Japan Coca-Cola is constantly innovating: it introduces and withdraws products at high speed. In March 2016 alone, it launched five new products: mineral water, green tea, a vitamin drink and two coffees.[387] It has over 190 brands in Japan; the core Coca-Cola brand represents less than one-third of revenues. These products are far removed from the original Coca-Cola: what ties the firm together is not the brand, but the firm. This means Coca-Cola operates in two ways at the same time: the brand is clearly global with global messaging, global positioning and a global formula. But the firm is acting as an international firm, similar to P&G under Lingle: its strength is in replicating its management systems and practices worldwide. Coca-Cola the firm is integrating and differentiating at the same time; it is globalising and internationalising at the same time.

Globalisation is pulling firms in two directions at the same time. The first pressure is to integrate and globalise; the second pressure is to differentiate and respond to local needs. This is the multilocal approach of international firms.

The classic work on the structure of global firms is *Managing Across Borders*, by Ghoshal and Bartlett.[388] They proposed that the key challenge for managing across borders is to balance the need for integration with the need for differentiation (local responsiveness). For many global firms, such as Coca-Cola and McDonald's, there is no choice between integration and differentiation:

There is no choice between integration and differentiation: you have to do both.

you have to do both. And global teams are at the forefront of having to bridge these two opposing forces.

In practice, integrating and differentiating varies across the value chain. This means that some firms can operate globally but from a very strong central hub with minimal local presence or differentiation. Coca-Cola and McDonald's see the need to market and adapt globally. The opposite is true of SABIC (Saudi Arabia Basic Industries Corporation): it is a petrochemicals giant with significant steel-making capacity and annual revenues of over $50 billion. When it first set up its marketing operations, it had no production facilities outside Saudi Arabia.[389] The job of marketing was not to adapt to local markets. Its job was to work out how to serve a global market most effectively. It had to balance supply between regions as well as balance long-term customers and contracts with short-term spot market trades. That pointed to one centralised and global marketing function.[390] The rest of its value chain was also highly centralised with minimal need to adapt to local needs, as seen in the diagram below.

Integration and responsiveness is consistent along the SABIC value chain:

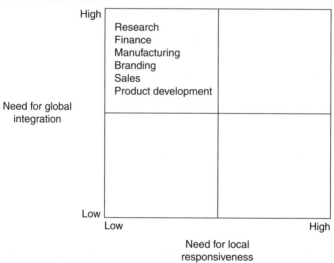

SABIC has a business with global scale and reach. Each of its functional teams had a global mandate, and they could all co-locate in the head office. SABIC marketing in its early days was global, but suffered none of the problems of global teams because they were co-located.

In contrast, P&G represents a much more complex business. Some parts of its value chain have to be localised, others have to be globalised as follows:

▶ Sales is inherently local, given that it sells to chains which are mainly national or buy along national lines (with some notable exceptions such as Walmart-Asda).

▶ Branding, as noted above, has moved from being a series of national operations creating unique solutions (1 in the diagram below) towards a more integrated group of global brands managed regionally (2 in the diagram below).

▶ Fundamental research is a global effort and P&G tries to harness the best capabilities around the world, both from within the firm and beyond. Its P&G Connect and Develop[391] is an open innovation programme which draws on the principles of crowdsourcing and co-creation.

▶ Product development is still required locally, at least in part, to respond to different types of water, regulations and consumer habits.

▶ Finance and IT is inherently global. If every country operates with different systems and different sorts of controls, then chaos ensues. It is also global to the extent that core operations can be outsourced around the world, to minimise costs.

▶ Manufacturing is also becoming more integrated. Unlike SABIC, it will never have one country serve the rest of the world, but economies of scale are driving consolidation across borders.

Integration and responsiveness needs vary along the value chain: P&G detergents

P&G's firm structure creates the need for global teams which can achieve both integration and responsiveness to local markets. They do not want a trade-off between integration and differentiation: they want both at the same time. This is the challenge which global teams have to address.

Conclusions

All organisation structures are a compromise: the search for the perfect solution is an exercise in futility because the perfect solution does not exist and the world is always changing, which means that even the preferred solution is always changing too.

In an imperfect world, there are four priorities for making the organisation structure work with global teams.

▶ Choose your structure
▶ Listen to the voice of the customer
▶ Manage the conflict
▶ Invest in the people and the culture.

Choose your structure

Do not worry about finding the perfect structure. Find the structure which gives focus where you want it: industry, customer, geography or function. A good re-organisation will achieve three things which are not just about structures:

▶ send a clear message to every team about the new focus and priorities of the firm
▶ challenge vested interests, power barons and the status quo
▶ reset expectations and the psychological contract with each member of your team.

In other words, restructuring is as much about the process as the outcome. Done well, it is a chance to re-energise and re-focus teams and individuals. Done poorly, it is a recipe for fear, uncertainty, doubt and loss of morale and momentum.

Listen to the voice of the customer

The more complex a firm becomes, the easier it is to lose the voice of the customer. Teams start arguing with each other over internal matters which are vital to them, but not to the market. The way to drive through this is to make sure that the voice of the customer is heard and respected throughout the firm. If there is a question about how to organise, or about priorities, listening to the customer normally blows away the fog of internal thinking.

> **The more complex a firm becomes, the easier it is to lose the voice of the customer.**

Manage the conflict

Organisations are set up for conflict. Each part of the firm has its own perspectives and priorities, so differences and conflict are inevitable. It is through the pro-

> **Organisations are set up for conflict.**

cess of constructive conflict that the priorities and budgets of the firm are decided. The conflict between the hub and the rim will always exist, and both sides lack trust in each other.

The conflict is greatest when it comes to goal setting and decision making: the rim is often excluded and overlooked by teams in the hub. When goals and decisions are made without reference to the rim, passive resistance and demoralisation quickly follow. Part of the solution is to ensure goal-setting and decision-making processes are seen to be fair processes. But formal processes are easily bypassed by the informal processes, where individual networks of influence and power make the decision in private. Given this reality, the firm has to ensure that global teams are hooked into the informal networks of power and influence: the best way of doing this is to rotate people through the rim and the hub and to ensure that each global team is led by someone who has the required personal networks at the centre.

Invest in the people and the culture

Successful global firms work hard to create a cohesive culture which transcends nationality, location and function: the goal is to have one firm working together, not to have many competing power barons and warlords.

Cohesiveness comes from people who understand 'global'. The only way to truly understand global is to work globally. The firm has to invest in a global talent pool and move people between the hub and the rim. The movement has to be two-way: it is not enough to export expats from head office to the regions. Great talent needs to come from the regions to the hub: this not only helps build cohesiveness and a global mindset, but is also a good way of attracting and retaining the best global talent.

PART FOUR
Rising to the global challenge: lead, trust and support

11

Conclusions

Before starting the research for this book it was not clear whether there was a challenge for global teams. At first glance, it would seem that all teams have the same needs: clear goals, roles and processes, and effective team members who trust each other and communicate well. The big question was: 'Are global teams really different?'

The answer was emphatic: global teams are fundamentally different from domestic teams. It also became clear that global teams are the oil which makes globalisation work and helps global firms perform.

Global teams are fundamentally different from domestic teams.

Plenty of research has been done on the structure of global firms, and that research focuses on the global–local trade-off. If you are designing a global structure for a firm, the global–local trade-off is an interesting intellectual challenge. If you are working on a global team, the global–local trade-off is not just an interesting trade-off: it is a daily reality where you have to balance the demand to be global with the need to respond to local requirements. No amount of clever organisation design can help you through that messy reality.

Many books have already been written about cultural differences between nations, and the world does not need another book like that. The challenges of making global teams work go far beyond learning how to exchange *meishi* (business cards) when you are in Japan. Global teams represent a fundamentally different management challenge from running a domestic team.

Why global teams are different

The differences between global teams are obvious: distance, time zone, culture and language. The consequences of these differences are significant:

Distance and the invisibility challenge

When you cannot see the rest of your team, team work becomes a challenge:

▶ How do you know whether someone is struggling or idling when you cannot see them?

▶ How can you manage workloads effectively when you don't know how they are coping?

▶ How can you coach or performance manage people when you cannot see how they are doing?

▶ How do you know whether you are communicating effectively when you cannot see their body language – how do you know whether they really agree with you or not?

▶ How can everyone understand what is happening and the context for decisions and goals when they are not part of the office chatter?

▶ How can you influence people and decisions remotely when you do not see the people and you do not know what their needs and wants are?

When you see millions of people stuck in traffic jams or crowded on public transport as they commute to work daily, it is reasonable to ask: 'What is the point of going to all this time and expense to put people together under one roof to work, when technology allows for remote working?' But the benefits of co-location only really become apparent when you are no longer co-located. When you are co-located, there is a constant dialogue and constant informal mutual adjustment which minimises misunderstandings. When you are no longer co-located, these informal methods of communicating, coaching, managing performance, making decisions and allocating workloads no longer work. Everything has to be more structured and systematised.

The challenges of distance arise even if you have a team working at opposite sides of the same city. The challenges of time zones, language and culture simply make the distance challenge even greater.

Time zones and the trust challenge

Time zone differences accentuate the problem of distance. It makes it harder for team members to communicate because they are not available at the same time as each other. The time zone difference also raises a fundamental issue of trust. If people are working on a different time zone, you have to trust that they will make the right decisions and do the right things in your absence. Controls stop them making decisions without authority, but cannot stop them making dumb decisions. The trust issue then drives a series of challenges for the global team:

▶ How can I recruit and retain good people with the skills required to perform well in my absence?

▶ How can the firm manage its development and promotion systems so that the best people globally will join? Or should the firm rely on sending trusted home nation expatriates out to lead teams around the world?

▶ How far can you really delegate tasks to a team you cannot monitor in real time?

▶ What processes and systems are required in place of informal trust?

Culture: knowledge or intelligence?

Learning one culture can take an anthropologist an entire lifetime. Teams and team leaders have to do far more: they have to learn to work with, not just observe, many cultures in the space of a few weeks. The anthropologist may acquire deep cultural knowledge, which the team can never hope to match. Instead, your team has to acquire deep cultural intelligence. Cultural intelligence is not about knowing the finer details of other cultures: it is about being able to learn and adapt personally and fast to very different ways of working and thinking. Culturally intelligent teams are not fixed on their own way of working – 'my way or no way': that way leads to a dead end of team conflict.

Global Teams identified 20 major categories of cultural differences which matter when working across the world. In practice, there are hundreds of major and minor differences which can surprise, delight or annoy when working in a new culture. Instead of attempting to summarise all these differences here, it is worth spelling out the consequences of these differences for how you manage global teams:

▶ How can you build cultural intelligence across the whole team?

▶ How can you avoid or minimise the cultural noise which leads to miscommunication and misunderstanding?

▶ How do you build cultural cohesion across the firm: do you export the home nation culture around the world, or do you create a culture which is global and above any one nation? What does that imply for how you recruit, train, develop and promote people?

▶ When problems arise, how do you know that they are substantive, not cultural?

Language: common language, common values

At the start of the research, I assumed language would be a big issue. I was half right and half wrong. Having a common language, normally English, is seen as a pre-condition for working on a global team. This immediately poses some challenges:

▶ How can team members communicate well when some are fluent and use complex, colloquial language while others have English as a second or third language and use simple and direct language only? How can the two sides learn to adjust to each other's language needs?

▶ How do you bridge the gap between an English speaking global team and a non-English speaking headquarters, where all the decisions will be made in a different language?

▶ How do you build trust when key decisions around budgets, resources, promotions and strategy are made in a different language from that of the team?

When global teams say that they want a common language, what they mean is that they want shared values across the whole team.

▶ How far should language proficiency and cultural intelligence be a recruiting or promotion requirement within head office as well as within the firm? Should the firm become officially bilingual?

The major language challenge turned out to be cultural. When global teams say that they want a common language, what they mean is that they want shared values across the whole team. This raises questions for the team and the firm:

▶ How do you create a common set of values across the team, which transcends any one nation?

▶ What are the core values which any global team member needs to have?

▶ How far do you recruit the team around talent or values?

▶ How do you deal with talented individuals when they have good values but not the global values you want?

Emerging global solutions

Making global teams work is not a new challenge. Countless firms have been finding ways of working across borders for many years. The research showed that there are emerging solutions. The purpose of this book has been to draw together that collective knowledge which is the result of hard-won experience. The solutions are still emerging: there is no universal three-step formula which can be applied like magic. This, unfortunately, breaks the central rule of any popular management book: it must offer a simplistic solution to a complex problem. Usually, the solution turns out to be as reliable as the miracle medicines sold by quack doctors in the Wild West.

Following the rule of three that most popular books follow, making global teams work involves three perspectives:

▶ The team leader: raising the bar and changing the game

▶ The team: building trust and communication

▶ The firm: creating the context for success.

These three perspectives are summarised below.

The team leader: raising the bar and changing the game

During the course of the research a distinct profile of the successful team leader emerged. To succeed in a global context, you need three qualities:

▶ High-level traditional and technical skills. The traditional skills of motivating, managing performance, communicating, coaching and delegating become far harder in a global context: you are separated from your team by distance, time zones, language and culture. In a domestic team, co-location means that any misunderstandings are quickly picked up and the problem is resolved. There is no safety net on a global team: you have to get it right first time, every time. That is a high bar to clear.

▶ Specific skills for managing globally. On a global team you have to influence decisions, stakeholders and team members remotely. You will not have direct control over your destiny: this means that the art of influence becomes more important. With your team, influence means building trust and commitment instead of command and control. With key stakeholders, influence means building alliances, aligning agendas and persuading people remotely. The art of influence is part of the domestic manager's tool kit: it is a vital part of the global leader's skill set.

▶ Distinctive mindset. Successful leaders in a domestic context will have a tried and tested success model. They would be unwise to change that success model, unless the context changes. The global context changes everything, and your domestic success model will be of limited use to you. The successful global team leader has to be highly adaptable to different ways of working; has to be excellent at listening and learning; and has to have high cultural intelligence. This is sometimes referred to as the 'growth' mindset.[392] Being fixed in your ways is dangerous on a global team.

These skills and mindset are demanding. The good news is that these are the skills that all leaders will need in future. The future is not going to be based on the certainties of command and control style leadership. The future will require leaders who can cope with ambiguity, uncertainty and changing conditions; it will require leaders who can exert influence far beyond their formal authority; it will require leaders who can lead people who are not like themselves. So if you want to be a successful leader, leading a global team is the perfect way to stretch yourself and grow the skills you need.

So if you want to be a successful leader, leading a global team is the perfect way to grow the skills you need.

The team: building trust and communication

Trust and communication is important on any team, domestic or global. But it is harder and more important to achieve on a global team. Trust and communication were the two most important factors which global team members focused on.

Trust is vital because you have to trust people who are acting in a different time zone to decide the right way. You have to delegate to them, and delegation requires trust. No one wants to work with people they do not trust. The team leader has to trust the team in order to delegate; the team has to trust that the team leader will look after their interests, and team members have to trust that they will not let each other down. This trust has to be built remotely by people who do not see each other, and have different cultures and ways of working. The trust challenge is higher on a global team than on a domestic team.

> **No one wants to work with people they do not trust.**

The solution to building trust is given in part by the trust equation (where t = trust):

$$t = \frac{i \times c}{s \times r}$$

The first stage in building trust is to build intimacy (i), or affective trust: let the team discover shared values, needs and interests. Time and again, teams reported that meeting face to face was transformative. Investing in a global team meeting costs time and money, but pays huge dividends. Meeting in the initial stages of working as a global team is when you achieve the highest return on investment: it enables a fast start and allows the team to overcome the teething problems of how they will work together. The overt purpose of the meeting might be training or planning: the big benefit is in building trust across the team. Once the trust is established, communication also flows more easily.

The second part of building trust is to build credibility (c). Credibility comes from always doing what you say. That means having potentially difficult conversations early about expectations and what can and cannot be achieved. Difficult conversations are avoided in more hierarchical and deferential societies, which raises a communication challenge.

You can also build trust by building a culture of selflessness on the team. Selfishness (s) destroys trust and teamwork. And you have to manage risk (r), which is always personal. Even simple things like asking for feedback can be a source of unexpected risk: in hierarchical cultures team members never 'give the boss bad medicine'. Understand what you are asking for and manage the risk accordingly.

Trust and communication walk hand in hand on a global team. High levels of trust encourage open conversations; open conversations enable the team to avoid misunderstandings and that builds trust. Teams consistently have a hierarchy of preferred forms of communication:

▶ Face to face physically

▶ Face to face remotely: Skype, Facetime, Hangouts

▶ Phone

▶ Open communication platforms: Slack, Whatsapp, google.docs, Trello

▶ Email.

Teams prefer rich communication formats where they can see and hear the context of not just what people say, but also how they say it and how they feel. The visual and aural cues are vital parts of communicating. Email was more or less universally reviled: there is too much 'reply all' and use of email to leave an evidence trail; it is a time sink which often results in misunderstanding and loss of trust.

All teams complain that they could spend their entire time communicating and never doing any actual work. This is a particular challenge for global teams where the communications needs are particularly high. Teams which manage this well establish a clear rhythm of predictable communications, so that team members know when and what and how to communicate. Co-located teams can rely on informal and ad hoc communication: global teams need more structure to make communications work.

The firm: creating the context for success

The core challenge for global firms is to maintain cohesiveness across the world. Cohesiveness includes creating a common culture, a shared set of values, a co-ordinated approach to the market, an integrated use of resources across borders, and common systems and processes: IT systems, performance management, talent management and communications.

Firms have to choose how they achieve cohesiveness. There are broadly two success models: replicate or integrate. Both can work, but they work very differently.

Replicate

Replication is the original version of globalisation. It requires replicating the home country success model globally. The main requirement for this model is that the firm has a very strong product or service or business model which can be copied around the world. Some products and brands have global reach: Facebook, Amazon, McDonald's, BMW, Toyota, Starbucks. They require low levels of local customisation. No one is in any doubt about the home nation of these firms and it is very clear where the control lies. The overwhelming culture and control of these firms remains rooted in the home nation.

The main variation on the replication model is where a business model is being replicated globally. This was how P&G originally globalised: they replicated their entire brand management in each and every country they expanded to. The brands would fit local tastes, but the system was global.

Maintaining the home country culture and controls makes it relatively easy to maintain the culture of the firm. The challenge is often around talent. A firm which is very prestigious in its home market will be able to recruit the best local talent, but unless it is also very prestigious globally it will struggle to attract the best talent globally. The best talent does not want to work for a firm where there is a 'pyramid of passports' and they have a second-class passport which limits their ability to rise to the top. Many top Japanese firms struggle with this: they attract the best talent in Japan, but struggle overseas. They maintain a cohesive Japanese culture globally, but at the expense of finding the best non-Japanese talent. Chinese firms are likely to encounter the same challenge as they globalise: they have a strong local culture which has served them well domestically.

Integrate

The main difference between the 'integrate' and 'replicate' models is how far the firm maintains its home nation origins around the world. Integrators are at least semi-detached from their home nation. There is no 'pyramid of passports' where home nation talent is promoted ahead of global talent. The advantage of the integrators is that they can access the best of the global talent pool. The challenge is how to achieve a cohesive culture when drawing on talent from many different cultures. The solution, invariably, is to create a firm-wide culture which transcends any single nation. This is done through selection, training, frequent cross-border gatherings and endless reinforcement through communications and the evaluation system. The message to staff is simple: you can be any culture you want at home, but you follow the one firm culture at work.

Integrators and replicators have different views about learning and innovation. Replicators centralise their innovation efforts. The bulk of Apple's innovation comes from Cupertino. P&G, which is now more of an integrator, scours the world both within and beyond the firm for new ideas and solutions to technical challenges. Both approaches can work.

Many firms are migrating to the integrate model, so that they can attract global talent, organise on global lines and deploy resources globally in the most effective way. Not surprisingly, the firms which are at the forefront of the integration approach are those which depend most heavily on talent. Professional services firms, financial services and systems integration require the best talent at the lowest cost. IBM, McKinsey, Goldman Sachs and others are slowly becoming more global and less American.

Both the integrators and the replicators have to create the context in which the global team can succeed. You have to 'keep chopping wood: it's very hard but it's not rocket science'.[393] The challenges which are hardest for a global firm are the following:

▶ Talent management: do you focus on the domestic or global talent pool?

▶ Culture: how do you create a cohesive culture across diverse national cultures?

▶ Goal setting: how do you ensure goals are not just clear, but also shared and that their context is understood so that teams understand the 'why' as well as the 'what'? Building commitment and understanding is vital to moving to action fast in the right way.

▶ Decision making: how do you ensure fair process and buy-in when access to stakeholders and agendas is very uneven across the world?

▶ Communications: what is the right rhythm of communications to ensure enough is communicated the right way without causing overload?

Even in a domestic setting, creating the context for success is hard work. But at least everyone has a broadly similar cultural background and similar ways of working. Where there are problems, they are relatively easy to spot and resolve. In a global setting it is easier for misunderstandings to arise, but harder to spot them and resolve them. That makes it more important but more difficult for the firm to create the context for success: keep chopping wood.

The future of global teams

Global teams are only going to become more important. The relentless logic of globalisation means that firms will have to seek the best talent, ideas and value wherever they may be. Firms then have to harness these global capabilities through effective teams working across borders on supply chains, product development, sales, marketing, service, research, innovation, finance, IT, HR and more.

> **The relentless logic of globalisation means that firms will have to seek the best talent, ideas and value wherever they may be.**

Global teams are not just the preserve of giant global firms. This research showed that start-ups increasingly think global from day one. Some of the most innovative ways of making global teams work occur in micro-global firms of fewer than 20 people.

For firms, global teams are a huge opportunity and threat. Firms which embrace global teams will get access to the best talent, ideas and value. Firms which ignore the opportunity will be overtaken or taken over.

For individuals, working on global teams is a great opportunity to grow personally and professionally. It is a personal journey of discovery: often hard, always interesting. But whatever your global journey is, enjoy it.

What did you think of this book?

We're really keen to hear from you about this book, so that we can make our publishing even better.

Please log on to the following website and leave us your feedback.

It will only take a few minutes and your thoughts are invaluable to us.

www.pearsoned.co.uk/bookfeedback

Glossary

Wherever possible, I have tried to avoid using jargon or clichés. The research shows that people value simple words and simple language. That is what I have aimed for. Doubtless I will have failed occasionally, in which case accept my apologies. But in a book on global teams you have to find a way of describing some unique and complex ideas. To minimise misunderstanding, this glossary summarises some of the key words and phrases I have used and what they mean in the context of this book.

Most terms I have explained as they arise. For instance 'victim' and 'accountable' mindsets are explained where they are used and do not require a second explanation here. This glossary covers more common terms which arise frequently in the book.

Anglo (and Anglo world). This refers to a culturally distinct group of countries: USA, United Kingdom, Australia, New Zealand and Canada, among others. These nations have cultural differences which they cherish, but from a global leadership perspective they have much in common.

Cultural intelligence. I use this specifically to draw a difference with cultural knowledge. Cultural knowledge relates to knowing everything about how a different culture works. That is akin to anthropology. Cultural intelligence does not mean that you know everything about another culture, but that you have the intelligence to learn, adjust and adapt fast to different cultures and conditions.

Domestic. I use this to refer to any team which is purely within one country.

EQ. This is a popular term used to describe 'the capacity of individuals to recognise their own, and other people's emotions, to discriminate between different feelings and label them appropriately, and to use emotional information to guide thinking and behaviour'.[395]

Firm. I use the word loosely to describe all types of global organisation, including NGOs and not-for-profit organisations, except where the difference is significant. Ease of reading takes precedence over precision in this case.

Global. I use the word loosely to refer to any team which is cross-border. Some of the research involved teams across ten countries. Some of the research looked at teams which worked in just two countries, in the same language: that was a useful way of isolating some of the variables of distance, culture, language and time zones. I refer to all of them as global.

Hub. This normally refers to the headquarters or home base of a team, and is normally used in the context of hub and spoke, or hub and rim.

IQ. This normally refers to a standardised assessment of human intelligence, where 100 is the mean score for the population. Management IQ is about judgement and pattern recognition in ambiguous situations, and does not necessarily correlate with the traditional form of IQ.

Mindset. This is now a commonly used word, and also one that is commonly abused. I use it here as a shorthand for 'habits of mind' which may be personal or culturally conditioned. They are normally unconscious habits, which makes them dangerous.

NGO. Non-governmental organisations. These are normally charities or other not-for-profit organisations which are not controlled by government.

PQ. Political quotient. This is an informal measure of a manager's ability to make things happen beyond their formal area of authority: across and beyond the organisation. Influencing skills are at the heart of PQ, and are essential on global teams.

Region/regional. I use region in the global sense of the word, where a region might be Europe or North America or South Asia.

Spoke. Anyone working on a team away from the headquarters or home nation (the hub) is considered to be working at one of the spokes of the team.

Western. Normally used to refer to western business practices which broadly encompass North America and Europe, which makes it wider than the Anglo world.

Notes

Chapter 1

1. http://www.worldeconomics.com/papers/Global%20Growth%20Monitor_7c66ffca-ff86-4e4c-979d-7c5d7a22ef21.paper

2. http://ourworldindata.org/data/global-interconnections/international-trade/

3. This is true until the financial crisis of 2007–8. Trade grew as a percentage of global GDP from 20 per cent to 50 per cent between 1990 and 2007, and then slipped back to 40 per cent in 2015. The change has been driven by intra-firm trade: firms increasingly reshoring some activities. See http://data.worldbank.org/indicator/NE.TRD.GNFS.ZS and http://www.ft.com/cms/s/0/0e0e6960-da17-11e5-98fd-06d75973fe09.html#axzz41jdAoDl2

4. UNSD Annual Totals Table 2000–2014.

5. https://www.telegeography.com/research-services/telegeography-report-database/

6. www.internetworldstats.com and elsewhere.

7. Bartlett and Ghoshal (1998). *Managing Across Borders*, Random House.

8. Erin Meyer is an Affiliate Professor in the Organisational Behaviour Department at INSEAD and specialises in the field of cross-cultural management. http://www.insead.edu/faculty-research/faculty/erin-meyer

9. Erin Meyer (2015). 'Getting to Si, Ja, Oui, Hai, and Da'. *Harvard Business Review* 93(12): 74–80.

10. Over the years firms merge and change their names: in each case I have taken the current name of the firm to make recognition easier.

11. Prominent Social Media firm requires complete privacy, except from its users.

12. Tetsuo Yanagi NRI.

13. W. Edwards Deming (2000). *Out of the Crisis.* MIT Press.

14. https://en.wikipedia.org/wiki/History_of_Facebook

15. http://edge.media-server.com/m/p/r63ian8u

Chapter 3

16. Daniel Goleman (1996). *Emotional Intelligence: Why it Can Matter More Than IQ.* Bloomsbury.

17. Jo Owen (2015). *How to Manage: The Definitive Guide to Effective Management.* Fourth edition, Pearson.

18. http://er.jsc.nasa.gov/seh/ricetalk.htm

19. Toshi Sakatsume, Senior Economist, EBRD.

20. Shane Pearlman, CEO, Modern Tribe.

21. Hiroshi Mikitani, Founder of e-commerce platform Rakuten. *Financial Times* 11 January 2016.

22. Hiroaki Nakanishi, CEO Hitachi. *Financial Times* 11 January 2016.

23. Hiroaki Nakanishi, CEO Hitachi. *Financial Times* 11 January 2016.

24. Graham Sheffield, Director Arts, British Council.

25. James Coltman, COO, Arrowgrass.

26. Bernadine Brocker, Founder, Vastari.

27. Attributed to John Wanamaker, but uncertain. https://en.wikipedia.org/wiki/John_Wanamaker. Also widely attributed to David Ogilvy, albeit much later.

28. DAR (Day After Recall) asked viewers who were watching the relevant TV programme what advertisements they remember, and without prompting them about which advertisements were aired. If no one remembers the advertisement, it is no use. Other research methods cost less and judge engagement better now.

29. Daniel Goleman notes that Mayer and Salovey offered the first formulation of a concept they called 'emotional intelligence' in 1990. http://www.danielgoleman.info/topics/emotional-intelligence/

30. BBC broadcast 1 October 1939. http://www.churchill-society-london. org.uk/RusnEnig.html

31. Daniel Goleman (1996). *Emotional Intelligence: Why it Can Matter More Than IQ*. Bloomsbury.

32. The original formulation of EQ excluded this attribute.

33. Zhen Gao, Managing Partner, Mandarin Capital Partners.

34. Shane Pearlman, CEO, Modern Tribe.

35. Paul Robinson, Director, CRU Group.

36. Bhavit Mehta, Senior Programme Officer, The Commonwealth Foundation.

37. Simon van Blerk, Chief Technology Officer, The House.

38. Yuko Tanaka, ICP Product Development Director, Canon.

39. Koji Agatsuma, Head of Technical, Hitachi Rail Europe.

40. Anonymous by request. Interview Notes on file p. 109.

41. PQ was originally formulated in Jo Owen (2006). *How to Manage*. Pearson. Currently in its fourth edition (2015).

42. Derived from Jo Owen (2012). *How to Influence and Persuade*. Pearson, second edition.

43. See Elaine Chan and Jaideep Sengupta (2010). 'Insincere Flattery Actually Works: A Dual Attitudes Perspective'. *Journal of Marketing Research* 47(1). http://www.bm.ust.hk/~mark/staff/Jaideep/ Jaideep%20JMR-Feb%202010.pdf

44. This is the staple of transactional analysis. Eric Berne (1964). *Games People Play – The Basic Hand Book of Transactional Analysis*. Ballantine Books.

45. Lesbian, Bisexual, Gay, Transexual.

46. http://film.britishcouncil.org/our-projects/2015/fivefilms4freedom

47. Middle Office, US investment bank, Notes p. 6. Anonymous by request, as with most banks.

48. Bhavit Mehta, Commonwealth Foundation, describing projects with previous employers.

49. Anonymous, to prevent discord in the respondent's team. Notes retained on file p. 122.

50. Reeva Bakhshi, CFO, Hiscox Re, Bermuda.

51. Graham Sheffield, Director Arts, British Council.

52. Masaaki Moribayashi, Managing Director at NTT Europe.

53. Paul Abrahams, Head of Global Corporate Communications, RELX Group.

54. Eddie Tay, Country Manager for Singapore, Malaysia and SE Asia, Electrolux.

55. Professor, Northwestern University, Dept of Psychology.

56. http://www.hbs.edu/faculty/conferences/2013-w50-research-symposium/Documents/eagly.pdf

57. Rolf Deusinger, Senior Advisor, Miles Partnership.

58. Carolyn Koenig, Head of HR, Laird.

59. David Jones, previously senior regional management, Pepsico and P&G.

60. Masaaki Moribayashi, Managing Director, NTT Europe, when interviewed. Now Member of the Board and Senior Vice President, Cloud Services NTT communications.

61. Paresh Thakrar, Chief Operating Officer, Hiscox Re.

62. Richard Harpham, Managing Director, Harris & Hoole.

63. Toshi Sakatsume, Senior Economist, EBRD.

Chapter 4

64. The trust equation has its roots in the MAC Group, which was absorbed into Cap Gemini. There is no academic research on it, so it may well not work in theory. But it has worked in practice over the past 30 years. There are several minor variations on it.

65. Yuval Abraham, South African financial controller, on working with one of the major consulting firms.

66. https://hbr.org/2015/12/getting-to-si-ja-oui-hai-and-da Erin Meyer

67. Anonymous by request. Notes on file p. 81.

68. Carolyn Koenig, Head of HR, Laird.

69. There is even an ISO standard on risk vocabulary: it ignores personal risk completely. http://www.iso.org/iso/catalogue_detail?csnumber=44651. ISO 73:2009

70. Kishore Agarwala, Senior Release Manager, IBM.

71. http://workingwithmckinsey.blogspot.co.uk/2013/11/Obligation-to-Dissent.html

72. Many examples of this are available, for instance: http://thepersonaldevelopmentcafe.com/images/stories/Desert_Survival.pdf

73. Željko Jovanović, Acting Director Marketing, Digital and Communications, Wider Europe. British Council, Serbia.

74. North America Underwriter, Hiscox Re

75. Geoffrey Longfellow, Thai citizen and government advisor.

76. Gopal Sriram, Solution Engineer, OMDC, IBM.

77. Anonymous by request. Notes on file p. 88.

78. Anonymous by request. Notes on file p. 110.

79. Financial Services. Anonymous by request. Notes on file p. 85.

80. Chief Investment Officer ILS (Insurance Linked Strategies).

81. Helen Murley, Global HR Director, British Council.

82. Cortina Butler, Head of Literature, British Council.

83. Elaine Chan and Jaideep Sengupta (2010). 'Insincere Flattery Actually Works: A Dual Attitudes Perspective'. Journal of Marketing Research 47(1). http://www.bm.ust.hk/~mark/staff/Jaideep/Jaideep%20JMR-Feb%202010.pdf
Also: Sho K. Sugawara, Satoshi Tanaka, Shuntaro Okazaki, Katsumi Watanabe, Norihiro Sadato. 'Social Rewards Enhance Offline Improvements in Motor Skill'. PLoS ONE, 2012; 7(11): e48174 DOI: 10.1371/journal.pone.0048174

84. http://www.thehousemedia.com/ and www.tri.be

85. Scrum is project management software which is part of the Agile movement. http://scrummethodology.com/

86. *Tomorrow Never Dies*, 1997. http://www.imdb.com/character/ch0000305/quotes

87. Anonymous by request. Notes p. 3.

88. Kim Underhill, Regional Head, Electrolux SEA Pte Ltd, Singapore.

89. North America Underwriter, Hiscox Re.

90. Reeva Bakhshi, CFO, Hiscox Re Bermuda.

91. Nenad Jelovac, Senior Web Developer, The House, Serbia.

92. Philipp von Bieberstein, Google, Business Development.

93. Shane Pearlman, CEO, Modern Tribe.

94. Nenad Jelovac, Senior Web Developer, The House, Serbia.

95. IPSOS MORI veracity index 2015. https://www.ipsos-mori.com/researchpublications/researcharchive/3685/Politicians-are-still-trusted-less-than-estate-agents-journalists-and-bankers.aspx#gallery[m]/1/

96. 'Carry interest' is a percentage of a fund's profits that fund managers keep on top of their management fees, and is a significant component of private equity compensation. Carry typically averages about 20 per cent of the fund's profits. It is meant to align managers' and investors' interests and often has tax advantages.

97. Minoru Takezawa, Managing Director, SECOM plc.

98. Japanese banking executive, anonymous by request. Notes p. 19.

99. IESE is a leading business school, based in Barcelona.

100. Haruki Katayama, Director of Product Management, NTT Europe.

101. Yuko Tanaka, ICP Product Development Director, Canon.

102. Alberto Forchielli, Managing Partner, Mandarin Capital Partners.

103. Paul Robinson, Director, CRU Group.

104. Zhen Gao, Managing Partner, Mandarin Capital Partners.

105. Head of Mergers and Acquisitions, Singapore.

106. Purnima Kochikar, Head of Games and Apps, Google.

107. Philipp von Bieberstein, Google, Business Development.

108. Laura Dawson, Chief Information Officer, British Council.

109. Shane Pearlman, CEO, Modern Tribe.

110. Myers–Briggs Type Indicators. http://www.myersbriggs.org/my-mbti-personality-type/mbti-basics/

111. MOL: Mitsui OSK Lines.

112. Goro Yamashita, Channel General Manager, Mitsui OSK Bulk Shipping (Europe) Ltd, car shipping carrier division.

113. Bertrand Lavayssière, Partner, Ares & Co., Paris and London.

114. Head of Mergers and Acquisitions, Singapore.

115. Nearly 200,000 MBAs graduate every year in the USA alone: http://fortune.com/2014/05/31/mba-popular-masters-degree/, and a further 350,000 graduate from Indian MBA courses of variable quality: http://articles.economictimes.indiatimes.com/2015-01-13/news/58024327_1_aicte-institutes-parag-kalkar

116. https://www.ge.com/sites/default/files/GE_Crotonville_Future_of_Leadership.pdf

117. This is the modern corporate equivalent of Machiavelli's advice in *The Prince*, Chapter XVII (first published in 1532): 'It is better to be feared than loved, if you cannot be both.'

Chapter 5

118. Kim Underhill, Regional Head, SE Asia and India, Electrolux professional services. Originally from John C. Maxwell (2010), *Everyone Communicates, Few Connect*. Jaico Publishing House.

119. The author worked with the late C. K. Prahalad for two years on deploying satrategic intent and core competence across a global electronics firm, and was taught by Gary Hamel at business school. C. K. Prahalad and Gary Hamel were the creators of these two concepts. The productised and popularised versions of strategic intent and core competence are weak imitations of their original formulation.

120. Carolyn Koenig, Head of HR, Laird.

121. Anonymous by request. Notes p. 99.

122. This is attributed to George Bernard Shaw, from a *Readers' Digest* article of November 1942. Other attributions include Oscar Wilde and Winston Churchill.

123. Study conducted by Jo Owen with Marshall Young of Said Business School, Oxford University, reported by CNN among others: http://edition.cnn.com/2007/BUSINESS/04/30/execed.anglofrench/

124. A *chef de cabinet* is the most senior civil servant responsible for the running of a government department.

125. Erin Meyer has worked extensively on mapping cultural differences for global teams. A good and free summary resource is available online at: http://erinmeyer.com/tools/interactive-culture-map-exhibit/

126. Purnima Kochikar, Head of Games and Apps, Google.

127. Head of Mergers and Acquisitions, Singapore.

128. Reported in the *Financial Times*: http://www.ft.com/cms/s/0/a9e2be7e-d1b4-11e5-92a1-c5e23ef99c77.html#axzz42rflTGyS

129. George Bernard Shaw, *Pygmalion*, 1916 which later became the film *My Fair Lady*. It explores accent and status in England.

130. Manager at a social media site. Anonymous by demand.

131. Alberto Forchielli, Managing Partner, Mandarin Capital Partners.

132. Geoffrey Longfellow, Thai citizen and government advisor.

133. Manager at a social media site. Anonymous by demand.

134. Anonymous by request. Notes p. 165.

135. Zhen Gao, Managing Partner, Mandarin Capital Partners.

136. The annual data of China's GDP, published on China NBS: National data - annual - national accounts - Gross Domestic Product. The 2015 figure is based on the *Statistical Communiqué of the People's Republic of China on the 2015 National Economic and Social Development* and uses market exchange rates, not PPP.

137. Myers–Briggs Type Indicators. http://www.myersbriggs.org/my-mbti-personality-type/mbti-basics/

138. Rob Watson, Chief of Staff, Rolls-Royce plc.

139. This formula is for an undirected graph, which means that there are two possible connections between nodes a and b: from a to b and from b to a.

140. Queen (1989), 'The Miracle', composed by Brian May.

141. https://www.atlassian.com/time-wasting-at-work-infographic

142. http://www.ft.com/cms/s/0/60ba520a-d0b2-11e5-92a1-c5e23ef99c77.html#axzz42rflTGyS

143. Bertrand Lavayssière, Partner, Ares & Co., Paris and London.

144. Head of Mergers and Acquisitions, Singapore.

145. Over 200 billion emails sent daily in total: http://www.radicati.com/wp/wp-content/uploads/2015/02/Email-Statistics-Report-2015-2019-Executive-Summary.pdf

146. https://medium.com/@lindsaytrinkle/business-email-its-bigger-than-you-think-1d927d67b1e#.e7b7nox9v

147. Michael Murdoch, Founder and CEO, The House.

148. Mike Krefta, Chief Underwriting Officer, Hiscox Re.

149. Laura Dawson, Chief Information Officer, British Council.

150. Paul Robinson, Director, CRU Group.

151. Goro Yamashita, Channel General Manager, Mitsui OSK Bulk Shipping (Europe) Line Ltd, car shipping carrier division.

152. Simon van Blerk, Chief Technology Officer, The House.

153. Yuko Tanaka, ICP Product Development Director, Canon.

154. Christine Hounsell, Contract Wording Specialist, Hiscox Re.

155. Lucy Kellaway, *Financial Times*. http://www.ft.com/cms/s/0/dee75f5e-e635-11e5-a09b-1f8b0d268c39.html#axzz42rflTGyS

156. Linda Walker, Senior Account Director, Warner Music.

157. IT, Banking, India. Anonymous by request. Commenting on email is the sort of thing which causes regulators, media, PR, communications, risk, legal and compliance to go into a flap.

158. Alex Hirst, co-founder and joint chief executive of Huckleberry Partners, a marketing and office support services company. https://next.ft.com/content/60ba520a-d0b2-11e5-92a1-c5e23ef99c77

159. Michael Murdoch, Founder and CEO, The House.

160. Study by Oxford Economics, reported in *Wall Street Journal*. http://online.wsj.com/ad/article/globaltravel-face

161. The Groove provides help desk software for small businesses to help them manage their online customer support. With just nine staff spread across Colorado, Maryland, Malta, Poland, Russia, Scotland and three more US cities, Groove is one of the smallest truly global firms.

162. Estimates vary. This source estimates that there are 375 million people who speak English as their mother tongue, although 1.5 billion speak it with reasonable competence. http://www.statista.com/statistics/266808/the-most-spoken-languages-worldwide/

163. http://www.globish.com/

164. http://www.basicglobalenglish.com/

165. Marmite is a spread made from yeast extract, widely sold in the UK. Even the makers admit that it is a love it or hate it product.

166. Hiroaki Okada, Managing Director, Milestone Chemical Tankers.

Chapter 6

167. This is a classic analytical tool for strategy: Michael E. Porter (1979). 'How Competitive Forces Shape Strategy'. *Harvard Business Review* 57(2).

168. Another classic tool named after the Boston Consulting Group who originated the idea. BCG have moved on since then. Also known as the growth-share matrix. See https://en.wikipedia.org/wiki/Growth%E2%80%93share_matrix

169. Yuki Hoashi, Senior Manager, Strategy, HERE, Chicago.

170. https://www.google.com/intl/gb/about/

171. http://www.coca-colacompany.com/stories/the-chronicle-of-coca-cola-a-global-business/

172. President Kennedy, 25 May 1961. http://www.jfklibrary.org/JFK/JFK-Legacy/NASA-Moon-Landing.aspx

173. Anonymous by request. Notes p. 3.

174. Rolf Deusinger, Senior Advisor, Miles Partnership.

175. Robert S. Kaplan and David Norton (1992). 'The Balanced Scorecard. Measures that Drive Performance'. Harvard Business Review 70(1): 71–79. https://hbr.org/2005/07/the-balanced-scorecard-measures-that-drive-performance

176. The author was present at this meeting. The minister involved is no longer part of the government.

177. Donald H Rumsfeld, US Secretary of State, was ridiculed for talking about 'known unknowns' and 'unknown unknowns' at a US Department of Defense (DoD) news briefing on 12 February, 2002, but this is a useful distinction of long standing; see Statement of Evidence of E. D'Appolonia, D'Appolonia Consulting Engineers, Pittsburgh, Pennsylvania. Proceedings of the British Columbia Royal Commission of Inquiry into Uranium Mining, Phase V: Waste Disposal, which dates from 1979.

178. Richard Harpham, who was Strategy Director of Pret at the time and is now MD of Harris & Hoole.

179. The German General Manager of one of the largest American banks.

180. Kim Underhill, Regional Head, SE Asia and India, Electrolux professional services.

181. EMEIA: Europe, Middle East, India and Africa.

182. Duncan Tait, Corporate Executive Officer, EVP and Head of EMEIA at Fujitsu.

183. SMART is an acronym which appears to have been first used in 1981: G. T. Doran (1981). 'There's a S.M.A.R.T. Way to Write Management's Goals and Objectives'. *Management Review* (AMA FORUM) 70(11): 35–36.

184. Zhen Gao, Managing Partner, Mandarin Capital Partners.

185. Carry interest is a right that entitles a partner of a private investment fund to a share of the fund's profits.

186. Yuko Tanaka, ICP Product Development Director, Canon.

187. John Ridding, CEO, Financial Times.

188. Kim Underhill, Regional Head at Electrolux SEA Pte Ltd, Singapore.

189. For more on World Faith's work, see http://worldfaith.org/Frank Fredericks is the founder and executive director.

190. Ross Nottingham, Head of America and Caribbean, Hiscox Re.

191. http://www.ifpi.org/facts-and-stats.php

192. Linda Walker, Senior Account Director, Warner Music.

193. http://blogs.timesofindia.indiatimes.com/Tech-a-tete/if-cognizant-is-indian-so-are-ibm-and-accenture/

194. http://timesofindia.indiatimes.com/tech/tech-news/New-age-IT-skills-can-double-your-pay/articleshow/51386706.cms

195. https://www.quora.com/What-is-the-typical-hourly-consultant-rate-for-a-good-software-engineer

196. If you assume that the Indian employees are billed out at four times salary, that gives them an annual cost of $20,000 to $60,000, versus $65,000 to $200,000 for their US counterpart. It is hard to compete when you cost three times as much.

197. http://www.officechai.com/stories/biggest-it-companies-in-india/

198. BPO: business process outsourcing. This is where a firm may outsource routine processes such as expense management, accounts payable and receivable, claims management, etc. to a specialist in that area.

199. http://www.tata.com/company/profile/Tata-Consultancy-Services. End 2015. These are global headcount figures, not just Indian; the same applies for Infosys and Wipro.

200. https://www.infosys.com/about/ March 2016.

201. http://www.wipro.com/about-Wipro/ March 2016.

Chapter 7

202. Ross Nottingham, Head of America and Caribbean, Hiscox Re.

203. Note: team members might rate several systems issues in their top five.

204. Louise Reid, Head of HR, Hiscox Re.

205. Global Bank. Notes p. 8.

206. Alikeh Doyle, Claims Analyst–Team Leader, Hiscox Re, Bermuda.

207. Shane Pearlman, CEO, Modern Tribe.

208. Jason, Global telecoms firm. Notes p. 45.

209. Alikeh Doyle, Claims Analyst–Team Leader, Hiscox Re, Bermuda.

210. Thirty per cent of interviewees from the spokes mentioned processes and protocols as one of their top five issues, versus only 20 per cent at the hub.

211. Twenty per cent of bosses mentioned processes and procedures as a top five issue versus 33 per cent for more junior staff.

212. BT was privatised in 1984, one of the first major privatisations in the UK (and Europe). https://en.wikipedia.org/wiki/BT_Group

213. Anonymous by request. Global financial services. Notes p. 130.

214. Eddie Tay, Electrolux country manager for Singapore, Malaysia and SE Asia.

215. Anna Searle, Director of English Language, British Council.

216. Mike Krefta, Chief Underwriting Officer, Hiscox Re.

217. Anonymous by request. Notes p. 137.

218. Jim Hollington, Director Arts, South Asia. British Council.

219. Debobrata Das, Country Manager, Electrolux Professional – India.

220. Douglas Lee, Electrolux Financial Controller, SE Asia.

221. Geoffrey Longfellow, Thai citizen and government advisor.

222. The author was personally involved in helping this transition. The case is kept anonymous by request.

223. The accountability mindset is explored more completely in Jo Owen (2015). *Mindset of Success*. Kogan Page.

224. Anonymous by request. Notes p. 122.

225. Noel M. Tichy and Stratford Sherman (2005). *Control Your Destiny or Someone Else Will*. Collins Business Essentials.

226. Tetsuo Yanagi, Senior Manager, IT, Banking.

227. Paul Abrahams, Head of Global Corporate Communications, RELX Group.

228. Vic Baines, previously at Europol.

229. RACI: responsible, accountable, consulted and informed. It is a standard tool for allocating responsibilities and has endless variations: the point is to have a clear framework to show who does what.

230. Anonymous by request. Notes p. 50.

231. Anonymous by request. Notes p. 77.

232. Anonymous by request. Notes p. 138.

233. Based on the author's personal experience.

234. TQM: total quality management. It was developed by Edward Deming and used by the Japanese to great effect before finally being adopted by the West. Many variations exist, but no one has really worked out yet how to apply TQM to the office.

235. For an example, see http://archive.teachfind.com/ttv/www.teachers.tv/videos/distributing-leadership.html. The author looks at TQM at a Range Rover factory in Solihull for a television programme.

236. Kishore Agarwala, Senior Release Manager, IBM India.

237. Augustin Landier, Vinay B. Nair, Julie Wulf (2007). 'Tradeoffs in Staying Close: Corporate Decision-Making and Geographic Dispersion'. *Review of Financial Studies* 22(3): 1119–1148. https://www.aeaweb.org/annual_mtg_papers/2007/0105_0800_1503.pdf

238. https://en.wikipedia.org/wiki/Bayesian_inference. But it really is not worth the effort . . .

239. Amos Tversky and Daniel Kahneman(1981). 'The Framing of Decisions and the Psychology of Choice'. *Science* 211(4481): 453–458. DOI: 10.1126/science.7455683

240. Yuko Tanaka, ICP Product Development Director, Canon.

241. Anonymous by request. Notes p. 23.

242. Anonymous by request. Notes p. 51.

243. Anonymous by request. Notes p. 47.

244. Anonymous by request. Notes p. 47.

245. Koji Agatsuma, Head of Technical, Hitachi Rail Europe.

246. Masaaki Moribayashi, Managing Director, NTT Europe.

247. NPV: net present value; ROI: return on investment; IRR: internal rate of return. These are just a few of the many TLA (three-letter abbreviations) used to describe different methods of assessing the financial viability of projects.

248. The German General Manager of one of the largest American banks. Notes p. 81.

249. Anonymous by request. Notes p. 146.

250. Tetsuo Yanagi, Senior Manager IT, Banking.

251. Zhen Gao, Managing Partner, Mandarin Capital Partners.

252. This follows Nonaka and Takeuchi in dividing knowledge into explicit and tacit knowledge. Hirotaka Takeuchi and Ikujiro Nonaka (1995). *The Knowledge-Creating Company: How Japanese Companies Create the Dynamics of Innovation*. Oxford University Press.

253. Kim Underhill, Regional Head at Electrolux SEA Pte Ltd, Singapore.

254. David Jones, previously senior regional management at Pepsico and P&G.

255. More on learning organisations from Peter Senge (2006). *The Fifth Discipline*. Random House, second edition; also Chris Argyris (1999). *On Organisational Learning*. Wiley-Blackwell, second edition.

256. Minoru Takezawa, Managing Director, SECOM plc.

257. http://www.secom.co.jp/english/ir/lib/AR/2015E_full.pdf

258. Paul Robinson, Director, CRU Group.

259. Clayton Christiansen (1997). *Innovator's Dilemma: When New Technologies Cause Great Firms to Fail*. Clayton Christiansen. HBR Press, reprint 2013; see also Francis J. Gouillart and Venkat Ramaswamy (2010). *The Power of Co-Creation: Build It with Them to Boost Growth, Productivity, and Profits*. Free Press.

260. See more at: https://www.researchgate.net/profile/Stuart_Hart4/publication/237379284_Innovation_From_the_Inside_Out/links/0a85e5320a7feba016000000.pdf#page=37

261. GUI: graphical user interface. This allows users to interact with electronic devices through graphical icons as opposed to text-based interfaces or typed command labels.

262. Purnima Kochikar, Head of Games and Apps, Google.

263. Under Tim Cook, Apple created a 104-word mission statement which describes their main product lines.

264. http://www.pg.com/en_UK/news-views/Inside_PG-Quarterly_Newsletter/issue2/innovation3.html

Chapter 8

265. David Jones, previously senior regional management, Pepsico and P&G.

266. http://sloanreview.mit.edu/article/the-onefirm-firm-what-makes-it-successful/. David Maister: Celebrating the success of firms such as McKinsey, Goldman Sachs and . . . Arthur Andersen.

267. American Express. https://www.americanexpress.com/au/content/careers/culture.html. There is even a Blue Box Values song.

268. Diversity helps business performance. http://www.mckinsey.com/business-functions/organization/our-insights/why-diversity-matters

269. Professor Ronald S. Burt is the Hobart W. Williams Professor of Sociology and Strategy at Chicago Booth.

270. http://snap.stanford.edu/class/cs224w-readings/Burt04StructureHole.pdf

271. http://www.nytimes.com/2004/05/22/arts/think-tank-where-to-get-a-good-idea-steal-it-outside-your-group.html?_r=2

272. Anonymous by request. Notes p. 2.

273. Purnima Kochikar, Head of Games and Apps, Google.

274. CEO and Chairman of Yum! Brands, which owns KFC, Taco Bell, Pizza Hut and many other restaurant formats, quoted in Forbes: http://www.forbes.com/sites/robertreiss/2012/03/05/driving-a-global-corporate-culture-of-1-4-million-employees/#55cf2525edc5

275. By 1838 the East India Company was exporting 1,400 tons of opium to China, enough to pay for all the tea in China which was exported back to the UK and beyond. The British went to war with their American colonies over tea taxation, and then went to war twice with China over the tea and opium trade. They took their tea seriously. They also burned down Beijing and Washington: how to win friends and influence people. https://en.wikipedia.org/wiki/East_India_Company

276. https://www.roberthalf.co.uk/news-insights/reports-guides/cfo-insights/robert-half-ftse-100-ceo-tracker

277. http://digitalcommons.ilr.cornell.edu/cgi/viewcontent.cgi?article=1022&context=student

278. http://knowledge.wharton.upenn.edu/article/talent-management-at-multinational-firms-in-china/

279. Russell Reynolds have produced a good description of this: http://www.russellreynolds.com/sites/default/files/LeadershipandTalent-BuildingaGlobalATeamAsianMNCs.pdf

280. Michael Murdoch, Founder and CEO, The House.

281. Eddie Tay, Electrolux country manager for Singapore, Malaysia and SE Asia.

282. Damien Smith, Director of Underwriting, Hiscox Re, Bermuda.

283. Nenad Jelovac, Senior Web Developer, The House, Serbia.

284. Goro Yamashita, Channel General Manager of Mitsui OSK Bulk Shipping (Europe) Ltd, car shipping carrier division.

285. Kim Underhill, Regional Head, SE Asia and India, Electrolux professional services.

286. Željko Jovanović, Director Marketing, Digital and Communications, Wider Europe. British Council, Serbia.

287. Bhavit Mehta, Senior Programme Officer, The Commonwealth Foundation.

288. As an author, I took exception to this comment. But I did not throw a tantrum, as that would have proven his point.

289. Zhen Gao, Managing Partner, Mandarin Capital Partners.

290. Shane Pearlman, CEO, Modern Tribe.

291. Paul Robinson, Director, CRU Group.

292. Rolf Deusinger, Senior Advisor, Miles Partnership.

293. Shane Pearlman, CEO, Modern Tribe.

294. Alberto Forchielli, Managing Partner, Mandarin Capital Partners.

295. Nick Niell, founder and CIO, Arrowgrass.

296. Enrica Sighinolfi, Opportunity Network. Head of HR and one of the founding team.

297. Yamashita Kisen merged into MOL in 1964. http://www.mol.co.jp/en/corporate/history/

298. Reeva Bakhshi, CFO, Hiscox Re, Bermuda.

299. John Ridding, CEO, Financial Times.

300. Kiram Nhayad, Senior Developer, IBM.

Chapter 9

301. http://www.geerthofstede.nl/

302. http://erinmeyer.com/tools/interactive-culture-map-exhibit/

303. Ricardo Semler (2001). *Maverick!: The Success Story Behind the World's Most Unusual Workplace*. Random House.

304. Unpublished original research and MBA essay by the author.

305. Original research in collaboration with Oxford University: http://edition.cnn.com/2007/BUSINESS/04/30/execed.anglofrench/

306. Cartesian thinking is based on the writings and methodology of French philosopher René Descartes (1596–1650).

307. D. Matsumoto, S. H. Yoo, S. Hirayama and G. Petrova (2005). 'Development and Validation of a Measure of Display Rule Knowledge: the Display Rule Assessment Inventory'. *Emotion* 5(1): 23–40. http://www.ncbi.nlm.nih.gov/pubmed/15755217

308. Nan M. Sussman and Howard M. Rosenfeld (1982). 'Influence of Culture, Language, and Sex on Conversational Distance'. *Journal of Personality and Social Psychology* 42(1): 66–74. http://dx.doi.org/10.1037/0022-3514.42.1.66

309. Amy Tan (1992). 'The Language of Discretion', in William H.Roberts and Gregoire Turgeon (eds) *About Language*. Houghton Mifflin, third edition.

310. Anonymous by request. Notes p. 20.

311. http://www.bbc.co.uk/news/business-33984961

312. Direct observation by the author. Names have been changed to protect the innocent.

313. http://uk.complex.com/pop-culture/2012/06/famous-tech-ceo-desks/6

314. Anonymous by request. Notes p. 176.

315. https://yougov.co.uk/news/2016/01/05/chinese-people-are-most-optimistic-world/

316. https://www.authentichappiness.sas.upenn.edu/testcenter

317. The study is summarised here: http://www.forbes.com/sites/jimkeenan/2015/12/05/the-proven-predictor-of-sales-success-few-are-using/#526802125d60

318. Douglas McGregor (1960). *The Human Side of Enterprise*. McGraw-Hill.

319. Fred E. Fiedler (1964). 'A Contingency Model of Leadership Effectiveness'. *Advances in Experimental Social Psychology* 1(1): 149–190. doi:10.1016/s0065-2601(08)60051-9 See also: Martin M. Chemers and George J. Skrzypek (1972). 'Experimental Test of the Contingency Model of Leadership Effectiveness'. *Journal of Personality and Social Psychology* 24(2): 172–177. doi:10.1037/h0033371

320. C. Shawn Burke, Kevin C. Stagl, Cameron Klein, Gerald F. Goodwin, Eduardo Salas and Stanley M. Halpin (2006). 'What Type of Leadership Behaviors are Functional in Teams? A Meta-analysis'. *The Leadership Quarterly* 17(3): 288–307.

321. '2011 Census: Ethnic group, local authorities in England and Wales'. Office for National Statistics. 11 December 2012.

322. Leo Benedictus (2005). 'Every Race, Colour, Nation and Religion on Earth, part 1'. *The Guardian*, 21 January 2005. London: Guardian.

323. https://en.wikipedia.org/wiki/Names_of_China

324. https://news.starbucks.com/leadership March 2016

325. http://www.nissan-global.com/EN/COMPANY/PROFILE/EXECUTIVE/

326. Carol Dweck (2012). *Mindset: How You Can Fulfil Your Potential*. Robinson.

327. For more on the seven mindsets of success see Jo Owen (2015). *The Mindset of Success: From Good Management to Great Leadership*. Kogan Page.

328. La Délégation générale à la langue française et aux langues de France.

329. http://www.academie-francaise.fr/linstitution/lhistoire

330. http://www2.psych.ubc.ca/~ara/Manuscripts/Levine%26Norenzayan%20POL.pdf

331. Marc H. Bornstein and Helen G. Bornstein (1976). 'The Pace of Life'. *Nature* 259: 557–559. http://www.nature.com/nature/journal/v259/n5544/abs/259557a0.html

332. Fons Trompenaars and Charles Hampden-Turner (1997). *Riding the Waves of Culture.* McGraw-Hill, second edition.

333. Gary Hamel and C.K. Prahalad (2005). 'Strategic Intent'. *Harvard Business Review.* https://hbr.org/2005/07/strategic-intent

334. https://www.panasonic.com/global/corporate/ir/pdf/20130918_vision_note_e.pdf

335. Bill Gates, Nathan Myhrvold and Peter Rinearson (1996). *The Road Ahead.* Penguin Books, revised edition.

336. Peter Walker (2007). 'Crossing the Anglo-French Divide'. CNN.com, 8 May. http://edition.cnn.com/2007/BUSINESS/04/30/execed.anglo-french/

337. Ben Love, Head of Business Development, Hiscox Re.

338. The German General Manager of one of the largest American banks. Notes p. 81.

339. Alex Turnbull, CEO and Founder, The Groove.

340. Jason Tomlinson, Technical Product Manager, NTT Europe.

341. David Blundell, Global Social Media Manager, British Council Madrid.

342. Anonymous by request. Notes p. 105.

343. Jane Oliver-Jedrzejak, Digital Content Manager, British Council.

344. Koji Agatsuma, Head of Technical, Hitachi Rail Europe.

345. Anonymous by request. Notes p. 45.

346. Anonymous by request. Executive in China. Notes p. 69.

347. Case drawn from personal experience of author as a founder and board member of Teach First.

348. This is the home and the office of the UK Prime Minister: a call from 'Number 10' is always a big deal.

349. Banking, IT, India. Anonymous by request.

350. Carolyn Koenig, Head of HR, Laird.

Chapter 10

351. Alberto Forchielli, Managing Partner, Mandarin Capital Partners.

352. Minoru Takezawa, Managing Director, SECOM plc.

353. Richard Harpham.

354. Anonymous by request. Notes p. 62.

355. Anonymous by request. Notes p. 51.

356. Goro Yamashita, Channel General Manager of Mitsui OSK Bulk Shipping (Europe) Ltd, car shipping division.

357. Tadashi Yanai, President of Japanese retailer Fast Retailing. https://next.ft.com/content/80bb0344-78d6-11e5-a95a-27d368e1ddf7#axzz44qimaAmb

358. Anonymous by request. Notes p. 93.

359. Anonymous by request. Notes p. 122.

360. John Le Carré (2011). *Tinker Tailor Soldier Spy*. Sceptre Books.

361. http://www.forbes.com/sites/robertjordan/2012/11/01/how-to-be-a-better-leader-ditch-your-desk/#4f54154b624d

362. All these quotations are anonymous by request.

363. Anonymous by request. Notes p. 45.

364. Anonymous by request. Notes p. 53.

365. Cortina Butler, Head of Literature, British Council.

366. Yuko Tanaka, ICP Product Development Director, Canon.

367. Rolf Deusinger, Senior Advisor, Miles Partnership.

368. David Jones, previously senior regional management, Pepsico and P&G.

369. Mark Lucas, Director, Sales and Marketing Planning, Europe, Middle East and Africa at Japan Airlines (JAL).

370. http://www.pg.com/en_UK/company/our-heritage.shtml

371. *New York Times* obituary, 19 March 1994. http://www.nytimes.com/1994/03/19/obituaries/walter-lingle-jr-86-p-g-vice-president.html

372. Quoted in Christopher A. Bartlett and Sumantra Ghoshal (1998). *Managing Across Borders.*, Random House.

373. http://we.experiencepg.com/home/pg_switzerland.html

374. Europe, Middle East, India and Africa.

375. http://www.eetimes.com/document.asp?doc_id=1264577

376. http://www.bbc.co.uk/news/business-22803218

377. https://en.wikipedia.org/wiki/List_of_countries_by_largest_historical_ GDP, Source data: IMF, World Bank and United Nations.

378. http://www.smartinsights.com/social-media-marketing/social-media-strategy/new-global-social-media-research/

379. http://www.statista.com/statistics/272014/global-social-networks-ranked-by-number-of-users/

380. http://news.bbc.co.uk/today/hi/today/newsid_9708000/9708023.stm

381. Dugald Baird (2015). 'Mail Online Soars Past 200m Monthly Browsers as Newspaper Sites Bounce Back', *The Guardian*, 20 February 2015. http://www.theguardian.com/media/2015/feb/20/mail-online-gains-17m-unique-browsers-as-newspaper-sites-bounce-back

382. You can see a sample of the advertising here: https://www.youtube.com/watch?v=KDG2V4veQLU

383. Andrew B. Bernard, J. Bradford Jensen, Stephen J. Redding and Peter K. Schott (2010). 'Intra-Firm Trade and Product Contractibility'. http://www.princeton.edu/~reddings/papers/IFT_p&p_21_aeastyle.pdf

384. http://www.oecdilibrary.org/docserver/download/5kg9p39lrwnn. pdf?expires=1459008868&id=id&accname=guest&checksum= 2D2B7B54A20A28AE27B1FF65598F1349. Less advanced economies are exporting raw materials and basic goods, which tend to trade between firms, not within them.

385. http://www.aboutmcdonalds.com/mcd/our_company.html

386. From McDonald's websites in each country, 2016.

387. https://www.ccej.co.jp/en/

388. Christopher A. Bartlett and Sumantra Ghoshal (1998). *Managing Across Borders*. Random House.

389. SABIC has since bought operations in the UK and US. Source: http://www.sabic.com/corporate/en/

390. The author was responsible for designing the initial global marketing group for SABIC.

391. http://www.pgconnectdevelop.com/home/stories.html

Chapter 11

392. See Jo Owen (2015). *Mindset of Success*. Kogan Page.

393. Financial Services UK. Anonymous by request. Notes p. 129.

394. Social Media is a social media firm which requires total privacy, except from its users.

Index

① Trust Ramda.
p5?

$$t = \frac{I \times C}{S \times R}$$ intimacy + credibility
self orientation + risk (personal)

✻ intimacy = shared experiences - face & face → training > ways of planning working.

✻ Credibility = consistency + doing what say you will
→ difficult conversations · referrals + past
· expectation setting.   actual projects.

✻ Self orientation = being selfless - put interest of team ahead of own

✻ risk = personal risk — easy to feedback : understand what you are asking for. Teach how to ask for feedback
↓   not give feedback
Not everyone.
Comfortable to give like
has "had practice."   SEE QUESTIONS on PAGE 45

② Communication = more understanding + less noise
Trust = open conversations = avoid misunderstanding = build trust.

preferred
① f2f physically   needs clear rhythm
② f2f remotely   ⟹ predictable comms
③ phone   then, chart how to
④ open comms platform eg. WhatsApp   Communicate
⑤ Email.   needs structure

Methods to build trust   ① Spend time socially together.
- build mutual understanding + connections
SEE QUESTIONS   ② Look internally to understand each other.
on PAGE 44   - profiling tool MBTI
③ goals   - preference sorting exercises
③ discuss ⊕ and ⊖ of preferences

✻ Substance · Clarity on what trying to achieve → why, how, what?
have a vision + a mission
set broad goals + let the team pre-prioritise them for themselves   } Context & getting the buy in.
① what will it take to can
✻ Style - open = involve all.   ② how can we answer
forces discussion.
Much ambiguity = ask questions.

if do 1 thing = Be curious!

* understand comm - don't judge = build links → progress
* make te most of diverse talent — not just your own.

⇒ Chop up a project into smaller parts. SEE GOALS SECTION.

Problem isn't communication
the problem is misunderstanding
due to "noise".

⇒ "Have you say"! Conversations = build contracts.

① What went well?
② Even better if...
  ∨
lots of questions.

⇒ Purpose, Person, People → Identity
                               Simple language
                               Common language
                               Passive voice
                               Cultural competence (curiosity)
                                     ↓
                                  Learning

by   by
communicate,   platter of
                communication
            how, when, platform, why

• What the goal is
• why it is relevant
• How will it be measured
• Who is responsible for what
• How to handle likely blockers.

⇒ leadership from top down.
Create conversation on how to get there.